T0349002

You Can
Kill Each
Other After
I Leave

ALSO BY PATRICK STRICKLAND

*The Marauders: Standing Up to Vigilantes
in the American Borderlands*

Alerta! Alerta! Snapshots of Europe's Anti-Fascist Struggle

You Can Kill Each Other After I Leave

REFUGEES, FASCISM, AND BLOODSHED IN GREECE

PATRICK STRICKLAND

MELVILLE HOUSE
BROOKLYN · LONDON

You Can Kill Each Other After I Leave
Refugees, Fascism, and Bloodshed in Greece
Patrick Strickland

First published in 2025 by Melville House
Copyright © 2024 by Patrick Strickland
All rights reserved
First Melville House Printing: February 2025

Melville House Publishing
46 John Street
Brooklyn, NY 11201
and
Melville House UK
Suite 2000
16/18 Woodford Road
London E7 0HA

mhpbooks.com
@melvillehouse

ISBN: 978-1-68589-066-7
ISBN: 978-1-68589-067-4 (eBook)

Library of Congress Control Number: 2024947224

Designed by Beste Doğan

Printed in the United States of America
10 9 8 7 6 5 4 3 2 1

A catalog record for this book is available from the Library of Congress

This book is dedicated to everyone
who has lost loved ones to fascist violence.

But it makes an immigrant laugh to hear the fears of the nationalist, scared of infection, penetration, miscegenation, when this is small fry, peanuts, compared to what the immigrant fears—dissolution, disappearance.

—ZADIE SMITH, *WHITE TEETH*

"THE KNIVES WILL COME OUT"

May 23, 2017, marked the 156th day of the trial of Golden Dawn, the Greek neo-Nazi party that had, just five years earlier, made history when it entered the Hellenic Parliament for the first time. Even before its political successes, the party had shocked much of Greek society by terrorizing refugees and migrants and carrying out wanton violence against political opponents, most often leftists. Entering parliament with seven percent of the vote had not tampered the neo-Nazi party's tendency toward bloodshed. Threats compounded. The pogroms continued. Murders followed, brutal knifings in which victims were left to bleed out in the streets. Now, sixty-nine Golden Dawn members were on trial. After a Golden Dawn supporter stabbed and killed the Greek anti-fascist rapper Pavlos Fyssas in

September 2013, the state accused the defendants of operating a criminal organization.

That day, United Kingdom–based filmmaker Konstantinos Georgousis, who had followed Golden Dawn members for his documentary *The Cleaners*, arrived at Korydallos Prison near the capital, where the trial was taking place. Georgousis took the stand and spoke about what he had seen while documenting the party's campaigning some five years earlier.

During the lead-up to the parliamentary elections in May 2012, Georgousis had tailed party candidate Alekos Plomaritis as he campaigned in Athens. Golden Dawn surged in those elections and a subsequent vote later in the year. When the young documentary filmmaker took the stand, none of the defendants were present, an absence that would come to define much of the five-year trial. Plomaritis made several horrifying statements to Georgousis throughout the filming. At one point during the filming, Georgousis followed Plomaritis and others as they harassed non-Greek vendors in an open-air market. "Get out of here," he barked. "You're not Greek."

Addressing the camera, Plomaritis said of migrants: "These parasites drink our water, eat our food, and breathe our Greek air. And they kill us." He continued, "We are ready to open the ovens. We would turn them into soap, but we may get a rash. So, we'll only use it to wash cars and pavements." Of the statements that most haunted Georgousis, he later told the courtroom, was a threat that proved with time to be true: "The knives will come out after the elections."

Golden Dawn had already accumulated a terrifying track record of violence, which included highly organized pogroms carried out by well-trained attackers reminiscent of Nazi Germany's assault squads, but there was no doubt that the bloodshed reached a crescendo after the party entered the parliament. And while it was true that Golden Dawn had never had a monopoly on far-right violence or anti-migrant pogroms in Greece, there was no denying the party's concerted effort to till the soil for militant racists and neo-fascists who sought to "cleanse" Greece of groups whom Golden Dawn had always identified as enemies: refugees, migrants, minorities, members of the LGBTQ community, leftists, anarchists, and anti-fascists of all stripes.

Although Golden Dawn is an outlier in many respects, the neo-Nazi organization's catastrophic rise in Greece marked a worrisome development on a global scale. Throughout the party's existence, Golden Dawn imported white nationalist texts from abroad and often modeled its strategic operations on neo-Nazi groups outside of Greece. The success Golden Dawn enjoyed in a pair of 2012 legislative elections in Greece, however, changed everything. Around Europe, far-right groups had been growing for decades, but they eschewed the sort of unabashed Nazism that Golden Dawn celebrated. Landing in the Greek parliament while also commanding a terrifying presence in the streets represented something entirely new, and neo-Nazis and white nationalists the globe over took notice. The Greek party offered a blueprint for others that hoped to straddle parliamentary politics and street-level violence.

THROUGHOUT MUCH OF the time while I was writing and reporting this book, Golden Dawn's trial was ongoing—and it groaned along at a funeral pace. There were thousands of documents to trudge through, and a series of strikes by public sector workers and lawyers didn't help speed up the process. With proceedings repeatedly delayed, a verdict seemed distant, and clarity about the exact extent of the party's role in the wave of destruction and bloodshed that had gripped Greece for so long remained unclear. And the violence, though occasionally decreasing, had never been eradicated. Between 2012 and 2018, the Athens-based Racist Violence Recording Network documented 988 incidents of bigoted violence, more than half of them targeting refugees and migrants.

WHEN I FIRST started reporting in Greece, in 2015, I mostly focused on what was then called the refugee crisis. Hundreds of thousands of people were making risky—and often deadly—journeys to Europe, and Greece was (and is) one of the main entry points on the long passage to Western Europe. They fled bloodshed in Afghanistan, Syria, Iraq, and Palestine, and economic catastrophes in countries across South Asia and Africa. Some walked through mountains, many were exploited and abused by smugglers, and all had put their lives on the line for a shot at safety and stability. After such perilous journeys, some found themselves on the receiving end of racist violence, a fact that, a decade after I started reporting on the mass exodus, I cannot stomach.

By the time I made it to Greece, I had already spent years living and reporting in the Middle East, and because I had learned colloquial Arabic early on during my four years in Palestine, I was able to communicate with many of the people crossing the Mediterranean directly, without the help of translators or fixers. I had also spent years reporting on the very conflicts, displacement, and humanitarian catastrophes driving this new wave of exiles across borders—from Israeli raids on Palestinian refugee camps in the West Bank to the fallout of Israel's fifty-one-day war on the besieged Gaza Strip in 2014, from the plight of ever-maligned Syrian refugees in Lebanon to villagers taking up arms on the Lebanon-Syria border to defend their communities against any possible attacks by the Islamic State (or ISIS) militant group. In early 2015, I spent several weeks in the Gaza Strip, speaking to the families of people killed during the Israeli military offensive the year before, meeting people whose homes airstrikes had turned into nothing but rubble, and hearing the stories of people who didn't want to leave but felt they had no other option to keep themselves and their families alive.

Sometime early in the refugee crisis, I became intensely focused on the way far-right groups around Europe and the United States used migration as a rallying cry. But much of the reporting I read in news outlets, I began to feel, placed a tunnel-vision focus on the far right itself. In my view, it was just as important to tell the stories behind why people left their countries and the stories of the people fighting back against nationalism, fascism, and hatred. I started documenting much of what made its way into this book in 2015. At the time, the solidarity I witnessed in Greece—as well as elsewhere in Europe—left me hopeful. But by the time I neared the completion of this book, I had also witnessed the way that solidarity can crumble, the way that nationalism and fascism, even in veiled forms, can take root and poison a society, whether in the United States, Greece, or beyond. Even as a US passport holder, someone with the undeniable privilege of being able to travel with relative ease, I grew to understand that attacks on the right to cross a border are not merely attacks on *other people's* rights. When we allow closed borders and violence against people who cross imaginary boundaries, we also undermine the integrity of our own rights: after all, someone like me—maybe even someone like yourself—might have to flee home one day and leave behind a life.

Thus, *You Can Kill Each Other After I Leave* is not a comprehensive history of the Greek far right or migration to the country, nor is it a dispassionate account of the years I spent living and working in Greece, a country where I have encountered such immense hospitality and warmth that I will forever be grateful. In a way, this book is a series of dispatches about the human impact of displacement, borders, and fascism. In many parts, I hope, it's a record of racist violence that the world shouldn't be permitted to forget. It's also a love letter to the people fighting against the rise of fascism as much as it is a warning to readers the world over, a plea to understand that not stopping xenophobia in its tracks runs the risk of losing more human lives. I witnessed the consequences of fascism, but I also witnessed the way everyday people can rally behind one another and push back. Whether the people resisting hate win or not, their stories deserve to be preserved. *You Can Kill Each Other After I Leave*, I hope, documents those glimmers of resistance as much as it records the incredible violence.

You Can
Kill Each
Other After
I Leave

CHAPTER ONE

"THEY TOLD US TO GET OFF THE ISLAND": THE REFUGEE CRISIS ON GREEK ISLANDS

One morning in November 2015, day yawned across the horizon, mist hovered above the Aegean Sea, and sunlight snapped off the rough waters. Skala Skamnias, a tired village on Lesbos Island's northernmost tip, was only just waking up, but strewn all along the shore was evidence that the night before had been busy. Thermal blankets were crumpled up and tossed aside. Damp life jackets lay in the sand, deflated pool floaties nearby—the only protection some of those crossing the sea had against the possibility of drowning. Campfires still simmered on the beach. Who knew how many boats packed with refugees and migrants had reached dry land since sundown the day before? For months, desperate people had huddled together on rickety old vessels and decrepit dinghies, braving the sea and setting off for Europe. Many had fled airstrikes and gunshots and shrapnel.

Many had abandoned bombed-out houses, empty stomachs, and faded blueprints for their lives. Many had left behind countries, cities, and villages that hardly resembled the communities they had once been. They had waved goodbye to their families, their lives, their dreams.

That summer the world had locked its gaze on the crisis unfolding in the Mediterranean Sea. Many European politicians and officials had expressed solidarity with the people trying to outrun war and death, but many had also held out hope that winter chill would put a stop to the boats bound for the shores of countries like Greece, Italy, and Spain.

A dinghy now nodded through the waves. Through binoculars, you could see the people crowded against one another on the vessel: refugees and migrants, men and women, young children and infants. At some points, the distance from Turkey to Greece only spanned a few miles, but that didn't make it a safe journey. By the time I arrived in Lesbos for the first time that November, more than four hundred thousand refugees and migrants had already passed through the island since February of that year. Nearly all of them continued to Greece's mainland and then pressed north toward the border with the Republic of Macedonia. Even then, as winter tightened its frigid grip, even as the sea grew hungrier, boats kept floating toward the island's rock-studded coastline. Around the world, news headlines focused on the humanitarian response, the nauseating number of deaths at sea, and the pointless debate pitting the words *refugee* and *migrant* against each other, the latter more times than not treated as somehow less deserving of protection.

On Lesbos, a spokesperson for the mayor, Marios Andriotis, complained that the Greek government, then headed by the left-wing party known as Syriza, which had come to power earlier that year in January, hadn't provided local authorities with nearly enough resources to handle the number of people arriving each day. It was a failure for which the refugees and migrants ultimately paid, he argued. "We want to provide safe passage to the refugees," he said.[1] "We don't want to see more deaths in the Aegean." By the end of the year, more than 3,700 people would die or disappear crossing the Mediterranean, heading to countries including Greece, Cyprus, and parts of Italy, according to the United Nations.[2]

In the past, winter often saw Skala Skamnias's restaurants and hotels shutter until the tourist season started up again. Now, there were thousands of humanitarian aid volunteers, NGO workers, and activists in town, and businesses were booming, staying open throughout months when their income usually sputtered to a halt.

Back in Mytilene, the capital of Lesbos, refugees had camped out along the promenade, most of them trying to stay as close to the port as possible. Ferries were booked for days in advance. It was wet and cold. Both news and rumors spread about the borders along the journey to western Europe. The Republic of Macedonia (now the Republic of Northern Macedonia) had bulked up its border security in an attempt to prevent irregular crossings through its territory. In the meantime, many refugees and migrants were left stranded in Greece, a country whose migration services were undermanned and disorganized, and a place where years of economic crisis had left little hope for work and financial assistance.

A nineteen-year-old Iraqi man from Baghdad had a ferry ticket booked for two days ahead. His name was Ahmad, and he planned to go as far as Germany or Sweden. "I also heard that there are problems at the borders," he told me, "but we have to keep going. Really, we have nowhere to go back to."

*

NEARLY A MILLION refugees and migrants reached Europe that year. Around the continent, far-right parties and anti-Muslim movements seized the opportunity to rally their bases.[3] For decades, far-right extremists from France to the United Kingdom, from Greece to Sweden, had warned of the supposed dangers stemming from mass migration, cultural miscegenation, and Islam. Migration was an invasion, in their worldview, and that invasion threatened Europe as a cultural and geographic entity. In Greece, Golden Dawn had first clawed its way to parliamentary prominence by advocating a halt to immigration and preserving jobs and resources for ethnic Greeks. But starting in 2015, during the early years of what became known as the refugee crisis—some critics objected to the term, but surely it was a crisis for the people risking their lives at sea—the party failed to bulk up its base. It was true that Golden Dawn was the third largest in the Greek parliament, a distinction it had held on to after the September 2015 legislative elections, but a long list of crimes and violence, including murder, had left the party bogged down in legal troubles, hemorrhaging funds and struggling to maintain its street-level support.[4]

As elsewhere across Europe, anti-refugee xenophobia and racism remained rampant in Greece. Still, untold numbers of Greeks banded together to support the refugees. Those days, it was common to hear the belief that the same policies that left Greeks starving and jobless also abandoned refugees and migrants to risking death at sea. In Lesbos, locals fought back as Golden Dawn supporters verbally attacked the mayor for expressing solidarity with refugees, took to social media outlets to spread hoaxes about supposed refugee attacks on locals, and tried to incite riots near Moria, the island's main refugee camp. Those opposed to Golden Dawn's exclusivist worldview sought to push its supporters into a place of marginalization, and the party's attempts to capitalize on frustration over the management of the refugee crisis found little currency.[5] "There wasn't much room for the Golden Dawn party," Christina Chatzidaki, a sixty-five-year-old activist, told one reporter two years later. "We are peaceful people who don't like all of those kinds of troubles."

During that first visit to Lesbos, I drove a rental car up a winding hill until I reached the top, where local authorities had been dumping the life jackets and floatable devices left behind on the beaches. Altogether, the vests made a small mountain. I was with a Greek journalist and a Romanian photographer, and we spotted a shepherd sitting on a large stone nearby. His mustache was thick, bushy, and curled up on its sides, and he wore a black-and-white bandanna wrapped around his forehead. His name was Spiros, he was in his seventies, and he felt disappointed in the government's response to the crisis. Not enough was being done, he said. He felt that locals bore too much of the crisis's burden, but he didn't blame the refugees and migrants. "Whatever happens," he told me, "it's always the normal people who pay."[6]

A man operating a forklift drove across a patch of earth and dumped yet more on top of the mounds. Sixty-four years old, he went by Fotis. He woke up each morning before sunrise and gathered as many life jackets as possible from the shores, hauling them up the hill. He told me he understood why the refugees had no choice but to flee their countries, and he worried that the number of people perishing at sea would continue to increase. "It was easier in the summer, but now it is winter," he said. "When it's cold, people will be coming off the boats shivering. What will happen then?" He paused for a moment, chewing on his own question. "I don't know what happens next."

No one knew what would happen next. Radical right-wing populism was taking root in pockets around Europe, and the future looked grim. Outwardly, Europe had united under the mantra Refugees Welcome, but how long could that last, and how long would it be until far-right groups around the continent swung the pendulum back in the other direction?

On top of the NGOs and charities aiding refugees, anarchists, leftists, and other anti-fascists had spent the summer organizing in a variety of ways. Many traveled to the islands to help boats disembark, established food kitchens for new arrivals there on the shores, and gathered clothes and blankets to distribute to people whose belongings had gotten soaked in the Aegean.

By winter, new refugee squats cropped up all around the Greek capital, especially in the central Athens neighborhood Exarchia, where squatting was a longtime political tradition. During an early visit to the neighborhood, I visited Notara (sometimes called Notara 26), a squat that provided temporary housing to refugees and migrants passing through the city. At the time, most only stayed for a few days before moving on, but the squat had attracted a committed group of activists, mostly anarchists, who remained on site to welcome the next wave of people showing up in Athens. The building the activists had taken over belonged to the Greek Ministry of Labor, but it had been deserted. Mimi, a thirty-four-year-old activist and a member of the squat's solidarity committee, sat and smoked a cigarette one night that December. A general assembly—an open discussion between the Greek activists and the displaced people staying at the squat—had just concluded. The discussion ended with the consensus that they should do whatever they could to support others attempting to open new squats, especially in areas outside of Athens. In Thessaloniki, the next major stop for refugees leaving the capital to move north, there was an acute need for safe shelter, the activists agreed. "We had a full summer of experience under our belts and felt that refugees needed a safe space when they get to Athens, especially as the weather gets worse," Mimi told me. "From Athens, they still have a long journey ahead of them."[7]

For people fleeing wars and armed conflict in countries like Afghanistan, Iraq, and Syria, the difficult path to Western Europe, which many walked, was yet another barrier between them and the promise of safety. The nature of that long journey, however, would drastically change in the months that lay ahead. By early 2016, countries across the Balkans began sealing their borders, marooning tens of thousands of refugees and migrants in Greece. In March 2016, the European Union and Turkey reached an agreement to stem the flow of refugee boats to the continent.[8] In effect, refugees and migrants had two options: apply for asylum in Greece, or voluntarily return to Turkey or the home country they had escaped. Syriza, the ruling left-wing party, had come to power promising radical anti-austerity reforms in January 2015, but it had also vowed to overhaul the country's immigration policies. Shortly after Syriza's electoral victory—but before the refugee crisis reached the level of mass arrivals for which it later became known—the leftist party announced plans to abolish a measure that allowed the government to detain refugees and migrants for a period of up to eighteen months.[9] In lieu of detention, the party would establish open shelters and integration programs, a stark contrast to the policies of its predecessors.

In early 2016, Syriza faced pressure from the European Union as refugee boats continued to come from Turkey, and the party's migration policies weren't shaping up to be that much different from the right-wing New Democracy's or the center-left Panhellenic Socialist Movement's (PASOK). After the European Union-Turkey deal, the Syriza-led government barred refugees and migrants on Greek islands from traveling to the mainland until they completed several levels of the asylum process. An attempt to reduce people whose applications would likely receive a rejection elsewhere in Europe, the about-face was only one in a growing list of measures that increasingly brought Syriza under fire from the left. The same islands where so many Greeks and internationals had rallied together to help displaced children, women, and men safely reach Europe were now turning into warehouses where asylum seekers, the number of whom continued to grow by the day, lived in squalid camps. That new reality proved a test for local solidarity.

Pollsters and researchers had not yet detected a sharp rise in support for Golden Dawn since the refugee crisis started, but that didn't mean that its jackboots had abandoned organizing behind the scenes.[10] In a sense, Golden Dawn appeared more versatile than many other far-right parties in Europe. The party had decades of experience in organizing and violence, and several years under its belt of straddling both parliamentary politics and shows of force in the streets. Hate crimes and far-right assaults had slumped during the first years following anti-fascist rapper Pavlos Fyssas's 2013 murder. Still, anti-fascists remained vigilant, and much of their efforts focused on the immediate needs at hand, especially refugee solidarity work. In April 2016, the month after the EU-Turkey deal, squatters took over City Plaza, an abandoned hotel in Athens. They opened the hotel's rooms to hundreds of refugees and migrants. Notara 26 had also been refashioned to make its space more suitable for long-term accommodation. All throughout Exarchia and in some other parts of the city, new squats cropped up. During those early years of the refugee crisis, I often spent hours at squats, sitting in on general assembly meetings, and talking to residents and activists. I wanted to understand how building an alternative to the state's cruel refugee policies fit into a broader anti-fascist vision, a way of fighting the far right by taking small steps toward building a society in which everyone—no matter where they came from—lived together without hierarchy.

When the attack happened, some 130 people lived at Notara, now semi-permanently while they waited for asylum decisions. Around 3:45 a.m. on August 24, 2016, most of Notara 26's residents were fast asleep, but a handful stayed up and patrolled the perimeter. Such security details were meant to protect against fascist violence and police raids. Suddenly an explosion ripped through the quiet night.[11] Flames crawled up the side of the building. Molotov cocktails smashed into the walls. Residents and solidarity activists scrambled to their feet, tried to quell the flames with bucketfuls of water, and used fire extinguishers to fight the blaze. They had prepared for this scenario for nearly a year. Everyone had expected fascists would one day target the squat, and now that the time came, they were able to prevent serious injuries—or worse still, death. "Notara was up and running in one week, but we were very lucky that no one died," Marcos, an activist on the solidarity committee, who used a pseudonym for interviews, told me.

Around that time, I met with Rami, a Palestinian refugee from Syria, who lived in the Notara squat at the time it partially went up in flames.[12] He had survived the slaughter of Syria's civil war, and he gritted out the decay of life in the refugee camps. He was thirty-eight, and his children and parents had stayed back in Syria. Attack or no attack, he planned to stay at the squat. "The camps are isolated," he told me. "A lot of times they are outside the city. Here you are inside the city. You feel like a human being; you can go out and communicate with people . . . You don't feel alone here, like when the fascists attacked the camps and police did nothing."

The squat's solidarity committee released a statement not long after the attack, a promise to persist and strike back. "The fascist scum who prowl in the darkness are very well aware of the con-sequences they'll suffer," the statement read. The squats would "continue to exist and multiply, housing the damned of the world," and "crushing fascism."

But the arson that August night was not the first far-right at-tack on squats, and it wouldn't be the last attack on refugees and those who supported them.

THAT SAME SUMMER of 2016, on the island of Chios, Dipethe was more a last resort, an on-the-fly rest stop, than a refugee camp. A refugee camp is planned, equipped with facilities—showers, bath-rooms, offices, clinics—and Dipethe had none of those. It was a deserted theater, and around three hundred people, most of them Syrians and Iraqis, lived there. The luckier ones slept in tents, the rest beneath ramshackle shelters pieced together with tarps, scrap wood, and ropes—whatever they could find. The former provided a bit more security from the elements than the latter, but neither protected the people inside from the stones and Molotov cocktails hurled at them by right-wing locals.

Almost everyone in Dipethe had fled from Vial, Chios's only official refugee camp, a place the Greek government described as a "reception center," the United Nations refugee agency as a "hot spot," and rights groups as a "detention center." Reporters visit-ing the island routinely described Vial with phrases like "hell," "a vision of hell," and "a living hell in a piece of paradise," but no combination of adjectives, adverbs, and nouns that included a reference to hellfire could fully capture the misery. In any case, Vial was an enclosed facility, overcrowded, teeming with anger, and the frequent site of violence. In fact, that was why Ahmad

Hamdan, a Syrian refugee sharing a makeshift tent with nine relatives, ended up fleeing to Dipethe.

Hamdan was a lawyer back in Syria, had what he described as a good life, and brought home a decent paycheck each month. None of that mattered in Vial, where the forty-six-year-old father's days consisted of waiting in line for the toilet, waiting in line for the shower, waiting in line for food, and waiting in line to see a doctor, from whom he could usually get no more than a handful of ibuprofen tablets. The camp was crowded. The staff was shorthanded, the living conditions decrepit. In an environment like that, Hamdan told me, tensions ran high. Everyone grew impatient; everyone felt like they were in a race for supplies and food. Fights became the norm. Then sectarianism took root. Some of the Syrians hated Afghans because their government had imported Afghan mercenaries to fight opposition groups; some of the Syrians hated Iraqis because the Syrian government had imported Iraqi mercenaries to fight opposition groups; some of the Afghans didn't like the Syrians, either; none took too kindly to the Moroccans because they hadn't come from a war zone, because they felt the Moroccans took up space that should've been reserved for people who had no country to which they could return. In the end, no one got along, and the Greek authorities that had put them in a human warehouse and forbidden them from traveling onward to mainland Greece were quite possibly the only party that benefited from the discord.

One night in April 2016, it all became too much. The clashes started well after nightfall. No one seemed to remember how it started, but everyone agreed on the general trajectory of what happened next. Threats were issued. Mothers and sisters were cursed. Stones flew overhead and crashed into tents, children inside crying. Bystanders scattered. Beer bottles shattered on the pavement. Garbage bins blazed in the narrow walking paths weaving throughout the camp. Hamdan gathered up his family. They packed their bags in a panic and set off on foot with a few hundred Iraqis and fellow Syrians. They did not know where to go, so they just kept walking until they reached the port, around four and a half miles away.

At the port, they jammed poles into the earth, set up their tents, and waited, for what exactly no one knew. From there, they could see the Greek *tavernas* and tourist shops lining the promenade across the street, could smell the meat roasting on spits behind the restaurants, often packed with customers, but few of their group, if any, had enough cash to enjoy a good meal. They stayed for four days and four nights, until a group of locals showed up, which was when the real problems started. The locals were far-right activists who hurled bottles at Hamdan and the others, shot fireworks in their direction. Police officers arrived and told them they had to move. Hamdan and the others packed up their bags again and set off on foot once more, this time winding up a ten-minute walk down the road at Dipethe. They strung together the tarps, erected their tents in the pavement courtyard, unrolled their sleeping bags, and hoped that Dipethe, a little less central and a little less visible, would offer some respite from the locals. After all, the Greek police told them to come here.

Throughout Greece's nearly decade-long economic crisis, Chios's strong shipping industry, and the enduring demand for mastic elsewhere in Greece and beyond the country's borders kept the local economy afloat. To an extent, this spared the islanders the type of gruesome realities that unfolded in other parts of the country: the spike in homelessness, the soaring suicide rates, the plummeting wages. For the refugees and migrants whose boats washed up on Chios's stone-studded shores, however, the island was grim, a place where the far right, tapping into frustration with

the government's lack of a meaningful plan for the asylum seekers, launched into action and sought to shift the blame to people
fleeing war and economic collapse in their homelands, who now
found themselves staring back at the grimaced faces of locals who
considered them invaders.

THE RESPITE THE Hamdan family enjoyed during the first few
nights in Dipethe didn't last. A week before I arrived in Chios, a
group of fascists appeared on the street outside the camp.[13] The
men wore black and carried stones. They hollered at the refugees
inside, told them to leave Greece, told them to go back to "where
they came from." Police intervened at the last second and prevented the attack, but Hamdan was sure it wasn't the last run-in
the refugees on Chios would have with the people who wanted
them gone. "We didn't sleep that night," he told me.

His brother, a schoolteacher named Muhammad, agreed. He
explained that there had been a "strong fear," especially among
the children, in Dipethe that night. A week later, that fear hadn't
entirely dissipated. Ammar al-Ashaq, their twenty-seven-year-
old nephew, said they still preferred risking the fascist violence at
Dipethe to returning to Vial. "We are scared the police will move
us back to Vial at some point," he explained.[14] Ammar reached for
his cell phone and scrolled to a video he took on the night they
fled Vial: Two groups of young men with bandannas and T-shirts
wrapped around their faces chunked Molotov cocktails and stones
at each other.

Sure, attacks constituted a problem, but the bigger concern
was that Greek authorities had implemented a no-travel policy. If
they could leave Chios, they wouldn't have to deal with the angry
locals, the Golden Dawn supporters, the police that intervened

sometimes and sometimes didn't. But their boat had reached Chios's shores in late March 2016, around the same time that an agreement was made between the European Union and Turkey. That agreement, in effect, forbade refugees on the islands from traveling to the mainland until they had passed certain stages of the asylum process. When the agreement was implemented, countries across the Balkans—Macedonia, Serbia, Croatia, and others—slammed shut their borders, leaving the refugees in Greece with no option but to apply for asylum there or risk deportation. Recounting all this, Ammar frowned solemnly, as if realizing what he'd say next for the first time. "If we stayed in Syria with the bombs and violence, it would have been better than being imprisoned here on the island," he said.

We sat beneath their tarp for an hour or so, talking about all the hardship of surviving in Dipethe. It was steamy under the tarp, but the sun blazed outside. Hamdan boiled water, poured it into small plastic cups, and dropped tea bags in each of them. Outside, children shouted at one another. You could hear someone hacking, someone yelling, someone snoring from the tents next door. Every now and then somebody would bump into the tarp and its poles would shake. "Many of the kids here are sick, and people are very angry," Ammar added. Plus, their savings were running thin. Everyone had paid the smugglers exorbitant fees—several thousand euros, in many cases their life savings—to join the boat journeys and pay for life jackets, sleeping bags, and other supplies. Meanwhile, the food provided by the United Nations High Commissioner for Refugees (UNHCR)—small, prepackaged meals delivered three times a day—wasn't enough. Medicine, bottled water, and cell phone data all required cash, and cash wasn't a commodity in wide currency there in Dipethe. If you ran out of money, "the aid organizations are the only way to get food," Ammar said.

*

CHIOS WASN'T THE only place where the government's isolation policy was creating a climate of dread and rancor. Closed borders had bottlenecked more than 57,000 refugees and migrants in the country, with more than 8,400 trapped on the islands. That same summer, things were spiraling out of control on Leros Island. On July 10, sectarian clashes erupted, and around 150 Iraqis, almost all of them from the Yazidi religious minority, packed their bags and fled.[15] Carrying their babies and their suitcases, they set off on foot for the island's main port.

Catharina Kahane, an aid worker and cofounder of the Echo100 Plus humanitarian group, had been working on Leros Island for months as living conditions plummeted. She caught wind that the refugees were heading back to the camp after they had been attacked near the port. While riding in a car with her colleagues, she received an ominous phone call: The caller warned that she and her colleagues had to leave the island—or else. Then, as the vehicle chugged along around fifty yards from the camp, a group of locals appeared. They had blocked the road, arming themselves with sticks, shovels, and stones. The locals pounded the hood of their car, preventing it from advancing.

"They told us to get off the island," she later told me by phone. "They said if we didn't get the first boat off the island something terrible would happen. It was scary. The only reason we left the island was because the police weren't moving at all to help."

With the police allowing the attacks, Kahane saw no option but to relocate. Along with her fifteen volunteers, she took a ferry to another island and set up there. "It was clear that the police were on their side," she added.

Katerina Kitidi, the Greece-based UNHCR spokesperson, told me that the clashes on Leros had been a long time in the making. "There have been tensions which targeted both refugees and members of the humanitarian community," she said. "It all started from long-standing issues related to the situation on the island, which clearly shows that we need specific measures for people who have requested asylum."

I phoned Georgios Kyritsis, a Syriza parliamentarian and the government's spokesperson for migration at the time. I asked why the government insisted on warehousing refugees on the islands even as far-right violence fanned out across the Aegean. Evidence that the policy was fueling the far right didn't appeal to Kyritsis, who insisted that the measure was necessary. "They are free in the islands, but they cannot leave the islands until the applications are processed," he told me. "This is practical because the asylum committees must be able to locate the people."

BACK AT DIPETHE, we finished our tea in the Hamdan family's tent and stepped back outside into the camp. The sun was slinking behind the horizon, casting smears of orange and purple and red across the skies. A breeze passed through, sent shivers through the tents. A man cupped his hands and sang out the muezzin, and a handful of men knelt prostrate behind him on prayer rugs. A few kids played tag, chasing each other in circles until they ran out of breath, gave up, and plopped down cross-legged on the stone courtyard. Others washed their hands and feet at a spigot on the side of the building. Nick Paleologos, a photographer I was working with on that trip, and I chatted with whoever would speak to us. At one point, a circle of men surrounded us. Word spread fast in the camp, and they'd heard I was American, and that Nick was Greek. One man had questions, but they all came out in a rant. His face flashed red. Why had America created

endless wars in the Middle East? Why wouldn't Greece let him
and his family keep pushing onward to Germany? Neither of us
had answers, and that didn't do much to quell his anger. He wasn't
wrong. Later that night, we'd be sleeping in a motel room—albeit
a drab one about the size of a large storage closet, equipped with
two twin beds, a single lamp, and a small television that looked
like it survived since the eighties—but he'd still be there in the
camp, blinking up at his tarp late into the night hearing every
cough two tents over, every argument between relatives, maybe
even the guttural screams of far-right attackers gathering outside.

THE NEXT DAY, we went to Souda, another makeshift camp that,
like Dipethe, the Greek government hadn't officially recognized.
We walked through a maze of tents tossed up beneath the historic
ruins of a castle. Gray clouds hung low and thick in the sky, and
people used wrapped-up T-shirts to fan away the humidity, use-
lessly. We were sweating. Everyone was sweating. Around a thousand people lived there at the time, and garbage overflowed from
bins, spilling out onto the dirt pathways where people walked
from their tents to the food line, from the food line to the medical
tent, from the medical tent back to their own tents. Water leaked
out from beneath a row of portable toilets, soaking a layer of earth
and creating large patches of mud. A row of tents stretched for a
few hundred yards, sidled up against the stone castle walls, and
behind it, women hand-washed their clothes in a fountain that
looked like a trough. More coughs. More sneezing. More shouting.
　　Down on the shore, a Syrian boy in jean shorts and a cutoff
T-shirt did his best to skip stones, but the waves were too powerful.
His friend wore a white baseball cap and laughed at him. Another
group of kids kicked a soccer ball back and forth, just passing the

time. Nick snapped a photograph, and a group of young men appeared next to us. "How's the situation here?" I asked.

"You see the conditions here," one replied. His name was Achraf Zbir, and he'd left his hometown, Casablanca, Morocco, hoping to unite with distant relatives in Germany. He stuck out his arm, motioned to a putrid pile of garbage, and then to a long line of women, most of them holding babies in their arms, outside the food tent. "You see the trash, the lack of food."

Achraf was twenty-nine, and he'd spent more than a thousand euros to reach Greece. A month earlier, before climbing onto a dinghy that carried a few dozen people like him, he had no idea that the European Union and Turkey had struck up a deal that would leave him marooned on Chios. The smugglers never mentioned it. "I saw people die in front of me in the sea," he told me. He and his friends could still pay smugglers to get them to mainland Greece, but that was risky, expensive, and "our money ran out a long time ago."

That people were dying at sea was true. The UNHCR documented just south of six hundred deaths in the Eastern Mediterranean in 2015, around 30 percent of them children.[16] In 2015, international headlines had announced the death of Alan Kurdi, a two-year-old Syrian boy whose lifeless body washed up on Turkish shores after the boat carrying him went under. News outlets around the world broadcast photos of the boy lying face down on the coast, still wearing a red T-shirt, shorts, and little sneakers.[17] Across the entire Mediterranean, more than 3,500 people drowned while making the journey to Europe in 2015. Of that total, at least a thousand were children, who, unlike Alan Kurdi, most news consumers could not name. By the time 2016 concluded, more than five thousand people crossing from Turkey or North Africa, heading toward Greece or other countries in Southern Europe, drowned and died, making it the deadliest year on record.

Later that afternoon, I made the fifteen-minute drive to a cemetery perched atop a steep cliff north of town. Most of the graves belonged to Greeks, but in the back corner sat two freshly packed mounds of red dirt in front of small wooden headstones. One contained a Syrian man, the other an Afghan child. The child was called Ali Reza, and he died when he fell out of his boat—just a few feet from land—and hit his head on a rock. Tacked to his headstone was a handwritten note: OUR BELOVED ALI REZA, WE LOVE YOU AND WE CARRY YOU IN OUR HEARTS. Someone had left a teddy bear, small and white and lying face down, atop his grave. From up there, we could see all the way across the Aegean to Turkey. It looked like a short trip, but on those boats, some of which weren't equipped with motors, the trek could last several hours. We found six fresh graves, empty and gaping like wounds in the earth. An aid worker told us they were reserved for people who died at sea. They sat open, waiting for more dead—people whom Europe, rather than take in, doomed to spend their final moments with lungs full of water and hearts full of terror.

THE REFUGEES IN Souda had seen their share of horror, of angry locals barreling their way, issuing blood-curdling threats, armed with projectiles and makeshift weapons. The attacks then broadened, and now even humanitarians and government employees—like Yannis Koutsodonotis, beaten by a far-right attacker while trying to protect a Syrian boy outside Souda early that June—who worked or volunteered in the refugee camps found themselves looking over their shoulders while they went about their business in town.

Antonis Vorrias was one of them. At forty-nine years old, he wore long gray hair that parted down the middle and dangled to his shoulders, and some of the refugees had nicknamed him "the pirate." When the refugee crisis first erupted during the summer of 2015, he and a few others nodded out into the sea on Sea-Doos. The underinflated dinghies would start filling up with water long before they reached the coast, and several had gone under, their occupants either swimming to shore, if they were close enough, or drowning at sea. He couldn't bear to hear about people dying so close to safety, and he did what he could to save as many people as possible, pulling whomever he could onto his Sea-Doo and flooring the gas until they reached dry land. He'd drop them off, turn around, and head back into the waves. By the time I met Vorrias, the Greek coast guard and the European Union's border agency, Frontex, had cracked down on nonofficial rescue crews, blocking them from carrying out their operations. Rather, Frontex intercepted the boats and dinghies at sea, transferring the refugees directly to the Vial.

No longer able to conduct sea patrols, Vorrias passed his time in Dipethe and Souda. He didn't speak English, Dari, or Arabic, but he found ways to communicate with others. In Dipethe that June, I watched as a group of children jumped on him. Some crawled up his skinny torso, one girl hanging from his shoulder, a boy wrapping his legs around his waist, yet another tugging on his shirt sleeve.

One day, not long before we met, Vorrias was walking through town running errands when a man he didn't recognize stopped him. "Hello," he said.

"You're on the list. You'll get what's coming to you sometime soon," the man said, sternly, and then walked away briskly.

A list, Vorrias thought, could only mean one thing. Combined with the local police's apparent indifference, the growing number of right-wing protests, and the recent attacks on refugees, he sensed that the man had given him an encrypted death threat. That wouldn't stop him from doing what he felt was right, though. He had become good friends with the Hamdan family, with Ahmad and Muhammad and their eight relatives, since he saved them at sea earlier that year, and he continued showing up at Dipethe each day, drinking tea, kidding around with the children, and bringing whatever food he could scrounge up from his place.

Two months earlier, in April, he and Ahmad decided to brainstorm ways to ease the rising tensions between refugees and the locals. They thought about it for a few days and eventually settled on an idea. The Hamdan family, along with a handful of others from Dipethe, gathered up a few wreaths of flowers and walked to a Greek Orthodox church in town. "We wanted to say, in the name of Syrian people here: Happy Easter," they told the churchgoers. "We are brothers in humanity."

CHAPTER TWO

"WE WERE THOUSANDS & THEY WERE TENS": A HISTORY OF FASCISM

On November 14, 1973, Dimitris Psarras, a twenty-one-year-old architecture student, joined a freshly minted committee of left-wing students in their fight against the ruling military junta. At the Polytechnic University in Athens, the students launched a dramatic strike against the regime. Raised in Athens by a politically centrist family, Psarras had become a communist activist during his formative years living under the military dictatorship's suffocating grip. "We were against the regime, and we tried to make a new start," he said. "We learned from books because the political parties had been dissolved." The students refused to make a compromise with the junta. "Most of the parties, even the two communist parties, were against the uprising."

The students occupied the campus. Minor clashes between communists and anarchists broke out inside, but the occupation began to take an organized shape. Students rallied under the mantras People's Rule and The People Make Revolutions, among others.[1] They knew the stakes, understood the risks they were taking by facing off with the junta. Recent months had seen the regime bar large gatherings and arrest left-wing students. By the second day, they had created a pirate radio station to transmit their message to citizens around Athens, launched safety patrols, and set up a first aid department and a canteen for the strike participants.

Headed by far-right military figures, the government was known as the Regime of the Colonels. It first took power after an April 1967 coup d'état. The military regime had dissolved unions, abolished civil rights, banned political parties, and exiled, disappeared, and tortured thousands of dissidents, chiefly communists and socialists. Many of the colonels, such as junta leader Georgios Papadopoulos, had collaborated with the Nazis during World War II, and the regime was rife with wartime-era German sympathizers. By the time Polytechnic students decided to strike, the regime had introduced a process of liberalization meant to eventually return the country to civilian rule. But milquetoast reforms were not enough to quell the students' anger—stemming from the banning of student elections and interference in university political life—and tensions reached a boiling point. Calling themselves the "Free Besieged," the students barricaded themselves inside the university walls, used laboratory equipment for the pirate radio station, and braced for a violent crackdown. Thousands of workers and socialists gathered to support the uprising.

"It was something between Woodstock and *Strawberry Statement*," Psarras remembered, the latter referring to a 1970 American film about the US student revolt and the explosion of counterculture in the 1960s. "We didn't have a real strategy. We tried to organize as students, to be free as students, so the workers could be free as workers if they tried to organize . . . It was an example because that night tens of thousands, or even hundreds of thousands, of people tried to come to the Polytechnic. This is what made the junta decide to bring the military rule and the tanks and so on. They saw that every minute the people of Athens were coming out to support us."

Security forces gathered outside. A band of enthusiastic fascists saddled up behind rows of police to show their support for the regime. A few dozen fascists from the 4th of August Party's (K4A) youth wing posted outside the university, although their plans to invade the campus and attack the strikers did not pan out. On the frontline stood sixteen-year-old Nikolaos Michaloliakos, a bullheaded and enthusiastic young fascist with a proclivity for violence. Born in Athens and raised in Pangrati, a neighborhood in the city center, Michaloliakos's family lineage traced back to a prominent family in Mani, a peninsula jutting from the western fringe of the Peloponnese region in southern Greece. He grew up idolizing Georgios Papadopoulos, who would later serve as his mentor when the two met in prison. During the Polytechnic uprising, K4A activists made every effort to incite clashes with the striking students. "I saw a group of youngsters behind the police line. They were trying to provoke us with [pro-junta] slogans, and throwing stones, and there were some stones thrown from our side," Psarras remembered. "But we were a thousand, and they were tens."

At the time Psarras and Michaloliakos were unaware of each other, but they would, several decades on, find themselves on opposite sides of a trial that threatened to obliterate Golden Dawn, the neo-fascist party Michaloliakos went on to establish several years later.

Before dawn on November 17, 1973, the city lights flipped off, and generators buzzed in the charcoal night. Although the students were negotiating with the army, an AMX 30 tank was posted outside the campus. The students offered to leave the university if the army could guarantee that the police would not arrest them. On the campus, from the tank shot a sliver of light, Psarras recalled. "We expected the tank to fire on us," he said, "because its [turret] was pointed toward us."

At around 3:00 a.m., the tank crashed through the university's front gate. "When the tank came towards us, of course, it was a great shock for us. We tried to run back," Psarras said.

Nearby, Dutch journalist Albert Coerant secretly filmed the incident, capturing footage that would later be broadcasted across the world.[2] The campus morphed from a protest site to a crime scene when the regime's jackboots attacked the occupiers. "He was a very courageous man," Psarras said.

Soldiers opened fire on protesters attempting to flee. As the bodies dropped around him, Psarras fled through a side entrance, burst onto Stournari Street, and found safety in an apartment across the street, where "some good people" helped him and hundreds of others by opening their homes and allowing them to hide out to avoid arrest. "The problem was not at the time; it was the next morning," he said. "The next morning, many policemen and military were around the school and arrested everyone who appeared to be a student. But I was lucky."

By the time the dust cleared, they had killed at least forty people. "We know the names and the numbers of the dead people, but we don't know exactly who killed them," Psarras recalled.

Protests broke out in central Athens in the wake of the uprising, but the junta "tried to terrorize the population of Athens, even in [suburbs] several kilometers away. We had deaths around Kypseli, Pangrati, and Ambelokipi," Psarras said, referring to several neighborhoods around the city center. "They tried to make the impression that if anyone went to the streets at that time, they may die."

Going into hiding for four months, Psarras dodged arrest in the wake of the uprising. But he was eventually called to early military service. "They shaved my head and beard, and I was looking like a junta supporter."

Despite the brutal crackdown, the Polytechnic student uprising set into motion a series of events that led to the regime's collapse the following year. With the colonels overthrown, Psarras eventually graduated from the Polytechnic with a degree in architecture, and he went on to work in that field for years. By the early 1980s, he felt the need to participate in change, and in 1982 he traded architecture for journalism. The following year, he banded together with a group of colleagues, and they founded *Scholiastis*, a left-wing weekly magazine that published investigative reporting, political analysis, and social commentary. "My generation is between two other great generations, so this period of the dictatorship and the first years of democracy were very intense," he said. "Young people could not be indifferent. It was a time of great hope. Everybody tried to do something about the situation. I was disappointed by politics—even left politics—so I thought a critical left-wing magazine was important for that time. I shared this view with many others from my generation, and we made this magazine. It was very successful. It was the first left-wing magazine that tried to be critical in the time of lifestyle journalism. It was a kind of school for many new journalists."

It was there on the pages of *Scholiastis* that Psarras first eventually took aim at the country's new ilk of fascists.

BY 1980, THE young fascist brawler Michaloliakos had built an impressive résumé of far-right credentials and outlandish violence. Only in his early twenties at the time, he founded *Golden Dawn*, a national socialist journal and the namesake for the neo-Nazi party to come.

Michaloliakos had been one of the 4th of August fascists who taunted leftists inside the Polytechnic in 1973. Founded in 1965 by Konstantinos Plevris, an anti-Semitic lawyer and far-right author, K4A was a virulently nationalist and racist outfit that fashioned itself as the rightful heir to Ioannis Metaxas, the Greek dictator during the onset of World War II. As prime minister during the lead-up to and outbreak of the war, Metaxas ruled Greece with an iron fist from 1936 until 1941, when toxemia killed him. But the ruling ideology, Metaxism, lived on. Metaxism sought the realization of a culturally, religiously, and politically homogenous Greece rooted in fantastical notions of creating a "Third Hellenic Civilization." Some scholars of fascism have quibbled over ideological designations assigned to the 4th of August regime, but Metaxism's fascistic or quasi-fascist qualities were enough for some scholars, such as Aristotle Kallis, to situate it in a "much wider process of political elite radicalization within the conventional space of the European right in directions mapped by the 'fascist' regimes."[3]

For its part, the K4A group functioned in a military fashion, with strict disciplinary measures for those members or supporters who did not adhere to its rules. The party viewed itself as revolutionary, nationalist vanguard fighting for advent of a "Third Hellenic Civilization"—much like the regime from which it borrowed its name. The party set up offices in cities and towns across the country, where it also embedded combatant cells. K4A railed against communism, capitalism, and what it viewed as the "degeneracy" of western culture, parliamentary politics, and liberalism.

During the years of the military junta, K4A maintained a tenuous relationship with the regime. After the regime's collapse, however, the movement buried itself underground.

Three years after the junta's collapse, on February 25, 1977, a ranking member of K4A, twenty-five-year-old Aristotle Kalentzis, returned home from a *bouzoukia* bar to find a group of police officers waiting for him, the *Washington Post* reported later that year.[4] Shortly after, security forces scooped up a pair of his accomplices, Evangelos Christakis and Anargyros Kakavas, and whisked them off to interrogation. At the time, the *Post* reported that junta supporters had attacked at least sixteen Greek journalists and bombed dozens of left-wing bookstores in Athens. Rocked by political instability stemming from the regime's downfall, Greece struggled to contain a new wave of far-right violence carried out by perpetrators and groups who refused to accept the downfall of the military regime. Greek political parties, youth groups, and journalists investigated the violent outburst, but results came slowly. Citing leaked judicial transcripts, the report noted that although Kalentzis remained quiet in interrogations, his colleagues "painted a James Bond scenario of contacts with international fascists, circuitous routes to meeting places, safe houses where arms and cash are stashed, and a membership of more than 1,000 activists in the Fourth of August."

A court eventually sentenced Kalentzis, who maintained close ties with the Italian New Order fascist organization, to twelve years in prison. As of April 1977, Kalentzis, Christiakis, and Kakavas were the only ones identified in relation to the terror. Hundreds walked freely, as did many of those responsible for the bloodshed under the military regime. The freedom and impunity some radical right figures enjoyed in those years helped till the soil for Michaloliakos to birth a neo-Nazi movement that would shape Greece's future in ways no one could have imagined at the time.

*

IN THE YEARS that followed the junta's collapse, Michaloliakos gained an impressive if not infamous reputation. He was arrested in Athens on July 24, 1974, while protesting the United Kingdom's stance toward the Turkish invasion and occupation of Northern Cyprus.[5] In December 1976, while attending the funeral of Evangelos Mallios, a policeman and notorious torturer under the junta, he was arrested for assaulting journalists who were covering the event. Along with his cronies, Michaloliakos roughed up the reporters, sending five to the hospital. Police again arrested him in July 1978 for carrying explosive materials and illegal weapons during the bombing of a cinema popular with leftists, and he was dealt a brief prison sentence and kicked out of the military.[6] It was in lockup that he met key junta figures, including Georgios Papadopoulos.[7]

In 1980, fresh from prison, he founded the journal *Golden Dawn*. The ideology of *Golden Dawn* was markedly national socialist, and the publication regularly ran articles that praised Hitler and Nazi Germany.[8] He reportedly traveled to apartheid South Africa for several months in 1983, though the details of that trip remain unclear today. In the mid-1980s, the magazine ceased publication when Michaloliakos joined the National Political Union, a far-right party founded by former junta leader Georgios Papadopoulos; Michaloliakos took control of its youth wing. Michaloliakos, however, was not suited for secondary leadership roles, and his apparent need for the spotlight led to his break with the National Political Union within less than a year.

In 1985, he founded an organization called Popular National Movement—Golden Dawn. Photographs from that period depict Michaloliakos wearing a swastika armband and raising his arm in a fascistic salute while standing in front of a large Nazi-era German flag. Although Golden Dawn would later exert a great deal of energy in futile attempts to brand the party as "social nationalist" (rather than national socialist), Michaloliakos's own writing from the 1980s leaves little room for doubt. In a 1987 article titled "Hitler for 1,000 years," the Golden Dawn leader demonstrated a profound admiration for Nazism and white supremacy.[9] "We are the faithful soldiers of the National Socialist idea and nothing else," he proclaimed. That same year, on August 18, Golden Dawn published a cover story praising Rudolf Hess, Hitler's deputy, who committed suicide a day earlier in a German prison. RUDOLF HESS—IMMORTAL! read leaflets Golden Dawn hardliners distributed in central Athens at the time.

NEW DEMOCRACY DOMINATED the first two elections following the fall of the junta, governing the country between 1974 and 1981. During the October 1981 elections, the social democratic party PASOK defeated the self-described conservatives in New Democracy. Throughout the remainder of the eighties and the duration of the nineties, voters consistently put PASOK and New Democracy in the top two slots. The main political disagreement that defined those generations was the choice between PASOK's social democracy and New Democracy's conservative variety of classical European liberalism. Over the ensuing decades, however, New Democracy would serve as a big tent party, with plenty of space for center-rightists and the far right.

Established in 1984 by the jailed dictator Georgios Papadopoulos, the National Political Union represented the most radically right-wing presence in Greek politics, attracting both junta supporters and self-described fascists. The party never performed well in elections, however. Although it gained a seat in the European Parliament in 1984, the party never managed to land a representative in the Greek parliament. Throughout four

legislative elections between 1986 and 1996, when the party dissolved, the National Political Union only surpassed 1 percent
of the vote one time, during legislative elections in 1989. In the
eighties, a handful of significant anti-fascist actions material-
ized but the parliamentary-focused politics of the traditional
left-wing—the Communist Party of Greece (KKE) and others
like it, for instance—often "overshadowed" the militancy advocated by anarchists and other militant anti-fascists.[10] December 6,
1984, proved an important date. Jean-Marie Le Pen, the French
far-right leader and Holocaust denier, appeared at a conference
hosted at the Hotel Caravel in downtown Athens. Feeling the
need to confront a public event hosting a well-known fascist,
militant anti-fascists adopted militant strategies that would eventually be synonymous with black bloc tactics. That night, they
lobbed Molotov cocktails at the hotel, torched cars, and smashed
up banks, car dealerships, and boutiques. The few surviving videos show a chaotic scene.[11] Shattered glass was strewn across the
sidewalks in front of shops. Flames swallowed automobiles. Blue
police lights flashed in the night.

ONE MORNING IN February 1988, Dimitris Psarras arrived at the
office of *Scholiastis*, where he and his colleagues found a curious
package. Then in his mid-thirties and with five years of journalism experience under his belt, Psarras wondered what it could
be. Psarras opened the package and found a trove of documents:
a rambling, poorly written political manifesto, a breakdown of
protocols, and a few issues of *Golden Dawn*. Reluctant to serve
as a mouthpiece for a small band of attention-hungry neo-Nazis,
Psarras and his colleagues penned a short article explaining to
Scholiastis's readers that such an organization did exist, but that

they would not reprint the contents of the package or the group's propaganda.

Unable to contain their anger, the new Nazis took to the pages of *Golden Dawn* to denounce Psarras and his colleagues as good-for-nothing "Bolsheviks." At the time, Psarras could not have known that these accusations—and far more harrowing ones, often coupled with threats—would come to define much of his professional life. That exchange, in which Psarras and his colleagues rebuked the young national socialist outfit, and the party responded with outrage, was the first in a series of similar exchanges that would stretch more than three decades. During that period, Psarras became the foremost reporter tracking Golden Dawn and eventually a key witness in the trial that threatened the very existence of the far-right group; meanwhile, Golden Dawn would turn into the leading far-right party in the country, unleashing a reign of terroristic violence on its opponents and one day securing the distinction of being the third largest political party in Greece's parliament.

The party advocated an implausible and irredentist greater Greece that included swathes of Albania and Turkey, as well as all of Cyprus.[12] Inside present-day Greece, the party argued, Turkish-speaking citizens of Greece and other minorities constituted legitimate targets for mass expulsions.[13] From its earliest days as a political organization, Golden Dawn demonized Muslims and Islam, trafficked in intense racism, preached anti-Semitism, and branded itself as an outlier, an anti-systemic force that would use the system toward the goal of smashing and replacing the existing liberal parliamentary system.[14]

Though many Greeks and international onlookers cringed at Golden Dawn's desires for a race war and the mass expulsion of ethnic and religious minorities, few suspected the group would ever become an official political party, let alone achieve much electoral success. Psarras and a handful of dogged reporters, some of whom survived the horrors of the junta, however, kept a close eye on the party's activities. While Golden Dawn had yet to swell into the country's largest far-right party, its growth merited attention.

In May 1990, an Athens-based newspaper set up an investigative unit dubbed Ios ("Virus"), a three-person team that featured Psarras, Dimitris Trimis, and Tasos Kostopoulos. Five months later, Psarras wrote his first article examining the Golden Dawn documents he'd held on to since 1988. Ios investigated a wide array of topics, but over time, the reporters began to grasp the significance of the resurgent neo-Nazi activity. "We saw as a team that we had a problem as a society, as a democracy," Psarras said. "Even when some members of Golden Dawn were taken to court or put in jail, nobody saw that there is an organization behind [their crimes]. Everybody saw this as an individual act, or a personal problem . . . The problem was that nobody saw that there was an organization, which, through these ideas, tried to use this violence against other people, that it was a real terror organization not like the far left. This was an international problem. Until the mid-1990s, everybody, even researchers, thought the problem of terrorism was only the left or the liberation movements [across the world]."

SAVE FOR A few disparate articles, such as the *Scholiatsis* editorial and the early investigate reports Ios produced, Golden Dawn garnered little attention until the early 1990s, when much of the mainstream Greek media learned of its existence through its vocal—and violent—participation in rallies against Greece's northern neighbor, which declared its independence from Yugoslavia as the Republic of Macedonia in 1991. That country's independence lurked behind Golden Dawn's decision to register as a political party in 1993.

Spared the bloodshed that gripped several of the former socialist republics in Yugoslavia, the Socialist Federal Republic of Macedonia quietly became the Republic of Macedonia on September 8, 1991. In Greece, where a northern region of the country also bears the name Macedonia, the dispute emerged, and it was not quiet. It was a volatile breeding ground for ultra-nationalists and neo-fascists. Greek leaders accused Macedonia of harboring irredentist territorial claims, while the Republic maintained that its culture, language, and heritage were always Macedonian. In response to Greek objections, which would later prove to be a barrier to Macedonia's ascension to both the European Union and the North Atlantic Treaty Organization (NATO), it amended its constitution to explicitly declare that it "has no territorial pretensions towards any neighboring state" on January 6, 1992.[15]

The move did little to stem the tide of ultra-nationalist fury in Greece, and the jingoist sentiment infested political currents across the spectrum. The following month, more than a million Greeks—around 10 percent of the population—took to the streets of Thessaloniki, the northern coastal city and the second most populous in the country. "Greece seems hypnotized once again by its past," the *New York Times* reported at the time, "not in study of its glorious achievements, but in an extraordinary burst of nationalism set off by the disintegration of Yugoslavia to the north. The object of this passion is the name Macedonia. Marching in the streets, putting stickers on cars and shop windows, and waving flags, Greeks are heatedly proclaiming that the name Macedonia is exclusively Greek, that it has been for three thousand years and must remain so."[16]

Giorgos Pitas, a twenty-three-year-old university student, organized as an activist with the Socialist Workers Party (SEK),
a small but enthusiastic Trotskyist sect, at the time of the 1992
Macedonia rallies.[17] Along with his fellow comrades, he used
the week leading up to the demonstrations in Athens, given the
official seal of approval from the New Democracy–dominated
government, to pass out fliers arguing for resistance against the
fervently nationalist political climate. With the government providing buses to transport high school students to the rally, Pitas
and others were shuttling from one school to the next and urging
students to boycott the protests. "We went to the schools arguing
that nobody should go to the rally," Pitas remembered. Even amid
an uptick in jingoist sentiment, Pitas explained, leftists sought to
capitalize on general anger toward the government in order to
build their own ranks. "I remember it was quite good—we sold
more than thirty papers one day. It was [nationalist] hysteria, but
people hated the government, so we could use that issue to get
more people on our side."

A day before the demonstrations, when Pitas and four others
arrived in Athens's city center to distribute yet more leaflets, a
group of around ten far-right assailants confronted them. The angry men surrounded and pounced on Pitas and his fellow activists.
By the end of the attack, Pitas spat blood through several cracked
teeth, sprawled out on the ground with a small red puddle forming
on the pavement beneath him. When he went to the hospital after
the attack, the doctors informed him that a gash he sustained on
his leg was infected. Pitas and his comrades later confirmed the
identity of one of his attackers, and years later he became aware of
the assailant's involvement in Golden Dawn. "I don't know if he
was Golden Dawn at the time," Pitas reflected. "It's possible that
he joined them later."

*

GOLDEN DAWN, THOUGH still far from becoming a name known the world over, spent the nineties attempting to muscle its way into electoral politics, toning down the overtly National Socialist rhetoric and attempting to tap into a comparably mainstream strand of nationalism and xenophobia. The most important relationship the group managed to secure, however, was an apparent understanding with MAT, Greece's riot police unit. With Golden Dawn members quietly becoming MAT's foot soldiers, anarchists and anti-fascists introduced a mantra that would go on to ring true throughout the ensuing decades: Wherever the Cop's Baton Does Not Reach, the Fascist's Knife Is at Work.

On December 10, 1992, a Golden Dawn squad made its way to the Athens University of Economics and Business—not far from Exarchia—and attacked a group of left-wing students who had occupied the campus to protest a new law introduced by Education Minister Giorgos Souflias.[18] A handful of riot police watched from a distance but did not intervene. After the brawl, the thugs from Golden Dawn headed to a long-standing anarchist squat named after Lela Karagianni, a Greek resistance leader who fought the Nazis during World War II. By the time the assault was over, the fascists had injured an elderly woman and two leftist students that had reportedly been passing by at the wrong moment. Golden Dawn later claimed responsibility for the violence, which it said targeted "anti-nationalist elements." The police arrested nine individuals, but all were subsequently released without charge or reprimand.

A year and a half later, on June 6, 1994, far-right attackers allegedly joined riot police as they yet again attacked anarchists occupying a university campus. The following April, Golden Dawn members ambushed and beat Panteion University rector Emilios

Metaxopoulos outside the school, while police officers stationed nearby watched on with folded arms.

Later that year, in November, riot police drove Golden Dawn members to the gates of the National Technical University (Athens Polytechnic) and dispatched them to launch a brutal assault on squatters that had taken over a small campus building. (The campus asylum law, introduced in 1982, forbade police officers from entering university campuses without special permission. The measure was put in place to prevent a repeat of the deadly junta raids on the Polytechnic in 1973.) Similar violent assaults at the hands of Golden Dawn—targeting squats and leftists, among others—continued throughout the 1990s.

IN THE NINETIES, Greece's radical far-right landscape was crowded. New groups were cropping up. Although the far right had yet to thoroughly infiltrate the mainstream political discourse, the Macedonia name dispute had altered the political DNA of post-junta Greece, reintroducing a strand of nationalism that had been condemned to the fringes since the junta crumbled. With the collapse of communism in the Soviet Union and its satellite states, immigration from neighboring Albania picked up dramatically in the early nineties, and the far right's earliest anti-immigrant obsessions emerged.[19]

In 1994, Makis Voridis founded the ultra-nationalist Hellenic Front, a party that trafficked in economic protectionism, anti-immigrant paranoia, anti-communism, and a general nativism that sought to smash the social democratic consensus. The party advocated reinstituting the death penalty and adopted a sinister motto: Red Card to Illegal Immigrants.[20]

Born in Athens in 1964, Voridis first entered the political

fray during his time as a student at Athens University.[21] There he founded and led the far-right campus group Student Alternative. Some students recall Voridis and his followers spray-painting swastikas on campus walls and threatening Jewish students and left-wing political opponents. During a police operation in Exarchia, the central Athens neighborhood with an anarchist and left-wing bent, Voridis and other far-right students went on the hunt for students and activists protesting police repression in 1985. The photos that later emerged showed him wearing a leather jacket, denim blue jeans, and black military-like boots—he was also carrying an ax.[22] While former dictator Georgios Papadopoulos was imprisoned, Voridis struck up a relationship with him and often made the trip to Korydallos Prison to visit.[23] Also in 1985, after Golden Dawn founder Nikolaos Michaloliakos quit the youth front for the pro-junta National Political Union, Voridis stepped in and took his spot, a position he held until 1990.

It was Voridis who reportedly brought Jean-Marie Le Pen to Greece for a visit in the mid-1990s, and he got the type of confrontation he had been searching for.[24]

THE HELLENIC FRONT never took off with Greek voters, though.[25] In 1998, Voridis garnered just over half a percentage point when he ran for mayor of Athens. During European Parliament elections in 1999, the party secured less than a fifth of a single percentage point. The Hellenic Front's failures were repeated during parliamentary elections in 2000, when it gained 0.18 percent of a vote, and in local elections in 2002, when only 1.4 percent of Greeks voted for the party. After another massive underperformance in the 2004 legislative elections, Hellenic Front merged with Popular Orthodox Rally (LAOS), the far-right party that had been formed four years earlier. Like the Hellenic Front and Golden Dawn, LAOS advocated banning immigration from outside of Europe and took a hard line on the Macedonia name dispute. LAOS party chief Giorgos Karatzaferis, a former bodybuilder, was known for his deep-seated anti-Semitism. "They say that to get ahead you have to be one of three things: a Jew, a homosexual, or a communist," Karatzaferis said of his party on his television channel, TeleCity.[26] "We are none of these . . . Vote for a parliament without Masons, without homosexuals, without those dependent on Zionism."

ON FEBRUARY 18, 1998, after half a decade of Golden Dawn organizing squads of young men, often with weapons, to attack their political opponents, the party made its debut in the Greek parliament. Golden Dawn was not in parliament that day as an elected party but as the subject of a debate. Following questions from a left-wing politician, Justice Minister Evangelos Yiannopoulos, a member of the center-left PASOK party, said of the neo-Nazi party: "I have commissioned the staff of my ministry to collect data . . . [Golden Dawn] . . . is fascism, it is a murderous act, a murderous ideology levied against the constitution."[27] Nonetheless, he stopped short of calling for a major crackdown, explaining that there was no need to "rush into taking extreme measures, as people may say that in Greece, people are persecuted for their ideas."

Yiannopoulos proposed that lawmakers come up with questions for a general discussion on the gradual growth of the neo-Nazi party. Yet, as Dimitris Psarras observed in his book *Golden Dawn on Trial*, the general discussion never came to fruition. In hindsight, many came to realize that putting off that discussion turned out to be a nearly deadly decision.

ON JUNE 16, 1998, one of the most shocking displays of fascist violence to date took place. Antonis Androutsopoulos, known to his comrades as Periandros, led the way, a gang of Golden Dawn members following behind him, toward the Evelpidon courthouse in central Athens. There, this far-right mob attacked a group of students who had gathered for a protest outside the courthouse. The attackers swarmed around Dimitris Kousouris, who would later become a respected history professor at the University of Vienna, and two of his friends.

Years later, Kousouris testified that Androutsopoulos ordered the assault, telling his followers: "Beat them up."[28] Although a police officer dressed in plain clothes reportedly witnessed the assault, he didn't intervene while the Golden Dawn group beat Kousouris and others with wooden poles. The assault was so brutal that Kousouris spent the next month in an intensive care unit. Androutsopoulos went on the run. It took seven years to find and arrest him. He eventually received a twelve-year sentence for his role in the violence.[29] Throughout the attacker's pretrial detention, Psarras later observed, Golden Dawn's publications never mentioned Androutsopoulos, and the party chief Michaloliakos never showed up at the courthouse.[30]

IT WOULDN'T TAKE long until someone else, once again, made good on the fascist promise of bloodshed. Starting on October 19, 1999, Pantelis Kazakos, a twenty-three-year-old security guard employed by the state news broadcaster ERT, went on a three-day killing spree, hunting for migrants and foreign nationals in central Athens.

That first night, he lurked around the city center in pursuit of the victims. In Metaxourgeio, he found a group of three Iraqi Kurds. One died, and the other two were badly injured and hospitalized. They had only been in the country for a month and a half.

Starting around 9:00 p.m. the following evening, Kazakos again walked through the city, apparently following a route he believed would bring him into contact with as many refugees and migrants as possible. News reports later said that he shot anyone he found on the path with "tremendous precision and calm."[31] He continued opening fire on foreign nationals around the city until the following evening. A few hours before he was arrested, he shot dead Udesiani George, a young Georgian. By the time it was said and done, he had killed two and injured another seven. On the last night of the killings, far-right politician Makis Voridis's Hellenic Front reportedly scattered fliers promoting anti-immigrant propaganda around downtown Athens. That same day, Golden Dawn's newspaper had published a frontpage story titled "The Death of a Nation," in which the author railed against the "overpopulation" of migrants in Greece.[32]

When the police finally caught and arrested Kazakos, he admitted that he had executed the shooting spree. However, he insisted that his motivations were patriotic, his actions a duty to the nation. Later, while on trial, the evidence emerged: The killer was a Golden Dawn supporter. One of Kazakos's former teachers testified that the killer had long harbored far-right views. Former classmates said he had been a Golden Dawn supporter. Photos that later emerged showed Kazakos holding a Golden Dawn banner. His father, a police officer who denied that his son supported the neo-Nazi party, later made a startling admission. His son had told him that he carried out the deadly shooting spree because he believed "foreigners" had been burning the Greek flag. Before his military service, Kazakos had struggled with mental illness and drug abuse and had received treatment at a detoxification program, according to his father. Later, he would say that he left his home "with the pistol, determined to kill any foreigner I saw on the street."[33]

The court convicted him on two counts of intentional homicide and seven counts of attempted homicide and sentenced him to two life terms and twenty-five years in prison.[34] (In Greece, the maximum time one could spend in prison, even when dealt a life sentence, was twenty-five years at the time.) Even on trial, Kazakos declined to express any remorse. Later, he reportedly asked his father whether the world outside considered him a "hero or a murderer." His father replied, "They call you a murderer, my child."

WHEN WAR BROKE out in Yugoslavia, Greeks from across the political spectrum—from the anti-imperialist left to the extremist far right—harbored warm feelings for Serb forces.[35] For radical leftists, support for Serb groups stemmed from opposition to Western intervention in the region, while right-wing conservatives and hardline far-rightists resented an attack on fellow Orthodox Christians gripped in battle against the Muslim population in Bosnia. As Belgrade grew increasingly isolated, the Greek government maintained and fostered its relations with Slobodan Milošević and hardline Serb nationalist elements. In turn, Milošević backed Greece's position on Macedonian independence. He visited his Greek counterparts in 1992. Channeling the most expansionist and far-right figures in Greece, he declared: "There is only one solution—common borders with Serbia!"[36]

In June 1993, Archbishop Seraphim of Athens warmly received the genocidal Bosnian Serb leader Radovan Karadžić in the

Greek capital.[37] During that visit, Karadžić met with Greek Prime Minister Konstantinos Mitsotakis, who then led New Democracy, and Andreas Papandreou, then leader of the socialist PASOK party. In the Piraeus stadium, Karadžić addressed a pulsing crowd of thousands to their applause and cries of support. "Everybody is telling us to lay down our arms because we are alone," he declared, flanked by prominent Greek politicians and religious leaders. "We say no, we are not alone. We have with us God and the Greeks!"

Archbishop Seraphim underscored the Greek Orthodox Church's backing for the Serb-led war on Bosnians. "The Greek Church," he later said, "cannot but support together with the Greek people the struggle of the Serbs."[3839]

Meanwhile, Greek volunteers touched down in Bosnia that same year. Two years after socialism collapsed in Yugoslavia, the Serb-dominated Yugoslav army fought tooth and nail to preserve Belgrade's lordship over the restive regions that once comprised the socialist federation. By the time the Greeks arrived, Bosnia had been a blood-saturated battlefield for more than a year, and Serb forces had besieged Sarajevo. Bosnian Serbs had failed to break through the last lines of Bosnian Muslim forces, but clashes between the latter and once-allied Croats were also spiking. Meanwhile, rival Muslim factions battled it out in northern Bosnia, Bosnian Serbs fought to fend off advances on Serb villages, and Croats joined Serbs in their fight against Muslims in central Bosnia. With bloody rampages spiraling out of control, the UN created safe havens for Bosnian Muslim civilians in Sarajevo, Gorazde, and Srebrenica.

In March 1995, Bosnian Serb general Ratko Mladić, seeking to centralize foreign volunteers under the Serb Republic's oversight, requested the formation of the Greek Volunteer Guard (GVG). The Greeks came from varied political backgrounds, but their common motivations included solidarity with a fellow

Orthodox Christian population and a shared commitment to ultra-right-wing nationalism. The GVG boasted of at least a hundred participants, many of whom were later found to have links to Golden Dawn and other neo-fascist and far-right groups.

On July 11, 1995, tens of thousands of Muslim civilians amassed in Potočari, a village in the municipality of Srebrenica, which was then a besieged enclave, designated a safe haven for civilians. The sun blazed, food and water ran scarce, and the displaced masses hoped the Dutch contingent at the United Nations Protection Force compound could protect them from enduring yet more of the bloodshed they had already fled. Outside the compound, Serb forces tortured and slaughtered Bosnian Muslim men, raping women, setting fire to homes, engaging in summary executions, and stuffing lifeless bodies into mass graves while the UN forces watched on from afar.

At the time, the GVG was stationed in Vlasenica, an hour's drive from Srebrenica. Subsequent reports vary, but the consensus maintains that ten to twelve Greek fighters were present during the genocide in Srebrenica. In a photo taken on July 11, GVG Antonis Mitkos stood next to Zvonko Bajagic and Mladić, while an orgy of mass murder unraveled in the supposedly protected enclave. In communications intercepted from the Bosnian Serb army, Mladić ordered troops to raise a Greek flag to "the brave Greeks fighting on our side." By the time the bullets stopped flying, the killers had claimed the lives of at least 8,737 Bosnian Muslims, cramming their corpses into hastily dug pits.

Back in Athens, *Golden Dawn* published several photos of GVG fighters on the Bosnian battlefield. One caption read: "Greek patriots fight at the Bosnian front on the Serbs' side. Among them, members of Golden Dawn."[40]

Psarras and his Ios colleagues fought a lonely campaign trying to push back against the Greek media's overt sympathy for Serb forces, exposing the role of neo-fascists in the buoying Serb nationalists. "We were among the few journalists in Greece who tried to say that even the Serbs weren't so innocent," he told me. "It was very difficult in Greece at that time . . . The targets of Golden Dawn are mostly people who are already targeted or delegitimized."

"At that time, everybody in Greece thought the Serbs were our brothers, that we must help them, that we have to make an alliance with them," he added. "From the left to the far right, it was a national issue. That's why I say that Golden Dawn started out targeting only those who were already demonized."

"Even the politicians and journalists that were not extremists [backed Serb forces] . . . so it was very difficult to see Golden Dawn's involvement [in the war] as participation in a war crime like Srebrenica. But they were there."

IN 1994, GOLDEN Dawn worked diligently to win over Greek voters, albeit with little success, by trying to scrub the overtly national socialist rhetoric that imbued its founding ideology. In the 1994 European Parliament elections, the far-right party first tested the electoral waters, but the results were an embarrassment: Only 0.11 percent of voters cast their ballot for Golden Dawn. "They were a very small organization at the time," Psarras recalled, "only doing politics through their newspaper, and even their gatherings were inside homes and private."

Small though they were, Golden Dawn busied itself building international links throughout the 1990s. The party focused on importing white supremacist literature to help shape its own vision for Greece. Golden Dawn translated several influential German Nazi books and American white supremacist texts, including

The Turner Diaries, an infamously racist and dystopian novel that salivates over the prospect of an apocalyptic race war gripping North America. Golden Dawn also translated to Greek the texts of George Lincoln Rockwell, the founder of the American Nazi Party and leader of the World Union of National Socialists. Using the pseudonym N. Exarchos, Michaloliakos is believed to have authored *Strike Team Lance*, the crude, Greek-language mimicry of *The Turner Diaries*.[41] That novel depicts Greece enveloped in violence between nationalists and their opponents.

In 1994, Golden Dawn members traveled to Moscow to attend a meeting of far-right parties organized by Vladimir Zhirinovsky. According to Psarras, the links between Zhirinovsky and Greek neo-fascists were first forged in the trenches of Bosnia.[42] Dubbed the Patriotic International, that conference afforded Golden Dawn "the opportunity to gain an international reputation as the representative of Greek right-wing extremism."[43]

On October 24 and 25, 1998, William Luther Pierce III, a longtime neo-Nazi and author of the infamously racist and apocalyptic *Turner Diaries*, attended an international conference of ultra-nationalist groups in Thessaloniki, Greece's second-largest city. Hosted by Golden Dawn, the conference's other attendees included "representatives of groups in Greece, Portugal, Romania, Flanders [Belgium], Denmark, Netherlands, Germany, South Africa, and Austria," Pierce later wrote.[44]

Ostensibly fearing retribution from anti-fascists, the conference room was guarded by security with dogs and labeled as a gathering of tourism agencies. Several days passed before the Greek media learned of the true nature of the conference, where some 150 people from ten countries gathered "amidst swastikas and sieg-heil salutes" in secrecy "to hear a keynote speech from Dr. William Pierce."[45]

Golden Dawn's newspaper boasted of Pierce's presence at the

conference. Pierce, who was sixty-five at the time, represented nearly four decades of far-right, ultra-nationalist, white supremacist, and often violent politics. In 1974, he made history when he founded the National Alliance, which "was for decades the most dangerous and best organized neo-Nazi formation in America."[46]

For his part, Pierce envisioned an international far-right struggle in the future. "Cooperation across national borders will become increasingly important for progress—and perhaps even for survival—in the future," the aging white supremacist predicted, adding that he obtained a slew of contacts during the two-day meetup.[47] "Much of the ethnic consciousness in Greece is based on culture: language, traditions, etc. Nevertheless, Golden Dawn is an organization with a clear, genetically based racial policy." Despite a few observations that unsettled Pierce, such as his initial inability to distinguish between some Greeks and "gypsies," the conference appeared to have been one of many steps that laid the foundations for Golden Dawn's eventual ascendancy to fame on the international white supremacist scene. Furthermore, it contributed to Golden Dawn's lasting infatuation with the most radical and violent elements of North America's far-right fringes.

During the September 1996 legislative elections, Golden Dawn again tried its luck among the electorate. But the party failed to secure 3 percent of the overall vote, the minimum required for entry into the parliament. With its support base largely confined to hardline ideologues in isolated pockets, the party received around 4,500 votes nationwide—less than one-tenth of a percentage point. That vote saw the PASOK reelected, and the right-wing New Democracy party retained its spot as the main opposition party, which it had occupied since the previous elections three years earlier.

During that period, one event proved immensely helpful for Golden Dawn's efforts to shoehorn its fascist message into the political conversation. On December 29, 1995, Ankara, Turkey's capital, announced that Imia—a pair of uninhabited islets in the Aegean Sea—belonged to Turkey after a Turkish cargo ship crashed into the stone-studded shores a few days earlier. On January 9, 1996, Athens replied by insisting that Greece retained sovereignty over the disputed rocks. Two weeks later, the Greek mayor of Kalymnos, an island in the southeastern Aegean, and a priest planted a Greek flag on Imia. Tit-for-tat flag-raising operations followed, with Turkish journalists flying to the islet and planting their country's flag, and Greek forces removing and replacing the Turkish flag with a Greek one.[48] On January 31, a Greek helicopter hovered above Imia and reported that Turkish forces had occupied the islet. The helicopter crashed, and its three-person crew died. Both countries blamed the crash on dangerous weather, but Golden Dawn and similar groups lashed out, claiming that Turkish forces had gunned down the aircraft. The ultra-nationalist and far-right groups dismissed the bad weather claim as an excuse deployed to prevent the two countries from barreling into war. From that year on, Golden Dawn organized an annual commemoration for the incident.[49]

CHAPTER THREE

"I'M AFRAID THEY COULD KILL ME": RACIST VIOLENCE AGAINST MIGRANT WORKERS

One day in April 2017, Ashfak Mahmoud spotted four Greek men loitering on the edge of the field as he worked in Goritsa. The young men, he noticed, were whispering to each other, and peering his way from where they stood by a rusty chain-link fence. He couldn't be sure, but he thought he recognized them from town; perhaps he had seen them hanging out in the central square. The forty-year-old migrant worker had lived in Greece for several years; like tens of thousands of Pakistanis in the country, he had left his home and relocated to Europe to find work and help support his family back in Pakistan.

Since the 1970s, Pakistanis have migrated to Greece to work. In the early years, they came in relatively smaller waves, many finding employment in the shipping industry.[1] In the 1990s, the number of people trading Pakistan for Greece increased, and more found work in the construction, agricultural, and retail industries, among others. According to a 2011 census, more than thirty-four thousand Pakistanis resided in the country, although the true number was likely higher—many entered the country irregularly or stayed undocumented. Between 2009 and 2014, Hellenic Police data shows, more than forty-two thousand Pakistanis were apprehended, and more than a quarter of those were deported.[2]

Watching the men watching him, Mahmoud grew nervous. Could they be up to no good? He knew he stood little chance of defending himself; he had worked in agriculture for most of his life, and he was strong for his size, but he was wiry, his arms were thin, and they outnumbered him four-to-one. He tried to ignore them, focusing instead on his work: swing the dull knife and slice a bulb of lettuce from the damp earth; toss it in the burlap sack; repeat.

Goritsa sits on the outskirts of Aspropyrgos, a suburb located eleven miles from Athens. The area was home to many Pakistani workers, but it also hosted a large population of Pontics, ethnic Greeks who immigrated to the country from the former Soviet Union. The community was home to a sizable number of Roma, an ethnic group spread out across much of the map of Europe.[3] With a diverse population, tensions between neighbors were nothing new. Less than two decades earlier, Greek authorities had forcibly evicted many Roma from their homes, razing almost every structure in an Aspropyrgos settlement, leaving standing only a handful of ramshackle shacks resided in by elderly or ill Roma residents.[4] Almost a decade into Greece's economic crisis, an emaciated economy had taken its toll on the already poverty-stricken community. Where organized crime had not filled the void left behind by the crisis, resurgent nationalism had: An estimated one-third of voters supported the neo-fascist Golden Dawn party.[5]

Mahmoud witnessed the violence firsthand. He had never

been attacked, but several of his colleagues had, and the violence soared in the months leading up to that day. Between April 2016 and April 2017, the Pakistani Community in Greece association recorded between seventy and eighty attacks in Aspropyrgos and the surrounding villages.[6] With the violence rippling throughout the area, tensions climbed in Goritsa, and Mahmoud found himself on edge. Since 2016, he had stood on the frontlines of anti-racism protests in the area. Each time a colleague ended up bloodied and beaten, he went to the hospital to offer his support, something Greek government officials rarely did. He urged victims to file police reports and accompanied them to the police station. Had doing all that landed him in the crosshairs of the four men watching him? "There had been many racist attacks, and they [assailants] always saw me," he said. "I was going to the hospital with victims and to the police station when they filed police reports. How could I not help when people were being beaten in front of my eyes?"

He wanted to make sure the young men weren't planning anything, but he hesitated. If they weren't there to harm him, would he offend them by asking? If they were there with dubious intentions, would asking only provoke them? Then he looked up from his work just as one of the men snapped a photo of him with his iPhone. Enough, he thought, and worked up the courage to confront them. No, no, the men said. They had no qualms with foreigners. "They said that they like Pakistanis, that they are together with the Pakistanis, that they eat with Pakistanis often, and that they had no problem with me," Mahmoud later told me.

Over the next few days, he couldn't shake the feeling that something worse was lying in wait. But why had they stood there for so long, watching him and whispering? Why had they photographed him? Wasn't it suspicious? "I was one hundred percent sure that they were planning an attack," he said.

＊

ON OCTOBER 7, 2017, a cool but humid afternoon, the sun washed the fields a pale yellow. Ashfak Mahmoud had almost forgotten about the men standing at the edge of the field one day about six months earlier, six months through which he kept his head down, worked hard, and sent as much money as possible back to his family in Pakistan. He had probably misread the situation, he thought. The boys were probably telling the truth. Maybe they'd just been curious or bored. After all, half a year had passed, and no one had shown up looking for him.

Nearby, another Pakistani worker sliced lettuce from the ground. His name was Waqas Hussein, and Mahmoud counted him among his friends. They worked for the same boss, and they were often paired up in the fields. Mahmoud chopped his way up and down the field in rows. Then he looked up and saw them: five men, all masked and wearing black, standing on the edge of the field. Suddenly they leapt into action, barreling toward him. The attackers screamed through their masks. One threw a hail of wild punches, missing Mahmoud's face but landing on his chest. Something metallic appeared in one man's hand, the sunlight glinting off it. A knife. "One by one, we will cut your throats," one shouted.

"We will burn you alive in your houses," another screamed. "Don't think we'll leave you [alone]."

Hussein and Mahmoud bolted, but rain earlier in the week had left the ground wet. Mahmoud slipped and the soggy earth beneath him rose and slammed into his body. He rolled to his back. Five masked faces hunched over him. A fist slammed into his cheek. Brass knuckles hammered his forehead. A boot crashed into his side. A knife tore into his face, just beneath his right eye. A stone came down on his head. Blood flowed from his wounds,

spilled out everywhere, and soaked the soil beneath him. His vision went cloudy. "If you go to the police, you can be sure it will
be worse next time," a voice warned, and then as quickly as they
came, the men disappeared.

IN FEBRUARY 2018, I met Ashfak Mahmoud at the Pakistani
Community in Greece's office in Athens. He'd gone to the hospital after the attack, but the bolt-shaped scar where the knife had
gashed his face would likely stay there next to his eye for the rest
of his life. It still hurt him sometimes, he told me, a deep ache in
his right eye socket that caused headaches.

The attack captured the attention of the nation. Greek leftists
from the United Movement Against Racism and the Threat of
Fascism (KEERFA) rallied in Goritsa and Athens. The Pakistani
Community in Greece helped him file a police report and put out
a statement denouncing the violence in Goritsa and Aspropyrgos.
News crews showed up in town, interviewing him and several
others who had survived the surge in violence. Greek Migration
Minister Ioannis Mouzalas, a Syriza member, visited Mahmoud
in his shack, seizing the occasion for a photo opportunity. Posing
for the cameras, he put his arm around Mahmoud's shoulder and
smiled—and then he was gone. Mahmoud was flattered by the
attention, and surprised that a politician would visit him, but the
gesture rang hollow for most of the migrant workers in Goritsa.
For more than a year, they had filed police reports, organized
demonstrations, and called on the police to crack down on the
far-right youngsters besieging them.

Police later tracked down and arrested three teenagers, two
of whom were age seventeen and one eighteen, in connection
with the assault. All three were known to authorities: Earlier that

summer, the boys had participated in a spate of violence, including attacking police officers and hurling Molotov cocktails at participants of an anti-racist protest.[7] A police spokesperson described them as "supporters of the extreme right," but conceded that "no evidence officially link[ed] them to the Golden Dawn party or any other extreme right group." Three others were wanted for questioning.[8] Although the police divulged the occasional update to Greek reporters following the case, half a year passed, and no one had bothered to provide Mahmoud with any additional details about the progress of the case.

Throughout most of the surge in violence in Aspropyrgos and its surrounding villages, Golden Dawn remained silent. After the attack on Mahmoud and Hussein, however, the party issued a press release denying any involvement. In the statement, the far-right party dismissed the allegations as "slanderous attacks," adding: "We condemn violence—in total and not casually—and we continue our legitimate and righteous struggle for the liberation of Greece."

Golden Dawn chief Nikolaos Michaloliakos went so far as to meet with Khalid Usman Qaiser, Pakistan's ambassador to Greece. The far-right firebrand assured the Pakistani diplomat that his party was not responsible for the incident. But after overseeing a party that carried out decades of violence against refugees, migrants, and political opponents, there was little Michaloliakos could say to convince anyone.

The president of the Pakistani Community in Greece, Javed Aslam, came to Greece in the mid-nineties. He sat across the desk as Mahmoud recounted the violence in Goritsa. Every now and then, he interjected. For the better part of the last decade, he told me, he documented anti-migrant violence around the country. Whenever someone attacked a refugee or migrant around Athens, or in the agricultural fields where so many Pakistanis worked,

Aslam rushed to the scene of the crime. He helped the workers file police reports and organized protests.

During the months leading up to Mahmoud's attack, Javed Aslam fielded dozens of frantic phone calls, almost one per day, he estimated. In his eyes, it couldn't be clearer: Golden Dawn had carried out the attacks. "They want to kick Pakistanis out of this area," he told me, matter-of-factly.[9]

IN NIKAIA, A suburb of Piraeus, tensions were no lighter. On January 4, 2018, at around 11:00 p.m., Nawaz Muhammad heard something crash through his window. He rushed to his bedroom and found a stone on the floor, glass shards scattered around it. The twenty-seven-year-old walked to the shattered window and looked out. A group of men huddled in a cone of light beneath the streetlamp outside. They wore black masks, black shirts. An orange flew toward Muhammad. A bottle followed. Several stones bounced off the side of his apartment bloc. Slabs of concrete pounded the building. Another bottle came through the window, bursting into small fragments of glass. "Leave our country, you dirty Pakistanis," one shouted. "We won't let you stay here."

Nawaz Muhammad, who had come to Greece to help support his family back home, had expected this moment. During a two-week period, straddling Christmas 2017 and entering the New Year, masked men had attacked more than thirty homes in Nikaia and nearby Renti.

I sat in his living room a few days later. The number of attacks mounted by the day, he told me. Between November 2017 and January 2018, gangs of Greek men had shown up outside his apartment at least twenty times. "They have been trying to provoke us to come down," he said, "but we won't make that mistake."

Down the street, I stepped into a store and found Javed Nasser standing behind the register. He was forty-five, and he'd lived legally in Greece for years, he told me. Throughout the previous three months, youngsters had attacked his shop more than a dozen times, he guessed. A few had thrown tomatoes and sprayed ketchup on the mosque down the road. "I've called the police more than fifteen times, but they've only come once to take a report," he said.

A few days later, I met Tina Stavrinaki at her office in Athens. She worked for the Racist Violence Recording Network (RVRN), a nonprofit watchdog that monitored hate crimes in Greece. Throughout 2017, the Network documented 102 hate crimes, a spike that marked a 7 percent increase when compared to the previous year. By the end of 2018, that number would grow by another 14 percent. "It reminds us of so many [surges in violence] from before," she told me.[10] Hate crimes had slumped for a while after the murder of the rapper Pavlos Fyssas, but now they were back on the rise. "In general, we do not think we are back in a situation like 2013, but what we also have is this feeling that we are right before the big wave of violence by Golden Dawn."[11]

WHEN WE MET in early 2018, I asked Ashfak Mahmoud if Pakistani workers in Goritsa would be willing to speak to me, and he suggested that I visit the village the following Sunday, a day when the bosses usually passed time with their families and didn't watch them closely in the fields.

That Sunday, I took a taxi from Athens to Goritsa, a forty-five-minute trip. All around you while pulling into town, you could see evidence of the divide that had driven the spate of far-right violence. Someone had spray-painted a large black X over the graffiti on an abandoned concrete shack: Anti-Fascist Zone. Political mantras blanketed the walls. Twisting down the narrow roads leading to the fields, I saw where Golden Dawn supporters had once passed: tagged on a deserted factory were anti-migrant epithets, the party's signature crosshairs, and a Celtic cross; next to them, Golden Dawn—Aspropyrgos.

I found Mahmoud in the field. Errant rays of sunlight hacked through holes in the late winter clouds, gray and pregnant with rain. Snow crowned the mountaintops in the distance, knots of trees crawling up their faces. Mahmoud wore a billowy navy-blue raincoat and a black beanie. He slipped off his work gloves and turned his palms to show their calluses. He told me work in those fields wasn't easy, but that he didn't mind it much. He walked along the field, pointed out the spot where he first spotted his attackers. "That's where they were," he said.

We reached the border of that field and continued onto the next. Mahmoud paused and motioned to the frame of a shack where two Pakistani workers used to live. The shack had been perfectly square, made of concrete blocks. Now it was deserted, missing its rooftop, its walls charred and smeared with soot. "They left after their home was burned down," he said. He shook his head, a stern look spread across his face.

The violence had thinned over time, but many of the Pakistanis in Goritsa gathered their belongings and moved to safer areas. Mahmoud couldn't blame them, but he refused to leave. If he took off, wouldn't it send the wrong message? "If I go, hundreds of others could see it and leave also," he told me. And what would that tell the men who had tried to kill him that day? "In the end, they would've succeeded."

Mahmoud was adamant, almost defiant, but he still racked himself with worry. He now avoided crowds of young men in town. He tried not to show his face in public too often. His face had appeared on television, he'd spoken out, and he'd filed a police report—the very thing his attackers warned him not to do. For the most part, he said, he thought he'd done the right thing by taking a public stand against the violence, but sometimes, he wondered if he'd made too much noise, drawn too much attention. Could there still be a target on his back? "It's a big problem," he said. "Until now, I am afraid they could kill me."[12]

DOWN THE ROAD from the field where Ashfak Mahmoud worked, I found Latif Abdul Butt gathering garbage outside his home. He was forty-eight years old but looked much older. Manual labor had left his face slackened and exhausted. He came to Greece a decade earlier, and, like Mahmoud, lived in a shack on the outskirts of town: jerry-built and wobbly, he'd slapped together the building with cinder blocks, rotting sheets of wood, and mangled strands of scrap metal. I wondered how it didn't collapse on him.

By January 2017, Latif Abdul Butt was worried. It seemed like every day that he heard rumors of a new attack in town. A few field workers had warned him to keep an eye out for young men prowling Goritsa. If he saw someone in a mask, or dressed in all black, he should run for safety, they'd said. One day that month, he was walking not far from his place. He stopped in his tracks: A group of Greek men stood over a Pakistani, splayed out on his back in the field. Paralyzed, he watched as the blows thudded off the man. Then, one of the attackers looked up at him and shouted. He couldn't make out what the man said, but he knew it was a threat. He sprinted away, and when he reached home, he considered himself lucky for escaping without catching a beating. A close call, he thought.

One night two weeks later, Butt lay in bed blinking at the ramshackle rooftop above him. He drifted off for a while—he doesn't know how long—and then woke to the smell of smoke. He jumped to his feet, swung the door open, and rushed outside. From the flimsy roof of his shack, plumes of gray smoke drifted upward, twirling in the night sky. A noise came from the field nearby. His eyes darted in the direction of the sound. He saw several men, all wearing masks, sprinting off through the field. He filled buckets with water, extinguished the blaze, and got to work repairing his shack. Things had changed in Goritsa, and he knew he was no longer safe there.

A FEW MONTHS passed, and on a breezy April evening, Abdul Latif Butt awoke to the sound of his dogs barking. He stepped outside, but there was nothing out in his yard. He looked for the dogs to see what the commotion was about. As he turned to go back inside, someone struck him from behind, a powerful blow in the back of his skull. He rolled over and above him were several men, their faces masked. Brass knuckles slammed his face and torso. "Go back to your country, asshole," he heard. His vision grew blurrier with each punch, and then darkness all around him.

Later that night, Butt blinked into focus the hospital surrounding him. He regained consciousness, and his boss appeared at his bedside. After he checked out of the hospital, Butt and his boss drove to the police station. There the officers told him they couldn't do much beyond filing a police report. The men were masked, and he wouldn't be able to identify them in a lineup. An officer asked him for his residency documents, something he didn't possess, and then placed him in a holding cell for three days.

We sat in front of his shack as he recounted the attack, and Abdul Latif Butt still spoke with a stutter, a problem he said started after the beating. "I feel dizzy and sick sometimes, and I have trouble focusing," he told me. "When I can't work, I don't get paid, but my boss brings me some potatoes and onions. So, I can at least eat something."

His two guard dogs mulled around in the yard. He pointed at them and shook his head. He'd had five dogs, he said, but someone threw poisoned meat into his yard a few days earlier. The other three died. Maybe that meant someone wanted to attack him again, he suspected. "I've been here for ten years, and I've never hurt anyone," he said. His voice quivered. "All I do is collecting metal and cartons. They don't have any reason to do this; they're just assholes."

CHAPTER FOUR

"DISAPPEAR": GOLDEN DAWN'S RISE

I t was hard to say when and where exactly Yonous Muhammadi's journey to Greece started. Was it one day some two decades before I first met him in Athens, when, after a month in a decrepit and overcrowded cell, he followed other fellow prisoners out of a Taliban jail, climbing through the window and making a run for it? Was it when he first left behind the Afghan refugee camps in Iran and Pakistan, places he had spent years living in exile? Was it further back still, when he dropped out of medical school and fled the Taliban's advance in Afghanistan the first time?

By the time he set off for Greece, he was twenty-seven. He thought he'd left the worst of it behind him: He had survived war and exile, had been incarcerated and had crossed towering mountains, had sneaked across heavily fortified borders. Dreaming of security for his family, hoping for the freedom to continue his human rights work, and searching for the stability the war denied Afghans, Muhammadi arrived in Athens in September 2001.

The migrant-hunting gang he encountered on his third day in Athens, however, had their own designs: a Greece without non-Greeks. He camped in Pedion tou Areos, one of the capital's largest municipal parks, along with dozens of fellow refugees and migrants. They slept outside, often under the rain. Designed in 1936 and spilling across more than sixty acres in the city center, Pedion tou Areos consists of concrete walking paths coiling throughout the park, dirt paths slicing through the clots of wooded areas, basketball courts, and a playground. Later, thanks to the economic crisis that ravaged Greece and the 2015 refugee influx, the park morphed into a far grimmer setting: Child prostitution, drug peddling, homelessness, begging, and unaccompanied refugee children.[1]

At the time of Muhammadi's arrival, the park served as *de facto* meeting ground for asylum seekers and displaced people from the Middle East, South Asia, and Africa—and it presented other dangers. The people who congregated in the park arrived in Greece looking for a safe space after fleeing war and economic devastation. Many tore through their life savings to make the journey, carrying only the clothes on their backs and travel-worn knapsacks, often soaked with sea water and then dried by the sun. Three days after he reached the capital, Muhammadi sat in the park and chatted with other Afghans. When Muhammadi looked up, he spotted a band of men, their gaits ready for confrontation, hurtling in their direction. Police officers lingered near the young Greek men, who carried sticks and shouted in a language the refugees did not speak or understand.

The other refugees bolted, scattering through the trees, but Muhammadi was safe. He had his documents. He would explain that he'd fled Afghanistan, had been imprisoned by the Taliban. He raised his asylum application papers, cleared his throat.

He was face-to-face with the first man who reached him. The man snatched the papers from Muhammadi's hand and ripped them up. He tossed the papers to the damp earth, and then struck Muhammadi with a stick. "I'm a doctor," Muhammadi protested, although he'd fled the country for the first time before graduating. "And I have my documents also. Because of the documents, the Taliban didn't kill me."

But it was no use. The sticks kept belting him until he tore away from the mob. As he escaped, though, he caught a glimpse of one man's face. Nearly a decade later, that same face would pop up time and again—during anti-refugee assaults and on television news programs. The face belonged to a man who would go on to rail against migration, to quote *The Elders of the Protocols of Zion* in the parliament, to address throngs of torch-wielding Greeks demanding a migrant-free country. It was the face, Muhammadi felt certain, of eventual Golden Dawn spokesperson Ilias Kasidiaris.

BORN IN NOVEMBER 1980 in Piraeus, the port city adjacent to Athens, Kasidiaris first joined the Golden Dawn youth movement and later climbed the party's internal ranks.[2] Twenty-one years old at the time Yonous Muhammadi says he assaulted him, Kasidiaris went on to weather accusations of acting as a getaway driver during another attack against a university student in 2007. During that attack, Kasidiaris allegedly shuttled away five people who stabbed a student outside a residence hall and stole his identification card.[3] Kasidiaris denied the claims, and he was later found not guilty of the charges due to a lack of evidence. He earned a reputation as one of the party's most violence-prone public figures.

He authored a book titled *Sector X*, named after a group of war-time Greek Nazi collaborators who hunted down and executed partisans from the anti-fascist resistance.[4] Over time, his love for tango dancing, sun tanning, and culinary arts—he received a degree in agriculture with a special emphasis in food chemistry—turned him into an absurd news spectacle. But his naked racism and tendency to let his fury boil over into physical violence were also unquestionable and well-documented.

Some in the press dubiously dubbed him Greece's far-right "playboy." Kasidiaris became the source of thinly veiled journalistic fanfare and incessant controversy. In 2012, while partaking in a panel discussion on the ANT1 news program, the neo-Nazi "playboy" assaulted a female politician aligned with the Greek Communist Party. During the seven-person panel, the participants debated immigrant labor and Greek unemployment. Typical of his style, Kasidiaris escalated the discussion to a fiery argument. He screamed at his antagonists, accused them of national betrayal. Rena Dourou, a politician with the left-wing Syriza party, interjected and said Golden Dawn sought to "take the country back five hundred years."

"You circus act," Kasidiaris yelled. He jumped to his feet, snatched a glass of water, and flung its contents in Dourou's direction. Communist parliamentarian Liana Kanelli protested, calling Kasidiaris a "fascist." She stood and tossed a wad of papers at him. He lunged forward and shoved her. "No, no, no," talk show host Giorgos Papadakis screamed. Undeterred, Kasidiaris clobbered the side of Kanelli's head three times, using both of his open-palmed hands.[5] The television crew apprehended him and locked him in a room, but he busted the door and vanished from the studio.

In Athens, prosecutors ordered his arrest, but Kasidiaris locked himself in Golden Dawn's headquarters, hoping to wait out the warrant. Greek law demands that such warrants are served within forty-eight hours, and police couldn't track him down before it expired. "I did what millions of Greeks would have done—when you get hit in the face you have to defend yourself," he claimed. Kanelli never struck his face, however. She pressed charges, but a court later acquitted Kasidiaris.

Voters didn't recoil from his brazen violence against a female lawmaker, and support for Kasidiaris and Golden Dawn spiked in the proceeding days. A pro-Kasidiaris Facebook page gained more than six thousand followers.[6] A few weeks later, when Greece took the ballot box for the second time that year, voters catapulted Kasidiaris into the parliament yet again.

DURING THE EARLY 2000s, Muhammadi witnessed Golden Dawn in the streets several times, but nearly a decade would pass before they again targeted him. Throughout these years, Golden Dawn directed its violence mostly—though not exclusively—at left-wing political opponents. In the 2000s, however, the neo-Nazi party began to target migrants and refugees more and more. The party also expanded its strategies to penetrate youth culture, replicating tactics deployed by European and North American white nationalists and neo-Nazi skinheads. In the late 1990s, the party had founded the Youth Front and launched its magazine, *Counterattack*. In 1999, Blood and Honor Hellas, a local adaption of the international Blood and Honor white power music scene, was formed. Bands like Meandros and Pogrom performed and recorded songs that railed against migrants, Jews, anarchists, and leftists.[7]

Implementing a program that fits into a broader European context, Golden Dawn also inaugurated the Azure Army, a squad of soccer hooligans headed by longtime party member Ilias Panagiotaros.[8] In 2004, after Greece miraculously won the UEFA European Championships, the Azure Army "incited the first pogrom against foreigners in modern Greek history in Athens," according to academics Sofia Tipaldou and Katrin Uba. The hooligans mobbed migrants in Omonoia Square in downtown Athens—and the Greek police later said no one was arrested because the security cameras in the area had not been running that evening, a claim that investigative reporters dubbed dubious, given that it took place only two months before Athens hosted the Olympics.[9] That same year, as authorities continued their long manhunt for Periandros, a news report claimed that police had fostered an intimate relationship with Golden Dawn, even supplying the fascists with sticks and clubs and claiming that they were merely outraged citizens taking action into their own hands.

Violence against immigrants was gradually mounting, but the police force took an especially zealous pleasure in fomenting attacks on anarchists and leftists, whom authorities viewed as "terrorists" rather than legitimate political movements. When, in 2007, far-right attackers crashed the Greek Youth Festival and stabbed a young Greek and a Moroccan immigrant, seventeen fascist attacks had already taken place in the six-month period leading up to the incident.

Around Greece, life was growing more perilous for refugees and migrants. On top of the rising far-right violence, migrant laborers found themselves facing an increasingly hostile environment in the agricultural fields where tens of thousands of them worked, toiling through biting winters and broiling summers and sending money back to their families and friends in their home countries.

Since 2008, Greek reporters and human rights groups had paid close attention to the exploitation endured by the migrant workers in Manolada, a small farming village sitting in the middle of an expansive rural plain on the country's southwestern coast. Stretching along the edge of the Ionian Sea, the village is home to just over 1,100 people. It is located around twenty-five miles southwest of Patras, the third largest city in the country. On average, the migrant workers, most of whom hailed from Bangladesh, made only twenty-two euros per day, but the bosses often paid late or refused to pay them at all.[10]

By April 2013, the workers hadn't been paid in five months. They were all fed up, all had families that relied on their income, and many were penniless. They decided to fight back against the indentured servitude their bosses imposed upon them. Golden Dawn and other fascists were organizing lynch mobs and attack squads around the country, but in Manolada, the racist violence was perpetuated by the very people who had brought the migrant workers to the country: their bosses. Around two hundred people participated in a protest, and the bosses responded harshly and quickly. Tipu Chowdhury, one of the striking workers, didn't expect the men to shoot at them, even when the guns were raised and aimed in their direction. "When they pointed their guns at us, and there were around two hundred of us gathered in that space, we thought they were joking," he later told *The Guardian*.[11] Then the gunfire rang out, the bullets whizzed past him. By the time the bosses stopped firing, bullets had struck thirty-three workers.[12]

AS THE YEARS groaned past, Muhammadi learned Greek, became an established figure in the migrant community, and carved out a reputation as a prominent human rights defender. He didn't fear speaking out against racist violence, and he labored tirelessly. In 2009, the Afghan Community in Greece elected him president, a post he held for four years. He later founded the Greek Forum of Refugees, where he served as president, and worked doggedly to provide new arrivals and long-term migrants with the support the Greek government never did. His activism won him a handful of awards, and in 2016, Human Rights Watch awarded him the Alison Des Forges Award for Extraordinary Activism, citing "his unwavering courage and commitment to protecting the rights of refugees, asylum seekers, and migrants in Greece and throughout Europe."[13] And he named names. He railed against the government's glaring indifference in the face of far-right violence, which reached a fever pitch between 2009 and 2013. As the government ignored the violence, Muhammadi drew up maps of safe areas and no-go zones in Athens, distributing them to refugees and migrants so they knew the areas where they most risked violence.

His activism also attracted negative attention. Shortly after renting an office in the capital's Agios Panteleimonas neighborhood, which he described as "the reference place" for refugees and migrants at the time, residents of the building launched a petition demanding the Afghan Community's eviction. The petition was a bust, but the streets of Athens grew yet more dangerous by the day. "They wanted us out of [the office] just because we are refugees," Muhammadi said. "They couldn't [succeed]. But unfortunately, it was very dangerous because of the far right. They [fascists] started to beat our members when they walked in the streets. They broke the hand of one of our translators. It was bad."

One day in 2010, while still working as the Afghan Community in Greece's president, he was instructing a classroom of Afghan women and children. Having mastered Greek, he taught them the basics: the alphabet, a few greetings, some grammar. The students were taking notes when Muhammadi paused mid-sentence, a cluster of Golden Dawn members bursting through the door. Lugging sticks and knives, they spilled into the room and fanned out. They smashed tables and desks. They stomped on the broken furniture. Then the assailants turned to Muhammadi. The students watched, frozen in fear, as the men punched and kicked their instructor. "I was teaching the Greek language to small children and women," he recalled.[14] "The shock for me [at that time] was not the attack itself. The shocking thing for me was the behavior of the authorities. When I spoke to the police, they said they'd put me in a detention center if I filed a complaint."[15]

There in Agios Panteleimonas, under the shadow of the neighborhood's elaborate basilica, Golden Dawn and its allies turned the area into an epicenter of racist violence. There in the reference place for refugees, as elsewhere, the knives came out.

ANTI-MIGRANT VIOLENCE IN Agios Panteleimonas started to blossom some two years before the men stormed the Afghan Community in Greece's offices and attacked Muhammadi. On November 24, 2008, around two hundred Greeks assembled in the neighborhood's central square.[16] A densely populated area, Agios Panteleimonas had become popular with newly arrived refugees and migrants. The rent was cheaper than many other parts of town, and the neighborhood sat close to the city center, where refugees and migrants could access services. Possessed by rage, the demonstrators accused the New Democracy–led government of turning a blind eye to their neighborhood's "ghettoization." The worst of Greece's crushing economic crisis had yet to sweep the country, but the neighborhood suffered, they said, from plummeting real estate values, gutted public services, and most of all, what they perceived as the theft of its Greek identity.[17] That rally, brief though it was, turned out to be the first shot fired in what Golden Dawn would later celebrate as "great battles in the square."

Effectively operating as a front for Golden Dawn, local, exclusively Greek neighborhood committees sought to send a message
to the government. If the state and its police would not rid the
public space of migrants and refugees, the committees would do
their best to make sure the new arrivals did not feel welcome.[18]
In May 2009, one such group began shuttering local parks and
playgrounds to non-Greeks, reciting the baseless claim that foreign children spread illnesses and diseases. A few months later,
vigilante patrols popped up, policed the area, and often used force
when they encountered non-Greeks.

A three-year wave of bloodshed started to wash over Greece
in 2010, with Golden Dawn riding the tide and taking credit
for "cleansing" the streets of "invaders." Although Agios
Panteleimonas received the lion's share of attention, anti-migrant violence erupted across Athens and other cities. During
the first half of 2011, the international charity Doctors Without
Borders treated around three hundred victims of racist violence
in Athens. Many victims never reported these attacks to authorities—they feared arrest at the hands of police officers sympa-
thetic to Golden Dawn and its xenophobic program. In practice,
Greece had yet to implement a 2008 law designed to prosecute
racist violence, and authorities took little to no action to curb
the epidemic.[19]

Sometime in late 2010, not long after the attack that left
Muhammadi battered and bruised, several Agios Panteleimonas
residents approached Muhammadi. They asked him to partake
in a discussion with his neighbors. Suspicious, he demanded to
know with whom he would be speaking. Just neighbors, they assured him. He arrived and found Golden Dawn member Themis
Skordeli, along with some of her comrades. Muhammadi had seen
some of them at attacks, and here they were occupying the front

row. "I thought there was an attack on the meeting," he said. "But no, they were participating in the discussion."

He continued, "The first person who started to say stuff was Skordeli . . . She started to insult us very badly. 'We don't want you,' she said. 'Why are you here? You're stealing, you're dirty.'"

In his telling of the exchange, Skordeli shouted at him, "You come here telling us to exchange our cultures. You don't have culture. We have culture; we are Greeks."

Muhammadi didn't want to provoke an attack. He composed himself, replied with a measured response. "I never imposed my culture, and I also respect your culture," he told Skordeli. "You are a woman, and maybe you're a mom. You think that an Afghan woman with a two-month-old baby will come from her country to make your city and streets dirty? No, it's because she was forced to leave."

"All the sudden, I saw that they were listening to me so carefully," he said. "I was very joyful. But then I finished, put down the mic and said, 'I'm leaving.'"

He left the meeting feeling accomplished. He hadn't persuaded the far-rightists, but he had forced them to hear him out. The silver lining dissipated soon, though, and a few weeks later he arrived home and found a small slip of paper wedged behind the windshield wiper on his car. DIRTY AFGHANS, the hastily penned note threatened, DISAPPEAR OR WE WILL DISAPPEAR YOU.

The attacks mounting, the Afghan Community in Greece packed up their office and left the neighborhood for Exarchia a week later. There, between the anarchist squats and anti-fascist collectives, Yonous Muhammadi hoped their office would be safer.

✳

IN 2010, GOLDEN Dawn's electoral fortunes began to shift, albeit gradually. A year earlier, Golden Dawn received 0.29 percent of the vote in legislative elections swept by the center-left PASOK party.[20] Popular Orthodox Rally (LAOS), an ultra-nationalist party, enjoyed near monopoly on the Greek far-right vote. Raking in more than 386,000 votes, LAOS secured fifteen seats in the parliament.

In November 2010, however, Greeks cast their ballots in local elections around the country, and Golden Dawn chief Nikolaos Michaloliakos landed a seat on the municipal council.[21] One in twenty Athenian voters showed up for Golden Dawn, enough for a single seat. During its early electoral rise, the party had the advantage of secrecy, and many observers didn't know the identities of many of its key members. As one analyst told Reuters, "Golden Dawn has the advantage of being invisible."

Later in 2010, while still fresh to the municipal council, Michaloliakos took the microphone during a session. "Be happy with the Pakistanis and Bangladeshis you turned into Greek citizens," he said.[22]

Petros Constantinou, a left-wing city councilor and anti-fascist activist, lunged to his feet. "We will have no fascist propaganda," he screamed, flinging an accusatory finger in Michaloliakos's direction. With his bodyguards huddled up next to him, the Golden Dawn chief locked eyes with Constantinou. He let go of the microphone and stiffened his back. He then threw up a fascist salute.

DURING GOLDEN DAWN'S political ascent, street attacks continued to mount at a breakneck pace. In Agios Panteleimonas, the citizens committees continued organizing, locking the gates of playgrounds, spray-painting racist graffiti, and beating refugees and migrants. "Greece our homeland," read a message spray-painted in large blue-and-white letters, the colors of the country's national flag, on the bricked pavement in the main square: "Immigrants Out of Greece."

On October 22, 2010, left-wing politician Alekos Alavanos visited Agios Panteleimonas for a campaign event.[23] Residents hurled yogurt at the Syriza politician, and several Golden Dawn supporters—Themis Skordeli, Aliki Papadaki, Andreas-Iason Sofias, Georgios Dimou, and Spyridon Giannatos—attacked him. Prosecutors later slapped the bunch with charges related to slander, threats, and non-accidental injuries.[24]

In late October 2011, Mina Ahmed, a twenty-year-old Somali, was walking in Agios Panteleimonas with her infant daughter. Ahmed was eight months pregnant.[25] As she waited at a crosswalk for the light to turn green, a group of men approached her and asked where she was from. "Somalia," she replied. The men tried to snatch her daughter, but she fought back, struggling to keep a grip on the girl. One of the attackers whacked her head with a wooden stick, and she fell to the ground, bleeding on the pavement. "All the people [witnesses] . . . were watching, but nobody helped me," she later recalled, speaking to Human Rights Watch. Although aching and frightened, she was relieved her worst fear had not been actualized: They did not hit, or make off with, her daughter. "It didn't matter if I was hurt. I just thought about the baby and my daughter."

The following month, between ten and fifteen far-right attackers stabbed Ali Rahimi, who had come to Greece from Afghanistan, five times in the torso.[26] Not long after that incident, a fifteen-person mob ambushed Mehdi Naderi, a twenty-year-old Afghan refugee, and two others in the nearby Attica Square, beating him with sticks and iron bars, Naderi told Human Rights Watch. "They have hit me everywhere, and in my body also," he remembered, adding: "It is not only my nose and my head . . . I started running but there was a lot of blood flowing. Suddenly, I felt dizzy and then I stopped, and my friends caught me. They were chasing us for a long time. They were behind us. At the time they attacked, my two friends escaped. I ran a lot."

Between October and December 2011, in Athens and Patras alone, human rights groups documented a staggering sixty attacks against migrants and refugees.

AROUND 8:00 P.M. on December 23, 2011, twenty-nine-year-old asylum seeker Safar Haidari, the president of an Afghan cultural association called Nour, walked along the sidewalk in Agios Panteleimonas. Only two hundred and twenty yards from the police station, he was accosted by a group of hooded and masked men. One punched him, knocking him to the ground, and the others quickly appeared over him. They beat him with sticks and kicked him. When they were done, the attackers made off with his cell phone and cigarettes, splitting up and disappearing into the night. Haidari used a spare phone to call the police, but the officers who came were more interested in scrutinizing his residency documents. Eventually, they sent him to the police station to file a complaint, where the officers on shift told him they were too busy and urged him to take a seat and wait. "But I saw the five policemen in the office drinking coffee and chatting," he said. "I made a remark to them. They told me again to wait." With his body aching and the officers showing no interest in helping him, Haidari left. When Haidari went to file a complaint four days later, the police officers on shift replied with the same disinterest.

That same month, eighteen-year-old Yasser Abdurrahman, a Somali asylum seeker, spotted a gang of black-clad men on motorcycles as he walked home at 2:00 a.m. one night. They stopped and called him over. "Come on, come on, Africa, Africa," they said. He approached them, and one of the men smashed a beer bottle on his head. The rest beat him for several minutes. He later recounted the incident to Human Rights Watch:

"They punched me in the face, cracked a tooth, and my nose. I don't know why they did this. They didn't say anything after they started hitting me. The police came, and they ran off on their motorcycles. I showed them [the police] my wrist and I said, 'Box, box' [to indicate he had been beaten] and they said, 'Hey Africa' and made a face and left. I didn't go back to the police . . . They don't do anything for people like me."

On June 22, 2012, as Golden Dawn campaigned nation-wide, five men chased down and beat twenty-two-year-old Sahel Ibrahim, a Somali refugee who worked as a translator for Human Rights Watch, the NGO detailed in its report. He tried to block the blows as the men pummeled him with a large wooden stick, but it was little use. By the time his attackers relented, Ibrahim's hand was broken. "I don't believe they [the police] can help me," Ibrahim said. "They know the situation, they know all the problems. Why are they still sitting [around]? We need some rules. We need big steps. This country needs it, this country deserves it."

Refugees knew police ignored—and worse still, sometimes participated in—the attacks. A 2014 lawsuit alleged that much of the violence "was carried out in cooperation with the district's police department and its deputy chief, Athanasios Skaras."[27] Filing police reports was often out of the question, especially for those who lived in the country without legal documents, but refugee rights advocates felt an even bigger betrayal from the institutions that purported to support them. Few nonprofits and international rights charities, Muhammadi said, seriously confronted the epidemic, and the local media couldn't have cared less, even as the victims piled up. "The media, the NGOs, the authorities, and even UNHCR—somehow, they didn't believe us when there were attacks on refugees. The whole climate was against us."[28]

THE FINANCIAL MELTDOWN that started in late 2009 sent Greece into a downward economic crisis that would crush much of the country's industry and leave its most vulnerable citizens reeling for nearly a decade. Political crisis accompanied economic hardship; strikes and demonstrations had become part and parcel of daily life. The old European socialist guard, long co-opted by neoliberalism, and Greece's ruling party, PASOK, was no exception. The failure of the institutional center left prompted many voters to seek out alternatives. It was against this backdrop that Golden Dawn began to thrive.

In December 2009, the Fitch ratings agency downgraded Greece's credit rating, prompting other agencies—S&P and Moody's—to classify Greek debts as "junk."[29] That move followed then Prime Minister George Papandreou's earlier admission that the government's budget deficit would be twice as large as expected, topping 12 percent.

On March 4, 2010, Greece introduced its first austerity package, which increased the sales tax and upped taxes on cigarettes and alcohol while also freezing pensions and capping civil servants' salaries. With swelling pressure from European lenders, Papandreou urged the Eurozone and the International Monetary Fund to bail out Greece in April. On May 2, finance ministers representing countries across the Eurozone settled on a 110-billion-euro (nearly $145 billion) loan package[30]. But the money came with conditions, and the Eurozone and lenders insisted that

Greece slash public funds.[31] Greece obliged, but not without resistance in the streets.

On May 5, unions, left-wing parties, and activist groups called for a nationwide strike. Between a hundred thousand and a half million people flooded the capital, according to various estimates, and staged what *The Guardian* described as one of the largest demonstrations since the junta collapsed in 1974.[32] The crowd swelled throughout the day. Anger coursed through Athens. Carrying banners emblazoned with anti-capitalist slogans and chanting against the "thieves" who had robbed the working class, demonstrators set banks ablaze and clashed with police officers, and the Greek Finance Ministry went up in flames.[33] Trash bins burned, bottles flew, and rocks shattered windows around the city. All around Syntagma Square plumes of smoke drifted in the sky. When a group of protesters tried to storm the parliament building, riot police fired a volley of tear gas and flash bangs, pushing them back.

The explosion of resistance sent chills throughout the European Union's ruling class. In Germany, Chancellor Angela Merkel urged that country's parliament to approve a bailout for Greece. "Quite simply," she pleaded, "Europe's future is at stake."[34]

Greek lawmakers approved the package, but Europe buckled down, demanding that Greece tighten its belt until the point of suffocation. In February 2011, Merkel and Germany pushed for the renewal of the loan program. Again, the Greek government conceded, and protesters swarmed the streets. A series of demonstrations erupted, and strikes paralyzed the country. While a broad assortment of leftists, anarchists, and trade unions led the resistance, Golden Dawn, too, saw an opportunity to broadcast its xenophobia to a broader audience. Since the 1990s, the party had sought to pin the blame for most of the country's woes on immigrants, but years of economic suffering had tilled the soil. Their message was now ripe for consumption. After loitering on the political fringe for three decades, Golden Dawn now branded itself as a political outsider, a vanguard of resistance that had been sounding the alarm since long before austerity stripped many Greeks of their livelihoods. Behind the scenes, the neo-fascist outfit plotted. Throughout 2011 and 2012, the crisis deepened, sending soaring already dismal poverty, unemployment, and suicide rates. The crisis also fueled pre-existing anti-immigrant attitudes.

Greek politicians from across the spectrum had no solution, and Europe's resolve was firm. In 2012, as the elections neared, Golden Dawn deployed its squads into poverty-stricken neighborhoods to enact supposed relief programs and mobilize voters. LAOS's decision to back the bailout program in 2010 and participate in the coalition government of PASOK's Lucas Papademos left it shedding support among voters. By December 2011, fewer than one in ten Greeks viewed LAOS favorably. Golden Dawn had already begun to snatch up more support than in the past, but the results of the May 2012 vote sent tremors throughout the country and much of Europe. Centering its 2012 campaign message on immigration, poverty, and austerity, Golden Dawn obtained 7 percent of the overall vote in the first round of elections, earning twenty-one seats in the parliament.

Another election was called for June 2012, and the party repeated its success, albeit losing three seats. But with eighteen seats in the parliament, Golden Dawn had made history as the first outwardly fascist party—though it now dismissed that label—to enter the legislative body since the military dictatorship imploded nearly four decades prior. The results hit Yonous Muhammadi hard. How, he wondered, could Golden Dawn gain the backing of so many Greeks as it unleashed violence across the country?

"There was generally a social tension, people were angry, society was angry, and it was a good excuse for Golden Dawn," he remembered. "Golden Dawn, when they attack, they don't care if someone is killed. That's clear."

Emboldened by its successes, Golden Dawn spotted the opportunity to fill the gaps left behind by the welfare state with a markedly racist solution. In the past, the party had provided poverty-ravaged Greek families with food and clothes. Between 2011 and 2013, however, Golden Dawn bulked up its social activism, dispatching members and supporters to down-and-out neighborhoods and towns nationwide. The party hosted a series of blood banks, soup kitchens, and clothing drives, among other charity-focused projects, that came with an important caveat: Greeks only. One project that caught the eye of media was the Jobs for Greeks initiative. Party members visited factories and pressured employers to hire ethnic Greeks rather than migrant workers.

In July 2012, the party organized a blood drive that sparked outrage from critics and opponents.[35] "All the bottles of blood we collect will be handed over to patients we choose and to no one else," a statement declared, echoing posters plastered across Athens that promised the blood would only be accepted from and distributed to Greeks. "This right to choose belongs not just to Golden Dawn members, but to all volunteer blood donors."

Politicians, hospitals, and medical facilities blasted the initiative. The move was "insane, unscientific, illegal, and racist action," said one of the largest medical workers unions in the capital, deriding Golden Dawn for violating the moral principles surrounding the "sacred procedure of blood donation."

On August 1, 2012, Golden Dawn set up shop in Syntagma Square, not far from the parliament. Unemployment had reached 23 percent over the summer, and tempers boiled. Crisis-punished Greeks lined up for pasta, milk, and olive oil, showing their identification card to prove their Greek heritage to the Golden Dawn volunteers manning the charity drive. Speaking to a reporter, the newly elected Kasidiaris boasted that the handouts were "exclusively from Greek producers to give to Greek people."[36]

Questioned by press, Golden Dawn parliamentarian Christos Pappas insisted, "We are in Greece, so Greeks have priority . . . The illegal immigrants that have come here, who enjoy, if you will, all the rights and privileges that come from Greek taxpayers, are illegal invaders. They are a threat to Greece."[37]

Although Golden Dawn staged several similar events in Athens and elsewhere, they appeared to do little to alleviate the suffering brought on by the crisis. But that did not matter: the goal, after all, was never to prevent Greek suffering; the goal was to provide cover for the suffering Golden Dawn sought to inflict on its opponents. In 2012, the party boasted of branches in areas spanning Greece, and some polls showed the party's support level topping 11 percent.[38]

CHAPTER FIVE

"NOT A SURPRISE FOR US": FASCIST MURDERS

For two days in January 2013, Khadam Hussain Luqman suspected that his eldest son, Faisal, had fallen ill or depressed. His home in Lalamusa, Pakistan, had always been lively, and none of his seven daughters appeared upset. Seized by worry, Khadam observed Faisal lumbering around in a sullen mood, unable to eat, and falling into sudden fits of crying. Late on the second day, Faisal fessed up: he had learned that his brother, Shahzad, had been killed by neo-Nazis in Greece. Faisal admitted that he had waited to pass the news on to his parents, fearing how it would impact them.

Sitting in the Pakistani Community of Greece union's office in Athens years later, seventy-five-year-old Khadam recounted the shock of his son's murder, blotting tears from beneath his eyes with a handkerchief. "I thought I was going to die," he told me. "I thought, I am an old person and cannot live through this shock."[1] In the months that followed, Khadam and his family struggled to cope with the loss. "That time was the most painful, and we were asking ourselves thousands of questions," he said, explaining that he worried he or his wife might die before seeing justice for the murder.

Throughout the same year Luqman was killed, the Athens-based Racist Violence Recording Network (RVRN) documented 166 attacks racking up 320 victims. Of that total, more than 86 percent targeted refugees and migrants.[2]

BEFORE LEAVING PAKISTAN, Shahzad, the seventh of Khadam's nine children, worked in their hometown as an apprentice under a local welder. "He loved to play cricket on the days when he wasn't learning to weld," Khadam said. Around the time Shahzad turned twenty-one in 2007, he first floated the idea of leaving home to find employment in Greece, where tens of thousands of Pakistanis work as migrant laborers. Khadam initially refused, encouraging his son to stay at home with his family. "I told him he couldn't go," he recalled. "The biggest reason was we didn't have enough money, but I'd also heard some rumors of groups attacking [migrants]."

But Khadam, who worked long hours in a brick factory, and his wife, Shugran, felt the financial pinch as they grew older and less able to work by the day. They eventually relented, and Shahzad set off for Greece in January 2008 after taking out a loan of 650,000 Pakistani rupees ($4,623) to pay smugglers.

Once in Greece, Shahzad worked several jobs, first picking fruits and vegetables in the agricultural fields of Aspropyrgos and later manning a booth at an open-air market in Petralona, a neighborhood in the capital. "He was a hard worker," Khadam says, explaining that Shahzad worked for less than thirty euros ($33.96) a day and sent back as much as he could, usually between two hundred and five hundred euros ($226–$565) a month. Shahzad's financial contributions kept the family afloat, and his parents were grateful. Khadam and Shugran divided the money up between living expenses, saving for their daughters' upcoming weddings, and paying back the loan they'd taken out to send Shahzad to Europe.

ONE DAY IN early January 2013, Shahzad, then twenty-seven, called Khadam for the second to last time. Six years later that conversation still haunted Khadam. Taking note of his son's shaky voice, he listened as Shahzad recounted the fear he felt while cycling to work each morning. Nearly every day, Shahzad heard news of attacks targeting Pakistanis and other migrant workers throughout Greece. A few months earlier, in August 2012, Golden Dawn supporters were suspected in the murder of a nineteen-year-old Iraqi migrant, who was stabbed to death by five men on motorbikes.[3] Shahzad didn't tell his father that he had been attacked only two days before their phone call, an incident that was thwarted when his boss intervened and broke up the scuffle, chasing off the man who'd badgered Shahzad. "I told my child, 'Please don't work at night anymore,'" he said. "I told him only one job is okay, that we were satisfied and that he was already sending us enough money."

A few days later, on the brisk winter morning of January 17, 2013, Shahzad woke early and readied himself. He dressed, stepped out, and hopped on his bicycle at around 3:00 a.m., pedaling to the market in Petralona. Darkness shrouded the streets, and lampposts provided slivers of light. Behind him, a motorbike bounced to a stop, and Christos Stergiopoulos and Dionysis Liakopoulos stepped off, each armed with a butterfly knife. The men seized Shahzad and plunged their blades into his torso and limbs. Altogether, the attackers stabbed him seven times, once in the heart. Witnesses later recalled hearing his cries for help, but he bled out and died in the street.

Parked nearby, a taxi driver jotted down the license plate number on the motorcycle and called the authorities. Police arrested Stergiopoulos and Liakopoulos only a few hours later, and both confessed to the crime.[4] Officers raided their homes, where they found Golden Dawn leaflets and a cache of weapons: knives and batons, among other banned items.

Yonous Muhammadi heard the harrowing news later that morning. "It was not a surprise for us," he said. "Every day we had attacks at the time, and we were insisting that one day these attacks will have victims who will be killed." Muhammadi had watched the violence unfold around him for years, and he sought to pressure Greek authorities to clamp down on far-right attackers. "One problem in Greece was that the judicial system didn't do its job," he told me. "No one was being punished."

Then in September 2013, the situation boiled over when a Golden Dawn member stabbed to death thirty-four-year-old anti-fascist rapper Pavlos Fyssas. That murder led prosecutors to file a litany of charges against the party, including operating a criminal organization. The trial of Shahzad Luqman's killers was, however, a separate legal case. Yet the murders sparked a wave of protests in Athens and elsewhere, many of them boiling over into clashes between Golden Dawn supporters and anti-fascists. "Pavlos Fyssas was important as a hero for us," explained Muhammadi. "He changed many things with what he started to do, with his singing, but also when he was killed."

WHEN SHAHZAD'S KILLERS went to trial in December 2013, Khadam flew to Greece for the first time, stepping out of the airport to find a throng of supporters. But the warmth he felt slipped away on the first day of the trial, watching the men who killed his son from across the gallery. "Seeing them in the court was like the same shock of Shahzad's death," he recalls. "I tried not to look at them because I felt something strange inside me." Four and a half months later, an Athens court sentenced both men to life behind bars, a charge in Greece that allows convicts to apply for parole after sixteen years. "Nothing can undo the murder of my son," Khadam explained, "but it was great to get justice, and I was satisfied."

*

WHILE SERVING THEIR time behind bars after their April 2014 conviction, Liakopoulos and Stergiopoulos filed appeals to overturn their life sentences, their lawyers arguing that the killing resulted from a dispute that had nothing to do with Luqman's national origin or ethnicity.[5] But the appeal process didn't start until 2018 and was still ongoing when I first met Khadam. With the help of the Pakistani Community of Greece and others, Khadam has traveled to Greece for every hearing.

On March 16, 2019, Khadam stood on a stage for a rally in central Athens. Flanked on both sides by migrants who were recently attacked, he held up a banner bearing Shahzad's face as he waited, one speaker after another addressing the crowd. Rows of apartment buildings eclipsed the sun, cast shade across the hundreds of anti-fascists, migrant workers, and refugees who crowded the street in front of him. They raised placards toward the cloud-carpeted sky. When Khadam's turn arrived, he adjusted the red-and-white scarf swaddling his head and approached the podium. "Golden Dawn members murdered my son, who was the only one supporting my family, and I want them to be resentenced," he said, speaking through a translator. Thick white sideburns framed his stoic face, and a salted beard drooped down to his chest. "If we are not on the streets, if we do not fight, we will not be able to stop them."

After pausing for a moment, he closed, "No to Golden Dawn, no to racism, no to fascism." The protesters set off to march through the city, bobbing above them placards calling on the Greek government to imprison the leadership of Golden Dawn. They chanted, "Never again fascism."

On March 22, 2019, the clouds rested low in the lead-colored sky over the Athens Court of Appeals, threatening rain. Dozens of anti-fascists gathered in front of the building where one of several appeals hearings was held. LIFE SENTENCES FOR THE NEO-NAZI MURDERERS OF SHAHZAD LUQMAN, read a banner stretched out in front of the activists. Inside in a courtroom on the sixth floor, Khadam sat in the second row, his arms folded on his lap as he listened to the prosecutor present the government's case in a language the loss-stricken father didn't understand. It was the seventh hearing, and he'd traveled from his home country for each of them. Stergiopoulos and Liakopoulos sat in an elevated box overlooking the court. Throughout the three-hour hearing, neither looked in Khadam's direction, neither directed their gaze toward a gallery teeming with anti-fascist activists.

Prosecutor Anastasios Skaras urged the panel of judges to uphold the life sentences and to uphold the guilty verdict on charges of murder with racist intent. If eyewitnesses had not come forward after the slaying, the convicted could've escaped without punishment, he argued. "My conclusion is that they had decided to find a foreigner that night, to show him that he is not welcome," Skaras said. "Not specifically Luqman, but any [foreigner]. That's why they had daggers with them."

Speaking to the killers' motivations, Skaras added, "A foolish, fanatical, and destructive obsession with racial superiority."

AFTER POLICE ROUNDED up Golden Dawn members following Fyssas's murder, the number of hate crimes in Greece plummeted the following year. Although many Greeks were aghast at the bloodshed, Golden Dawn repeated its electoral success in January 2015, becoming the third largest party in the parliament.[6]

But the trial had put the party under a spotlight, and for a time party leaders distanced themselves from racist attacks. After a handful of attackers stabbed and bludgeoned two Pakistani field hands in Goritsa in October 2017, Golden Dawn chief Nikolaos Michaloliakos met with Pakistan's ambassador to Greece to assure him that his party had no connection to the incident.[7] Damage control efforts withstanding, Golden Dawn's jackboots had never signed up for a strictly parliamentary party, and the 2015 influx of refugees and migrants to Europe had left many eager to return to the streets and fight.

In 2017, Greek police recorded a sharp spike in hate crimes, with attacks targeting people owing to their skin color or national origin nearly tripling when compared to the previous year. In 2018, as a surge in nationalism rattled the country and hundreds of thousands attended protests against a name accord with Greece's northern neighbor—now the Republic of North Macedonia—attacks on migrants, journalists, and opponents of the far right fanned out across the country at a breakneck pace.

Golden Dawn had never been the sole party behind far-right violence, however, and in 2018 a pair of little-known neo-Nazi groups exacted a spate of attacks and vandalism. In early March, police raids led to the arrest of several members of Combat 18 Hellas, a national socialist group that had attacked left-wing squats and vandalized several Jewish cemeteries across the country. Later that month, a shadowy group calling itself Crypteia firebombed the Afghan Community in Greece's offices in the capital.

The Racist Violence Recording Network released its annual hate crimes report for the year. Altogether the monitor documented 117 incidents in 2018, a 14 percent increase when compared to the Network's findings for 2017. "The support base for violent acts against refugees and migrants is expanding," the report observed, adding that the number of attacks targeting refugees or migrants more than doubled. The RVRN partially attributed the spike in hate crimes to the resurgence of "nationalist populism" and the "normalization of extreme messages of intolerance."

With European Parliament elections scheduled for May 26 and Greek elections slated to take place by October 20, the report warned that "far-right, neo-Nazi and extreme nationalist groups across Europe [are gaining] further strength," striking up alliances with each other and competing "in committing racist attacks."

The Hellenic Police, which kept its own tally, recorded 226 hate crimes; the disparity between RVRN's stats and the stats of the police partially stems from the latter's inclusion of hate speech in their statistics. But the numbers spoke for themselves. According to the police tally, nearly one in four victims were Pakistani nationals, a number that weighed heavy on Khadam's heart. "Whenever I hear about attacks, I am afraid," he told me. "I don't want to hear once again that somebody was murdered by fascist attacks. That's why I joined demonstrations [while in Greece] to express my feelings, to make some efforts to stop these racist attacks."

ON APRIL 17, 2019, during what was meant to be the eighth and final court hearing for the appeals of Shahzad Luqman's killers, lawyers for Stergiopoulos and Liakopoulos recycled arguments from the first trial, claiming that neither had links to Golden Dawn and that Luqman's death was the result of a commonplace street fight rather than a planned murder.[8] "On the one hand, a young man was killed and it does not matter whether he was a Greek or a foreigner," said Stergiopoulos's lawyer. "On the other hand, two young people are accused of [a crime] with serious consequences for them and their families."

"There are not many Greeks who believe that 'foreigners are destroying our homeland,'" he argued, insisting that the defendants "have nothing to do with" anti-migrant groups or Golden Dawn. But as the hearing wore on, the crowd grew rowdier. When one of the lawyers claimed police never found the "screwdriver" he suggested had killed Shahzad, several people in the gallery shouted: "With a knife."

Then a small but loud group of anarchists suddenly stormed the courtroom and hurled fliers across the gallery while chanting. The judges rescheduled the final hearing for May 6, delaying the final appeal decision for another three weeks. "I'm certain the punishment will remain the same," Khadam said.

Back in Lalamusa, the Luqman family had done their best to adjust to life without Shahzad. An anonymous Greek donated enough money for the Luqman family to open a corner store, and all of Khadam's daughters had since married. Each time Khadam traveled to Athens for hearings, the Pakistani Community in Greece and other unions raised the money to cover his trip and expenses. "I've felt unbelievable support from the Greeks. I never expected this, but they support me. I'll remember this for my whole life, and I have no words to express how I feel."

Despite the support he felt, he worried that young refugees and migrants were still at risk in Greece. Khadam now urged young Pakistani men not to leave their country and search for work in Europe. "There is no need to leave your homeland," he would advise them. "Please don't put your life in danger or cause pain for your parents."

ONE DAY IN May 2013, Magdalene Fyssa, who goes by Magda, and her only son, Pavlos, went for a stroll in their neighborhood, Keratsini. The working-class borough had been hit especially hard by Greece's economic crisis. For months, the mother and her son had discussed the political consequences of Greece's financial collapse, and they were both worried about its impact on their neighborhood. From time to time, they chatted about Golden Dawn. Neither Magda nor Pavlos, to her knowledge, had ever had a direct interaction with a Golden Dawn member, but she knew the group was no good. Because the group's Nikaia chapter was nearby, the party had been making a public show of their presence more frequently than in the past. "Of course, we all knew who they were," she told me.[9] "We talked about the rise of Golden Dawn, and we wondered how they were even able to become a party in the parliament."

That day, they strolled along the sidewalks lining the narrow streets, past the same kind of left-wing graffiti, ubiquitous on the walls of office buildings and homes, Pavlos had soaked up for his entire youth. There was plenty to be happy about. Born in 1979, Pavlos had turned thirty-four a month earlier. He was outgoing, funny, and enjoying his increasingly successful career as a rap artist, an artistic path he first started down in 1997, throwing himself into a rap scene known as Low Bap, a subgenre characterized by its slower beats and slower pace of rapping as well as its deeply political lyrics.[10] Several years had come and gone since Pavlos worked in the shipyards in Perama, an arduous job that his father had also worked. Beloved by young rap fans with left-wing politics, he went by the stage name Killah P, which, he often explained, meant *killer of the past*. He supported Antarsya, a left-wing movement, and had been an active member of the Syndicate of Metalworkers of Piraeus during his shipyard days. Adopting a logo of a mask-wearing dog, many of his songs were about love and everyday life, and he never mentioned Golden Dawn by name, but his lyrics were sharp, the themes deeply informed, his politics fiercely anti-fascist. In one track, he condemned the Greek police for the 2008 murder of fifteen-year-old Alexis Grigoropoulos. In another song, "Zoria," Fyssas railed against the increasingly popular fascist iconography and the nationalism that had gained ground in recent years:

> A DAY LIKE THIS IS A GOOD ONE TO DIE,
> GRACEFULLY AND ON PUBLIC DISPLAY.
> MY NAME IS PAVLOS FYSSAS FROM PIRAEUS,
> GREEK—WHATEVER THAT MEANS,
> NOT A FLAG, A BLACK-SHIRTED
> SPAWN OF ACHILLES AND KARAISKAKIS.

*

PAVLOS'S LYRICS HAD been improving during that period, and he was ambitious, his friends said. Along with his friend Athanasios Perrakis, who was a few years younger than him, he had been planning to launch a new collaborative group. Athanasios and Pavlos were already part of a squad, E-13, something that Athanasios—whose rap name was Tiny Jackal—described as a Greek version of the Wu-Tang Clan. For Tiny Jackal, Pavlos was a mentor. Today, he told me, people focus too much on Pavlos's anti-fascist songs. Pavlos was an anti-fascist, Tiny Jackal insisted, but he "was not only that . . . He had songs about friendship, family, life and what to do with society. He was the type of person who would help you with anything."[11]

While Magda and Pavlos walked that day in May, they heard a loud commotion from the main street nearby, the roar of engines revving, and walked in its direction. Something stopped them in their tracks: a motorcade of Golden Dawn members, wearing black shirts and waving blue-and-white flags. "We froze, just waiting, like everyone who was watching," Magda told me. "We were afraid of what was happening. We were afraid of what it meant, of how this was going to affect the country. We didn't feel safe by any means."

Five months had passed since Shahzad Luqman's gruesome murder, and Golden Dawn was still operating with impunity, still in the parliament, still building up legions of angry men and women willing to storm the streets. She couldn't escape a bad premonition at the time, but another four months went by before Magda came to understand the motorcade as an omen, as a warning from the universe that the worst was yet to come. "We felt like something bad was coming our way, but we didn't know it would touch our family directly," she said.

*

NEARLY FOUR MONTHS later, on the evening of September 12, 2013, activists with the All Workers Militant Front (PAME), a communist party–linked union, fanned out in the Piraeus area to put up posters and fliers announcing a festival. Throughout the far-right surge in recent years, PAME had made a point of calling on working-class people to organize against their bosses and reject the xenophobia Golden Dawn offered as a solution to their problems.

Unemployment topped 40 percent in Keratsini, where PAME enjoyed broad support among workers, and the entire area surrounding The Zone—where the city's port is located—was quickly turning into contested territory. Golden Dawn, hoping to chip away at local support for PAME and the Communist Party of Greece, had been agitating in the neighborhoods for months, and the party had allegedly made a dark alliance with the wealthy ship owners that had a vested interest in squashing advocates for workers' rights.[1213] Around the world, from the United States to Europe, far-right groups have long tried to appeal to the working class, framing their worldview as a battle against the elite. Golden Dawn was no different. The moment was prepped for violence, and with the PAME unionists in small numbers that night, Golden Dawn spotted an opportunity to strike. Communists, after all, represented one of the fascist party's largest political enemies, a threat to the nation and Greek heritage, as they saw it.

As the PAME activists pasted one poster after another, a group of men appeared. Armed with clubs and knives, they emerged from the alleyways in columns. Altogether, around fifty Golden Dawn members encircled the unionists. Two police officers, sitting on motorcycles, paid little attention as a spectacle of intense violence unfolded. As the neo-Nazis moved in, the unionists tried to defend themselves, but they were outnumbered and unprepared for a gang of knife-wielding extremists. A few of the fascists hurled stones, while others beat the unionists with their flagpoles and rods. "It was the first time they'd dared to attack us so openly," Thanassis Panagiotopoulos, a trade unionist present at the ambush, told reporter Maria Malagardis.[14]

The police officers "did nothing when the stones and the clubs rained down on us," Sotiris Poulikogiannis, head of the local metal workers union, told Malagardis. Nine unionists were injured, some badly enough to seek medical treatment at the hospital, by the time the violence ended. For the victims, there was never any doubt as to whether they had walked into a trap. Only a few months earlier, Golden Dawn parliamentarian Yiannis Lagos had given a speech in The Zone. He vowed to drive PAME from the streets and the shipyards, vowed to eradicate the support for the communists and socialists fighting the country's crippling austerity measures. Lagos had ordered the attack, party members would later confess. The same night as the attack, Lagos sent a message to Sotiris Develekos, a prominent member of Golden Dawn's Piraeus chapter. "We fucked those communists today in Nikaia and Perama. They went out to hang posters, and we slaughtered them," Lagos boasted.[15] They weren't finished, either. He added, "Forty of our people are hunting them down now."

"Is there a bone left for us?" Develekos replied.

ON THE NIGHT of September 17, Pavlos Fyssas joined his girlfriend, Chryssa, and her friends to watch a soccer match in the Coralie Café near his family home. Early on that night, he focused on the game: his favorite club, Olympiacos, was facing off against Paris Saint-Germain in a Champions League match. Along with his group, Fyssas drank a few beers during the game, complaining each time the rival team scored a goal. The café was lively, a bit rowdy even. People jumped to their feet and screamed when the Greek team missed a penalty kick. The scene was rambunctious, but the game passed without any brawls or heated arguments.[16] Fyssas didn't know that Ioannis Aggos, a Golden Dawn member from Nikaia, spotted him. Aggos stepped outside, rang Ioannis Kazantzoglou, a fellow chapter member outranking him. The information crawled up the chain until it reached Yiannis Lagos, who gave the green light. *Attack.*

Past midnight, after Paris Saint-Germain bested Fyssas's club four to one, a group of suspicious men had assembled outside. "It was only at the end of the evening, when everyone was leaving, that I saw the gang, which appeared out of nowhere on the other side of the street," the café owner later recalled.

From across the street, around twenty men hollered and cursed at Fyssas and his group while they were still inside the café. Tension hung in the air. A fight appeared imminent. Chryssa spotted a nearby group of police officers and pleaded with them to intervene. Her pleas failed to convince the officers, who simply watched from afar, keeping their distance and declining to step in. The crowd began to push Fyssas, and a few of his friends broke away. Attempting to defend his companions, Fyssas fought back until a car screeched to a stop in front of him. Behind the wheel was Giorgos Roupakias, a forty-five-year-old truck driver and cafeteria employee at Golden Dawn's office. Roupakias hopped out. He grabbed Fyssas and twice plunged a knife into the rapper's chest. He threw the knife into a gutter, but one policewoman intervened. She pointed her weapon at the killer, ordered him to freeze.

Pavlos's father phoned Magda. He'd been stabbed, he told his ex-wife, and she rushed out of the home. All throughout the ride to the hospital, Magda believed that Pavlos had been badly injured but that he was still alive. She didn't know who had hurt her son, or why. After rushing through the hospital entrance and finding a doctor, however, she learned that the truth was far graver than she could have imagined. "Pavlos has been murdered by a Golden Dawn member," the doctor told her.

It was only a few days after the murder when the graffiti appeared in central Athens: IF YOU'D CARED ABOUT IMMIGRANT DEATHS, PAVLOS MAY STILL BE ALIVE.

CHAPTER SIX

FRIENDS FROM THE UNITED STATES TO SWEDEN: FASCISM ACROSS BORDERS

During the summer of 2013, a then obscure American neo-Nazi called Andrew Anglin checked in at the Athens International Youth Hostel in the Greek capital. Born in 1984 and raised in the suburbs surrounding Columbus, Ohio, Anglin has described himself as someone who was committed to a liberal worldview during his youth. At one point during high school, he wore dreadlocks and adopted a vegan lifestyle.[1] His seemingly progressive phase didn't last long, though, and around the time he became a high school senior, he fell into a shadowy online world of conspiracy theories. After dropping out of Ohio State University in 2004, he launched a spate of short-lived websites that borrowed aesthetics and ideas heavily from the sort of paranoid fever dreams pushed by Alex Jones, founder of InfoWars, one of the world's most prominent conspiracy theory websites on the internet. By the time he touched down in Greece, he was already enjoying relative notoriety for his website, Total Fascism, an online publication dedicated to publishing poorly penned and highly ironic long-form essays about National Socialism.

The Athens International Youth Hostel was cheap spot for tourists in Greece, and many visitors likely booked a room without realizing that it sat in a crime-heavy neighborhood ravaged by Greece's economic crisis. Evidence of the economic downturn was present in the shuttered stores, understocked markets, and dusty cafés. Located on Victor Hugo 16, the hostel's cheap prices attracted young European and North American backpackers, among others, but during the refugee crisis that erupted in 2015, it began to also attract displaced people from war-torn countries, those who could afford a room rather than sleeping in tents or taking up in the overcrowded refugee camps popping up around Greece. At nighttime, the neighborhood is rife with drug peddlers and sex workers, despite its location near a police station. Also nearby, only a five-minute walk down a handful of residential streets and around a few bends, was one of Golden Dawn's largest offices in the capital.

Telemachos, a longtime front desk employee at the hostel, remembered Anglin well. They became friends during Anglin's time at the hostel. He thought the American was funny and kind— because Telemachos was vegan, Anglin even bought him an expensive juicer as a gift for all his hospitality. Telemachos noted Anglin's politics, but he didn't think much of it. The crisis had brought back a stripe of racism many once considered moribund in Greece, and Anglin's hatred for ethnic, racial, and religious minorities didn't appear to be all that serious, after all. "He is a smart businessman, and he sells his product well," Telemachos offered by way of explanation. We were sitting in the hostel lobby, and Telemachos stood up to buzz in guests every now and then.

I lived only a ten-minute walk from the hostel, but I had never seen it before that day in March 2018, when I showed up and found Telemachos behind the desk. Through an ongoing court case in the US, I had learned that Anglin listed the hostel as a previous place of employment. That initially puzzled me. I had been visiting Greece since 2015, and I knew the neighborhood was near Exarchia, the anarchist stronghold I later moved to, a place known for squats, demonstrations, and anti-fascist rebellion. Like Anglin, I am an American citizen, and I knew that the immigration process was not easy in Greece. Securing a Greek job as a non–European Union citizen was even trickier, and I wondered how a neo-Nazi blogger had landed a gig at a hostel in Athens. I plugged the address into Google Maps and, along with a colleague, walked to the Athens International Youth Hostel, passing some of the sullenest patches of the city center where austerity had taken its darkest toll. We rang the buzzer, and the man behind the counter, who turned out to be Telemachos, let us in. "I have a somewhat odd question," I said. "I'm not a guest. I'm a journalist from the United States, and I want to ask about someone who claims they used to work here."

I explained how I learned of the hostel, and I lifted my phone to show him an image of Anglin's face on the cover of *The Atlantic*. "The Making of an American Neo-Nazi," the title read. Telemachos started laughing. "*Ela, re malaka,*" he said, jokingly. *C'mon, asshole.* He was dumbfounded, couldn't believe that Anglin was "famous."

A few weeks after Anglin's arrival, Telemachos eventually offered his new pal a good deal: If Anglin gave English-language tours of the Acropolis to visitors hoping to soak up a bit of Athenian history, he could stay at the hostel for free. Anglin always behaved professionally as a tour guide, Telemachos said, and didn't treat any of the guests differently based on their race or ethnicity. But in conversations with Telemachos, Anglin wasn't shy about his views, the clerk said. "He said he left America because a black guy was president," Telemachos told me, referring to former US president Barack Obama. "He was a big fan of Golden Dawn. He also liked Trump, [French far-right leader Marine] Le Pen, and [Russian president Vladimir] Putin."

Telemachos insisted that he was no supporter of Golden Dawn—he had voted for Syriza, the country's largest left-wing party, at one point, and during the 2015 elections, he cast his ballot for far-right firebrand Kyriakos Velopoulos as a joke—but because he liked Anglin, he admitted, he offered to walk his American guest to the party's office one day. There he introduced Anglin to the people at the door, helped with translation. The party was thriving at the time. They were fresh to the Greek parliament, having surged in a pair of legislative elections a year earlier, and their black-clad supporters were cropping up in many impoverished neighborhoods in the capital, often donning their all-black uniforms and carrying out vigilante patrols. It was unlikely that the hostel clerk thought much of the introduction, but he was contributing to a long-standing relationship of mutual solidarity, ideological exchange, and strategy sharing between Golden Dawn and other figures and groups in the fascist international. Anglin subsequently began showing up at occasional Golden Dawn rallies in the capital, and he sometimes attended meetings at the party's office, where local supporters gathered to discuss political issues and planning.

It was there at the Athens International Youth Hostel, in July 2013, that Anglin launched the Daily Stormer, a neo-Nazi website that would later attain infamy in the United States for inciting bands of anonymous, white supremacist trolls to threaten or attack a multitude of targets, among them Jews and African Americans.[2] The website's name is a nod to *Der Stürmer*, the anti-Semitic paper founded by Julius Streicher, a Nazi war criminal who was convicted of war crimes in Nuremburg and hanged on October 16, 1946. Within a few years of its founding, Daily Stormer grew into what the Alabama-based hate monitor Southern Poverty Law Center described as the largest neo-Nazi website in the United States.

Anglin wrote about political issues all over the world. In his characteristically appalling and witty posts, he sang the praises of German Nazi leader Adolf Hitler, claimed Donald Trump represented the last hope for white Americans, and celebrated Syrian dictator Bashar al-Assad, among a lengthy list of unsavory criminals and despotic far-right political leaders. He warned of the impending race war and urged his followers to prepare accordingly. Overtly neo-Nazi and intensely anti-Semitic, he disparaged African Americans, Jews, Muslims, other religious minorities in the west, and wrote adoringly of far-right parties and groups across North America and Europe. His surroundings also influenced him, and when he wrote about Greece, he did so with an especially intense zeal. Many of his celebrations of the infamous neo-fascist group were buried in racist tirades about migrants in Greece. After scandal rocked the party following Pavlos Fyssas's killing, Anglin regularly wrote angry screeds in defense of Golden Dawn and denying its complicity in the murder. He seldom spoke openly about his own personal ties with Golden Dawn members, but he didn't hide it, either. Years later, photos of him standing at a Golden Dawn rally, the group's flag-waving supporters in a mass behind him, emerged online. In many of his Daily Stormer posts from that period, Anglin promoted Golden Dawn. He often accused Greek anarchists and anti-fascists of being funded by Jews, parroting conspiratorial, anti-Semitic claims often disseminated by the most extreme facets of Greece's far right. He was not the only Anglophone Golden Dawn fan, but he did his part in

disseminating the party's propaganda to an English-speaking audience. In turn, Golden Dawn–linked websites and publications
often translated, quoted, and cited Daily Stormer articles.

On August 29, 2013, Anglin was interviewed by a little-
known Holocaust denier and radio show host called Carolyn
Yeager, whom the Southern Poverty Law Center had described
as a "woman of leaden stupidity." Yeager had become a fan of his
writing, and she wanted to know more about his time in Greece
and his thoughts on Golden Dawn. "There's no way that a person
who hasn't witnessed it could really understand the feeling you
get when you see all these young men in black shirts, in very good
shape, all standing in a line, carrying flags, marching, and singing," he told Yeager. He praised the party's blood drives and soup
kitchens, publicity stunts that prompted widespread condemnation in Greece because they had been reserved for Greeks only.
"It's incredibly powerful . . . it's like a tribal thing, you know."

In September of that year, in the wake of the murder of rapper Pavlos Fyssas, the Daily Stormer quickly leapt to the party's
defense. Unsurprisingly, Anglin's publication claimed the murder
was part of a broader conspiracy targeting the National Socialist
movement. "The level of media coverage of the stabbing of the
Greek rapper Killah P is astonishing," one article claimed. "This
is exactly what the Jews were waiting for, as is evidenced by the
clearly premeditated manner in which the media is attacking the
Golden Dawn."

Five years later, Anglin's time in Greece would feature in a
legal dispute during a civil suit trial against the neo-Nazi pub-
lisher. The Southern Poverty Law Center and Tanya Gersh, a
Jewish realtor from Montana, were suing Anglin for inciting a
barrage of anti-Semitic harassment and death threats on his website. Anglin's lawyers attempted to have the case dismissed on the
grounds that he was not a domicile resident of the US, pointing

to the handful of countries he had been residing in for several years. "In 2013, I moved to Greece with the intent to live their permanently," Anglin said in the statement, adding that he "obtained employment as a tour guide for the Athens International Youth Hostel."

The declaration stated, "At that time, I considered Greece my permanent home, although I traveled to other countries in Europe from time to time."

His account of the following years was unclear, stating next that he moved to Cambodia in April 2017, the same month the lawsuit against him was filed.

Vasilis Nastos, owner of the Athens International Youth Hostel and several similar establishments, had less generous words for Anglin. He denied Anglin's claim that he was his employee, insisting that he did not sponsor Anglin for residency.[3] Nastos, who had worked in the hospitality industry for more than forty years, explained that some guests at his hostel provided English-language tours to visitors on a volunteer basis in exchange for free accommodation for a brief period. "I had no idea who he was, and I'd never heard his name before," Nastos told me by telephone, surprised by the question. "If I knew who he was, I wouldn't have even accepted him as a customer," he said. "These Golden Dawn guys are dangerous."

IT IS IMPOSSIBLE to measure Golden Dawn's influence on white nationalist and far-right groups abroad, but plenty such outfits have sang its praises over the years. The group built ties with violent organizations from Italy to Sweden, from Australia to the United States, and from Germany to Australia. After entering the Greek parliament in 2013, *The Guardian* warned that Golden

Dawn sought to go "global," founding chapters abroad among Greek immigrants in North America, Europe, and Australia.[4] "The extremist group, which forged links with British neo-Nazis when it was founded in the 1980s," wrote correspondent Helena Smith, "has begun opening offices in Germany, Australia, Canada, and the U.S."

In May 2014, Greek-Australian supporters of Golden Dawn and members of the far-right Australia First Party held a joint protest in Brisbane to support the neo-fascist organization in Greece. "We shall call on the Greek government to release from jail the illegally imprisoned Golden Dawn members of parliament," the Australia First Party wrote on its website ahead of the demonstration.[5] "Their protest was overshadowed by a counter, anti-fascist rally staged by up to two hundred unionists and members of the group Antifa," *Brisbane Times* reported.

In August 2014, Golden Dawn European Parliament member Georgios Epitideios and party organizer Michalis Giannagkonas announced plans to visit Australia. A backlash quickly ensued. A swath of groups representing ethnic and religious minorities sent a statement to Australian authorities demanding that they block the visit. "Australians have a proud record of bravery and sacrifice in fighting and defeating fascism in the twentieth century," read the letter, which was signed by honorary secretary of the Greek Orthodox Archdiocesan Council, Nicholas Pappas.[6] "We call on all Australians to unite once more to demonstrate their detestation of the message of hatred and the violent politics being propagated by groups like Golden Dawn." That visit was subsequently canceled.[7]

Back in Europe, Golden Dawn fostered friendly relations with far-right, populist, neo-Nazi, and white supremacist groups across the continent. Jonathan Leman, a researcher and journalist at the Sweden-based watchdog magazine *Expo*, told me that members of

Sweden's national socialist Nordic Resistance Movement (NRM) maintained an ongoing dialogue with Golden Dawn. "Some activists in NRM have contacts in Golden Dawn and visited them [in Greece]," he said.[8]

In May 2014, according to the NRM's website, group members visited Golden Dawn in Chania, a city on the island of Crete. In the blog post, a photo showed NRM members holding up their green-and-white flag and posing with the Golden Dawn members. "It was a very interesting meeting," the post read.[9] "The meeting ended with me telling them about our organization and even expressing our support for their comrades who were brutally executed," it continued, ostensibly referring to two Golden Dawn members who were allegedly shot dead by anti-fascists in the wake of Pavlos Fyssas's murder.

On the same day, a Golden Dawn–linked blog also hailed the ties between the two groups.[10] "It was an important moment when the head of the squad of Swedish nationalists said from the podium that Golden Dawn is a beacon of hope and a guide for all European nationalists and an example to be imitated," the post said. It was accompanied by several photos of Golden Dawn members posing with NRM activists.

In June 2016, Daily Stormer published an interview with Golden Dawn's New York division and NRM leader Simon Lindberg. In that discussion, Lindberg praised Golden Dawn's food banks and their frequent resort to force. "I can say that Golden Dawn, first of all, [is] a very good source of inspiration for us," he explained, "because nowhere else—at least in the twenty-first century—we can actually see a truly nationalistic and anti-Zionist organization grow like Golden Dawn has managed to do. They actually accomplished a lot of things."[11]

Lindberg proclaimed that Golden Dawn "lead[s] the way . . . I can also say I'm very impressed with your social activities, where you hand out food to your people and defend them physically in the suburbs." At the end of the interview, Lindberg offered these closing words. "Of course, white people throughout the world differ a bit from each other," he said. "We don't share the exact same DNA, all white people. We may have different cultures, we may have different religious beliefs, we may speak different languages, and so on. But I do believe that our thirst for freedom is the same within every white heart . . . Our enemy, the enemy of our people's freedom, is the same all over the world no matter which country you live in. Our struggle is global; we must all take our responsibility."[12]

In the United Kingdom, the far-right British National Party (BNP) threw its fervent support behind Golden Dawn, particularly in the wake of Fyssas's murder. In January 2014, its then leader Nick Griffin visited Athens with the stated goal of incorporating Golden Dawn into his plan to forge an alliance with several European far-right parties. "The relationship [with Golden Dawn] is still very much in its infancy," Griffin told a reporter.[13] "From what I've seen of them they are very similar to the other nationalists in Europe."

Griffin dismissed descriptions of Golden Dawn as a neo-Nazi group as a "ridiculous smear." In a joint press conference with Golden Dawn spokesperson and other party members, Griffin stated that the neo-Nazi outfit "has already won the moral victory . . . now they will move on to legal victory as well," referring to the charges piled on the Greek fascist party after Fyssas's murder.[14]

In May 2014, French far-right leader Marine Le Pen, who headed the National Front, denied reports that her party was seeking to sculpt an alliance with Golden Dawn after a flurry of news articles suggested such efforts were underway.[15]

Forza Nuova and CasaPound, a pair of Italian fascist groups, were also similarly linked to Golden Dawn.[16] CasaPound and

Golden Dawn established close ties. Michaloliakos visited CasaPound headquarters in 2015, and members from each group visited their counterparts from time to time to participate in joint events. In January 2018, for instance, Golden Dawn members trekked to Rome to join CasaPound in a commemoratory march dedicated to two teenage Italian neo-fascists shot dead in Rome in an incident that became known as the Acca Larentia killings in 1978. "Once again, Golden Dawn was present, reviving its relations with the CasaPound national and social movement and honoring the fallen comrades," the party wrote on its English-language website, likening the slain Italians to Manolis Kapelonis and Giorgos Fountoulis, the Golden Dawn members shot dead in Athens's Neo Irakleio area in an apparent anti-fascist revenge attack following the murder of Fyssas.[17]

Until 2017, Golden Dawn was a member of Alliance for Peace and Freedom, a coalition of far-right, Eurosceptic, and pro-Russian political parties from countries across Europe, including Slovakia's Kotleba—People's Party Our Slovakia, Italy's New Force, the National Democratic Party of Germany, Spain's National Democracy party, and others.

Among the most important friendships Golden Dawn maintained throughout the years was with Russia, a relationship largely manifested in the close ties with Aleksandr Dugin, the ultra-nationalist ideologue who popularized the concepts of Eurasianism and National Bolshevism. The crux to that friendship was the shared Orthodox Christian faith, a point repeatedly stressed in Golden Dawn propaganda praising Russian leader Vladimir Putin and Dugin.

In 2014, Golden Dawn functionaries Artemis Mattheopoulos and Eleni Zaroulia met with Dugin in Moscow, who was advising President Putin at the time. "Mr. Dugin believes the destiny of our country is the creation of a new empire with cultural content, based on ancient Greek values," Golden Dawn's New York branch subsequently wrote on its website.[18] "The Golden Dawn," it continued, "is a natural ally of Russia and is fighting American expansionist policies. Russia is perfectly aware of the political persecution against us and believes that this is precisely because we talk openly in favor of a geopolitical shift towards Russia."

A 2016 report by Political Capital, a Budapest-based research group, observed that the Golden Dawn–Russia connection was partially fueled by increasing antagonism toward the US during Greece's financial crisis. "Golden Dawn's heavy-handed xenophobic, anti-Muslim policies, and its intolerant ideology, fit the Kremlin's authoritative approach on many issues," the report explained.[19]

The party is nonetheless drawn more by the Russian regime's statism and authoritarian nationalism than by its orthodoxy. The pro-Russian far right is part of a broader far-right and far-left "patriotic subculture," apt to portray President Putin and Russia as a potential "savior" to Greece and the Greek economy.[20]

Over the years, Golden Dawn's respect and admiration for Russia's autocratic regime was echoed time and again in blogs, articles in its newspaper, and by its followers. In February 2014, Golden Dawn proclaimed support for its pro-Russian "compatriots" in Ukraine against what they characterized as the attempts to foment a civil war by the "ravens of international usury [in] Washington and Berlin."[21] Between February and March of that year, Golden Dawn's "compatriots" and their backers in Moscow took up arms in a bloody conflict that led to Russia's annexation of the Crimea.

UNSURPRISINGLY, GOLDEN DAWN had close ties with Germany's National Democratic Party (NPD) and other German neo-Nazis, chiefly in Bavaria.[22] These relationships were not merely gestural. Through its bloody pogroms in migrant-heavy neighborhoods, Golden Dawn emulated "the practices of the German neo-Nazi NPD party with its notorious 'nationally liberated zones,' especially in cities and regions of the former [German Democratic Republic]," Dimitris Psarras observed.[23]

Drawing on the tactics of Italy's *Ordine Nuovo*—New Order, an Italian far-right organization active between 1957 until its forcible dissolution in 1973—Psarras has argued that Golden Dawn's violence was designed to pressure leftists and anti-fascists into carrying out violent retribution.[24] In Italy, this practice gained notoriety as the "strategy of tension." From 1969 until 1974, Ordine Nuovo's splinter affiliates—namely, the New Order Political Movement—carried out several bombings, including a 1974 attack that left eight leftists dead during an anti-fascist rally in Brescia. "They [Golden Dawn] want to force the other side's hand into committing similar violent acts, just like during the strategy of tension in Italy in the seventies," Psarras argued in a 2013 interview.[25] During Italy's Anni di piombo ["Years of Lead"] its government was widely accused of exploiting alleged communist attacks to carry out mass arrests, while turning a blind eye to far-right violence. Thirty-five years later in Greece, the parallels were self-evident.

BY 2015, GOLDEN Dawn had gone from spray-painting swastikas in shadowy alleys of Athens three decades earlier to becoming the country's third largest party, all the while commanding the imagination and admiration of excitable fascists, ultra-nationalists, neo-Nazis, and white supremacists from Europe to North America, from Australia to Russia. Andrew Anglin wasn't the only American to travel to Greece to learn from the party's experience. Matthew Heimbach, founder of the Traditionalist Worker Party (TWP), represented the clearest example of an effort to re-create a Golden Dawn model in America. From 2014 until his March 2018 downfall as a leading white supremacist in the US, Heimbach was deeply invested in attempts to implement Golden Dawn's ideas, strategies, and models. Heimbach preached the necessity of coupling physical violence and street-level force with social programs—soup kitchens, drug addiction treatment, and donation drives—similar to the ones Golden Dawn enacted at the height of its popularity and the peak of Greece's economic crisis.[26]

In 2014, Heimbach began posting videos of interviews with leading Golden Dawn members on the group's YouTube channel after traveling to Athens. Among those Heimbach spoke with were Georgios Epitideios, a member of the European Parliament, and Irene Pappas, the wife of Greek parliamentarian Christos Pappas. At the time, Christos Pappas was locked up in pretrial detention as part of the trial against his party. "Golden Dawn is the edge of the knife fighting this war against modernity and globalism and that is why I have always and will always proudly say 'Hail the Golden Dawn!,'" Heimbach wrote after returning to the US.[27]

Later, authorities cut loose Pappas, Michaloliakos, and the rest of the detained party members, who had reached the maximum period—eighteen months—that the Greek justice system allots for pretrial detention.

Heimbach, a vocal convert to Orthodox Christianity, returned to Greece again in 2015, meeting with Michaloliakos and other leading party figures in the Hellenic Parliament and the party's offices. Afterward, he wrote fawningly that the presence of crucifixes in the party's offices represented a "true symbol of Golden Dawn fighting for the faith, family, and folk of Greece."[28]

Three years later, the practical influence of Golden Dawn on Heimbach's white nationalist organizing was on full display in Charlottesville, Virginia, where one of the largest white supremacist rallies in recent history culminated in the murder of thirty-two-year-old anti-fascist protester Heather Heyer in broad daylight. During that rally, dubbed Unite the Right by its organizers, white supremacists, white nationalists, and neo-Nazis attacked community members, anti-racists, and anti-fascists around Charlottesville on the night of Friday, August 11, and throughout the following day. Anti-fascists and others fought back, and Charlottesville was transformed into a battleground for two days.

On Saturday afternoon, as Heimbach and his cohorts were marching around the city and engaging anti-fascists and others in street brawls and attacking minorities, James Alex Fields plowed his car into a group of anti-racist marchers. Dozens were injured, and Heather Heyer was killed. Shortly after her murder, Heimbach spoke to VICE reporter Elle Reeve. When she asked about their "organizing tactics," he replied: "Sure, [we're] primarily following the European example of Golden Dawn, Nordic Resistance Movement, and other organizations that really are at the vanguard of nationalist organizations in the world."[29]

In Greece, just days after the bloodshed in Charlottesville, angry members of parliament pointed out that Golden Dawn hosted Heimbach in Athens. Golden Dawn had also published a glowing profile of the white supremacist on its website, including photos of him shaking hands with Michaloliakos, ahead of Unite the Right. In another statement, Golden Dawn celebrated the incident as a "dynamic demonstration against illegal immigration."[30]

Prominent though he was, Heimbach, who had racked up a mound of legal challenges throughout his activism career, was also a highly controversial figure within America's white nationalist movement. Heimbach labored exhaustively to gain media attention for TWP's supposed community outreach efforts, including a campaign to fight the opioid epidemic among rural Americans, with "job training, prison outreach, and environmental activism."[31] When police arrested Heimbach for domestic battery in Paoli, Indiana, in March 2018, his effort to build a Golden Dawn–like group in the US tumbled to an embarrassing end. Thanks to the trial in Greece, Golden Dawn was at risk of a similar fate.

CHAPTER SEVEN

"BURN THEM ALIVE":
THE POGROMS
CONTINUE

Two years had passed since my first visit to Lesbos when I returned to the island in December 2017. On that earlier trip, the refugee crisis was still new, and the far right had yet to seize the swell of refugee boats shoring up on the island to suit their own political desires. Much had changed throughout that period, and Lesbos was no longer a stopover for refugees and migrants; it was effectively a prison, an island where asylum seekers were forced to remain until their asylum applications were processed. If they were accepted, they could move on to mainland Greece, start a new life there. If they were rejected, they were doomed to stay on Lesbos until being shipped back to Turkey, back to another state of limbo.

On my first day back on Lesbos, I drove to Moria, the former military barracks that had been repurposed into a refugee camp designed to accommodate around three thousand people, maybe less, depending on who you asked. Two years earlier, refugees stayed there for a handful of nights and then moved on to Athens, to Berlin, to Stockholm. The changes that had taken place on Lesbos were apparent as I rolled up to the camp, searching for a spot to park the car within walking distance but also far enough to avoid damages should protests break out, should riot police lob tear gas and flash bangs, should the refugees there defend themselves with stones, with sticks, with bottles, with whatever they could find lying around in the fields spilling out around the camp.

Misery hung low in the air like a cloud. Queues of men and women, some of them with babies in arms, stretched around the camp. I learned that the camp had swelled to more than twice its capacity. In the fields surrounding it, refugees who couldn't find space inside the camp lived in tents that provided little protection from the winter chill. Diapers, shit, and small mounds of garbage flecked the fields around Moria. The smell of strange medleys—a goat stolen from a nearby farm, some potatoes and vegetables, rice—rose from cauldrons sitting atop bonfires. Barbwire adorned the fence squaring in the camp's interior, stretched as far as I could see.

A yellow shack with a tin roof was perched on the hillside olive grove, surrounded by tents and ramshackle shelters. OUR ONLY COUNTRY, OUR CHILDHOOD DREAMS, read graffiti tagged on its backside. I walked up the hill, toward a Syrian family sitting cross-legged around the fire. I found a man named Jalal Ahmed al-Talaa. The olive trees surrounding his tent weren't much different from the ones he remembered in Syria, the country he'd fled a month earlier, but he'd never imagined he'd live in an olive tree grove, especially not in Europe. During his final months in his home country, the Islamic State was in its final throes in Deir Azzour, the region where he and his family lived. Syrian government forces were rapidly advancing, leaving a trail of dead bodies in their wake. His plan then was simple: Make it to Idlib, a rebel stronghold, and then cross into Turkey. From there, take a boat to Greece and move onward to Germany, where his brother had received asylum two years earlier. Challenges mounted early on, though. His wife gave birth to another child, his newborn son, in an undersupplied clinic in Idlib, and traveling with an infant and a wife fresh from delivering was harder than he'd imagined. Worse still, Greek authorities placed the family in Moria, forbade them—like everyone else there—from moving on to the mainland until their asylum claim was processed.

Jalal was only thirty, but years of living under siege, of surviving the Islamic State's draconian rule, and watching neighbors and relatives gunned down around him, had taken their toll. Europe was their only hope, he thought, but arriving in Greece, he learned that hope was scarce in Europe. "I knew the island was bad, but I didn't imagine it was this awful," he told me.[1] I wondered how anyone could have imagined this. "I didn't imagine you had to wait two hours to go to the toilet."

Jalal had bribed rebels at checkpoints back in Syria, places where people crossing ran the risk of being whisked off to a dungeon, held until someone in their family could cough up enough money to cover a ransom. He'd paid smugglers, crossed the sea on a dinghy that, he felt, could have been swallowed by the Aegean at any moment. Now he spent his days resting in his tent, scavenging for food—the food provided by camp authorities often wasn't enough—and waiting in lines: queues to see the doctor, queues to see the camp authorities, queues to use the shower, queues for everything. "It's very bad here," he said, "and people with special cases, such as injuries or newborns, need to be allowed to move on to Athens . . . Whenever you tell the doctor something is wrong, they only say you should drink more water."

All around Jalal's tent, families banged hammers on tent posts, trying to batter them down into the hard earth beneath. Not far off, I found another man wearing an air-pollution mask, milling around the fence surrounding the camp. A muffled cough beneath his mask. The flu, he said. Three or four days now, he said. His name was Abu Mohammed al-Qallab, and he was forty-one. He told me Syrian government forces had tortured him for his pro-opposition activism back home. Now, life in Moria tortured him every day, he said. He drifted out into the field, searched for scraps of wood to burn that night. "It gets very cold here at night," he told me. Fierce charcoal clouds had gathered above, and he worried that it might rain, searched for stones to weigh down the base of his tent. "This is a big prison," he said, and a man passing by chimed in: "Moria is no good."

Pants and T-shirts, sweaters and winter coats, and underwear and bras were draped from the barbwire fence. WELCOME TO PRISON MORIA, someone had spray-painted on a concrete wall adorned with the gate's fence. I spent three days on Lesbos, and everyone I met had suffered, had bathed in frigid hose water, or had eaten rotten food that upset their stomachs. Some had been treated for food poisoning. Sitting on a bench at the bottom of the hill, not far from the camp's entrance, was Basil, a forty-one-year-old from Nigeria. Asylum applications were backlogged, and he'd already spent a year in Moria. "We came for help," he told me, "but this is a big ghetto. Only God sees what they are doing to us here."[2]

BACK IN MYTILENE, the capital of Lesbos, a few dozen refugees had decided to fight against their detention in Moria. That fall, they had occupied Sappho Square for more than a month until riot police swarmed their impromptu camp and tried to force them to return to Moria. Instead, they occupied a local office building belonging to Syriza, Greece's ruling left-wing party. There, thirty-four refugees and migrants, most of them Afghans, took over the building with the help of local anti-fascists. They fortified the windows, padlocked the gate. They issued a single demand: to be allowed to move to the mainland.

One night that December, I walked over to the office and loitered around the gate until someone came and let me in. Inside I found seventeen-year-old Karime Qias, an Afghan refugee whose family—she came to Greece with her mother and seven siblings—had been shocked when they arrived in Moria, when they found themselves effectively imprisoned. "The facilities were not hygienic," she told me, "and the food was not edible."

She was sitting in the office's kitchen area, a few fellow squatters sat beside her. Thirty-four people altogether, including a couple from Iran, had taken to sleeping in the office. The anti-fascist solidarity activists provided security, operated patrols to make sure police or Syriza supporters weren't moving to raid and evict them. "Because the food in Moria was not edible, we continuously suffered from vomiting, diarrhea, and constant dehydration," Karime said, but "when we would go to the doctor, the doctor would say everything is fine."[3]

Moria had attracted aid groups, humanitarians, and human rights observers from across the world. Time and again, they sounded the alarm on the plummeting conditions inside the camp, but it was all to no avail. Every now and then, the government announced plans to "decongest" the island and transferred a few hundred asylum seekers to camps on the mainland, but it was never enough to keep up with the steady pace of arrivals. "They are treating people like animals and slaves and in a very dehumanizing way," she added. "We didn't come to Europe to be imprisoned . . .

and have no agency. It's every human's right to have control of their choices."

I spoke with Arash Hampay, an Iranian whose father had been gunned down by the government back in Tehran. He'd helped in planning the occupation. Arash had spent several stints in prison, including a stretch in the notorious Evin Prison in Tehran, and he'd come to Greece with his brother more than a year earlier. Greek authorities granted him asylum, but at the time I met Arash, his brother had been rejected. Arash said they chose Syriza's office for one simple reason: That was the ruling party at the time, and they didn't much care if that party was left-wing or right-wing; all that mattered was that refugees and migrants were marooned on the islands and trying to forge an existence in the misery of the camps. Syriza, however, had responded harshly, issuing a statement accusing the occupiers of "adventurism" and providing cannon fodder to "xenophobic and racist voices" on Lesbos. "This extreme attitude of this small group of refugees does not reflect . . . the thousands of peaceful refugees and immigrants on our island," the local Syriza branch said.

As far as Arash saw it, the government's policy of warehousing people on the islands was what fueled the "xenophobic and racist voices" on Lesbos. Arash told me that "it is the 'leftist' government of Syriza that is implementing" the "dirty European policies" that "created these conditions for refugees," adding: "The Greek government has to be held responsible for turning this beautiful island into a concentration camp for refugees."

Karime's sister Ely came in and joined us. Her family had traversed the mountainous border between Iran and Turkey, she said, and braved an overcrowded boat from Turkish shores to Lesbos two months prior. They couldn't be expected to survive all that only to share a tent with twenty others, strangers, in Moria, could they? "Before people come to Moria, they aren't ill, but everyone becomes sick once they are there," she told me, "and at night, we were afraid to leave the tent because there were fights."

The fights are what first prompted the Qias family and other Afghan and Iranian refugees to occupy Sappho Square that fall. Hampay shook his head, chimed in. "If Europe wants to close its borders, can it also shut down the arms factories that create refugees as well?"

The occupation stretched on for a few more weeks. In the end, the government caved. Everyone moved on to camps and squats on Greece's mainland. But back on Lesbos, more people arrived, and more boats sidled up to Fortress Europe's shores, by the day.

The morning after I met the occupiers, I drove back out to Moria, only fifteen minutes from the promenade of Mytilene, and found Jalal Ahmed al-Talaa still sitting in the same spot, still wearing the same clothes, as the day before. Down the hill, a few men used a hose to splash water on their faces—it was too cold to bathe, and no one wanted to risk getting sicker than they already were. Jalal watched them, thought for a moment. "There isn't anyone here who didn't go into debt to get here," he told me. "Most of us already have relatives in Germany or elsewhere. Whenever you put everyone on the island and don't let them leave, you create big problems—and there are going to be more problems."

ALL THROUGHOUT THE rest of 2018, tensions mushroomed on Lesbos and the other islands hosting refugees and migrants. With no space in the already-packed Moria refugee camp, and few people able to get spots in the nearby Kara Tepe camp, more and more refugees found themselves sleeping in fields, public squares, and on sidewalks. When a Syrian family slipped out of Moria during clashes inside the camp one day in July 2018, a seventy-eight-year-old farmer with a history of brandishing a shotgun approached and opened fire, hitting a sixteen-year-old boy.[4] The boy was rushed to the hospital, and the police later detained the man, who claimed that the family had attempted to rob him. According to local media reports, the boy narrowly survived the gunshot injury.

Only a couple months before the Syrian boy was shot outside Moria, an omen had appeared on Lesbos. The island of Lesbos, celebrated for supposedly driving away the local Golden Dawn chapter early on during the refugee crisis that began in 2015 eventually felt the consequences, too. On the evening of April 22, 2018, refugees and solidarity activists staged a protest in Mytilene's central square, rallying against living conditions in the camps and the suffocating restrictions on movement.[5] Some two hundred far-rightists broke through the police barricades, hurling rocks and glass bottles, firing flares. Solidarity activists attempted to form a human chain around the asylum seekers, but the attackers kept pressing forward. Eventually police officers intervened, dispersing the attackers with volleys of tear gas and stun grenades. But the refugees and migrants who survived the incident would remember what their attackers had screamed that night in Lesbos, a chilling threat that echoed throughout Sappho Square: "Burn them alive."

CHAPTER EIGHT

"YOUR STORY BEGINS IN THE MOUNTAINS": NATIONALISM RISES AGAIN

On the night of February 3, 2018, Golden Dawn was planning to demonstrate in Athens. It was meant to be boisterous shows of strength, this time to mark the annual commemoration of the 1996 Imia incident, the crisis during which three Greek naval officers died near an uninhabited and disputed island in the Aegean Sea and almost brought the two countries to war. I took the metro from Syntagma Square toward a stop on Mesogeion Avenue, where Golden Dawn's headquarters were. Most of the passengers were everyday citizens, people heading home from work, others riding with their children to wherever they were heading. A few caught our eye: Greek flags, face masks in their grips. Greek photographer Nick Paleologos and I exited at our stop and stepped out into the night, taking a winding path

down residential streets carving through a shadowed neighborhood where the streetlights had yet to click on.

A few hundred yards off we could see Mesogeion Avenue.
Torches appeared in the distance, men and women marching in
unison toward the office where the rally was slated to take place.
"Blood, honor, Golden Dawn," we heard them chanting, their
words echoing through streets and alleyways.

Hearing that, Nick turned to me and said, "We have to stick
together tonight."

GOLDEN DAWN SUPPORTERS rallied for Imia every year, but
this year the protest had another source of fury, something that
overshadowed the deaths of those three Greek officers more than
two decades earlier. In recent months, the Syriza-led government
had re-launched negotiations with Skopje over the decades-long
name dispute between the Republic of Macedonia and Greece.
The left-wing government was prepared to concede the name
Macedonia with a qualifier—such as Northern Macedonia—and
the Republic of Macedonia was open to change, desperately hoping to enter the European Union and NATO. The negotiations
hadn't gone over well in Greece, where nationalists, right-wing
politicians, the far right, and a considerable number of centrists
considered any compromise on the name *Macedonia* a matter of
national betrayal. Only two weeks before the Golden Dawn rally
that night in Athens, a massive show of defiance erupted a five-
hour drive north in Thessaloniki, the country's second-largest city.

That protest, the first of several, took place on January 21, and
some three hundred thousand people flooded the squares and
streets of Thessaloniki. According to their estimation, Macedonia
was only Greek.[1] A decade of demonstrations against financial

crisis, years of crippling austerity, and lengthy periods of protracted violence against refugees and migrants had rarely been able to spur so many people to take to the streets, but here they were, raising blue-and-white Greek flags to the sky, singing the national anthem, and calling for the left-wing government to be toppled. An anti-fascist group in Athens described the mushrooming Macedonia protests as a "greenhouse" for neo-Nazi recruitment.[2]

Most opponents of the country's use of the name Macedonia were not—neither then, nor now—adherents of the far right. But from the outset Golden Dawn and others like it seized the opportunity to catapult themselves into the mainstream discourse by tapping into a deep well of nationalist sentiment. But these rallies served as a launching pad for the nascent Golden Dawn who joined the first protests and registered as a political party the following year, in 1993.[3] Rather than alienating everyday Greeks with Nazi salutes and fascist chants, Golden Dawn and likeminded groups appealed to a broader audience by fashioning themselves as sensible patriots, said journalist Dimitris Psarras. "They tried to use this opportunity to participate and recruit young people," explained Psarras. "After that, they had to show that they are not the same as all the other people who participated in the demonstration, so they made [several] attacks."

The two countries made little progress over the years, and the dispute appeared intractable until late 2017, when Macedonia's center-left party won elections and Zoran Zaev became prime minister. Unlike his right-wing predecessor, Nikola Gruevski, Zaev was open to compromise and eager to lead his country into the European Union. Talks resumed, and Zaev's government began removing road signs and renaming buildings named after Alexander the Great and other historical figures claimed by the Greeks. In Skopje, far-rightists and nationalists railed against the agreement, and in Greece, violence exploded onto the streets.

In 1992, Golden Dawn had joined the first protests against their northern neighbor's declaration of independence under the name Republic of Macedonia; the nascent group used the rallies as an incubator, an opportunity to carry out attacks on leftists and anarchists. Twenty-six years later, they were back in the fold of the anti-Macedonia camp, this time using the rallies as a last-resort effort as their party's pulse flatlined and support crumbled under the weight of the ongoing criminal organization trial. And Golden Dawn made no secret about their participation in the Thessaloniki protest, a reality that prompted little meaningful condemnation from New Democracy, the right-wing opposition party, or the Greek Orthodox Church. Although New Democracy and the Church issued milquetoast pleas for their followers to avoid the rallies, officials and acolytes of both claimed that the Macedonia name negotiations constituted a legitimate issue of national sovereignty, and they flocked to join the festivities, effectively stamping a seal of approval on the wave of militant nationalism washing over the country.

The far right festered among their ranks, and on January 21, they seized the rally as an opportunity to carry out violence against political opponents. As the rally wrapped up and the streets cleared out, a group of far-right participants set off toward a pair of anarchist squats in Thessaloniki's city center. Someone spray-painted GOLDEN DAWN on the city's Holocaust memorial.[4] Apparently furious about a counterdemonstration held by anti-fascists and anarchists, a rabble of far-right thugs set off from a statue of Alexander the Great and first attacked The School, one of the squats.

The anarchists at The School put up a fight, pushed the fascists back, and sent them back on their way. Their efforts thwarted, the attackers, accompanied by a group of soccer hooligans, regrouped and moved on to Libertatia, a three-story squatted social center in the Faliro quarter of the city. The building had survived the Nazi

occupation of Greece during World War II, and in 2008, a group
of anarchists squatted it and initially established a social center
for immigrants.

Over time, Libertatia grew into a larger operation, a squat
where several groups provided social services for people in the
city.[5] That day, it went up in flames. Dozens of far-right attackers
shot flares and hurled bottles at Libertatia. A blazing projectile
flew up above the front stairway, landed on the porch, and the
building caught on fire. Flames crawled up its face, incinerated
the shuttered windows, and spread throughout the rooms. Dark
plumes of smoke hovered over the street outside. Firefighters arrived, but it was too late. All that remained was the shell of a
building, its guts burned to ash. "It is a historical building: one
of the few that survived the Nazis, but unfortunately [it] was destroyed by their grandchildren," one Greek anarchist told the UK-
based website Freedom.

The organizers of the Thessaloniki rally saw it as a stun-
ning success. Three hundred thousand people had voiced their
opposition to the name negotiations, had taken to the streets
in a display of popular anger. The organizers hoped that a fol-
low-up demonstration in Athens on February 4 would draw the
participation of at least a million people. Three days before the
Athens demonstration, I attended a press conference at a hotel
in Omonoia, a neighborhood in the capital. Despite the organizers putting on an air of professionalism, it only took a few moments for the press conference to devolve into a colorful circus of
nationalist hubris and wild-eyed conspiracy theories. Around a
hundred people packed into the room, some standing against the
wall in the back. I sat in the last row and took notes, listening
to one speaker after another spout lines about the supposed plot
against Greece. "The only thing they're missing is tinfoil hats,"
someone sitting nearby muttered.

Nina Gatzoulis, a historian and member of the World Committee of Pan-Macedonian Associations, a civic group that promoted Greek Macedonian culture and trafficked in revisionist historical theories, launched into a bizarre tirade. Gatzoulis laid out a supposedly shadowy scheme to strip Greece of its sovereignty by erasing its historical and cultural connections to the name *Macedonia*. (To my knowledge, no one, not even the most ardent nationalists in Skopje, had ever denied or objected to the fact that Greece also had a region called Macedonia.) Gatzoulis pointed to United Nations negotiator Matthew Nimetz, whom she claimed had a spurious history of employment at nonprofit organizations funded by the Jewish, Hungarian-American billionaire and philanthropist George Soros. I'd covered the far right across Europe and North America for years, and Soros's name was a constant fixture, a man they viewed as so slick and conspiratorial that he could undermine entire nations. In the United States, fascists shouted time and again that Soros funded Antifa; in Hungary, the far-right prime minister Viktor Orbán repeatedly blamed Soros for the refugee crisis that started in 2015; here in Greece, Soros apparently lurked behind every supposed plot to spread anti-Hellenic propaganda and undermine the country's national sovereignty. At one point, Gatzoulis made the strange claim that Coca-Cola was somehow in cahoots with Soros's plan to steal Macedonia from Greece and hand it over to Skopje. "We should love our fatherland and do everything to get it," she said.[6] "Let us be all as one and fight bravely."

She also insisted that the organizers had no affiliations with political parties, a claim that rang hollow for anti-fascists, journalists, and other critics. That same day, Greek foreign minister Nikos Kotzias received a threatening letter that promised "three bullets" just for him.[7] It was, according to officials, only one of several death threats Kotzias had fielded in a span of just a few weeks.

＊

THAT NIGHT IN front of Golden Dawn's headquarters, the protest attracted around five hundred people. I stood near the front, keeping close to the other reporters, photographers, and videographers who'd shown up to cover the event. Up on stage a group of Golden Dawn supporters raised long flagpoles upward. The red flags, emblazoned with the party's swastika-like logo, had frilled decorative edges, shivered in the night breeze. The buzzing city lights had turned the night skies purple, but down on the ground, torches blazed above the crowd. Once enough people had amassed in the crowd, a Golden Dawn member invited a few photographers up to the podium, let them snap shots from the elevated platform. Golden Dawn members regularly mobbed reporters, smashed their equipment, and threatened to kill them, but here they were asking us all to come up and take a few panoramic shots. I wondered if they thought the crowd would look larger than it was from up there.

The rally got underway, and early on a speaker from the National Popular Front, a Golden Dawn offshoot party in Cyprus, addressed the audience with a screed about the links between the fight against the Macedonia name negotiations and their supposed struggle against the ongoing Turkish occupation of Northern Cyprus.

The torches were still blazing, and every now and then, the protesters broke into chant. "Blood, honor, Golden Dawn," was a frequent one. "Punks, politicians, traitors," another went. In the front row I saw several children, some of them wearing Golden Dawn T-shirts, some of them singing along with the nationalist mantras. A familiar lineup of Golden Dawn's high-ranking members and officials—spokesperson Ilias Kasidiaris, parliamentarian Ilias Panagiotaros, a few shaved heads I didn't recognize—took turns at the podium, recycling the same talking points about the sanctity of the nation, the moral imperative of nationalism, the persecution of nationalists, the criminalization of nationalism. They mobilized just about every synonym of *persecution* you could find in a thesaurus, coupled alongside every adjective, noun, and linguistic variant relating to the word *nation* that you could dream up. (Of course, every speaker made the requisite reference to Macedonia, that strip of land that had reinvigorated nationalists from Greece's southernmost tip to its northern frontier.) Each time a speaker thanked the protesters and finished their speech, rambunctious applause filled the air around us.

Nikolaos Michaloliakos, the party founder, stood with his hands folded over this crotch at the stairs attached to the podium, waiting his turn. He wore a black sport coat with no tie, a white button-up beneath it. He was only a few yards from me, but a security detail stood nearby like a wall of defense. Not without good reason—anti-fascists had attacked these headquarters and other Golden Dawn offices several times in the past, busted the joints up with flagpoles, tire irons, and sledgehammers, and scrawled less-than-polite messages on their walls: Once at the party's offices in central Athens, vandals edited the spray-painted slogan WE WANT OUR COUNTRY BACK to WE WANT OUR WELL BACK, a snarky reference to the Well of Meligalas, where communist guerilLas tossed the breathless bodies of dead fascists after gunning them down in a field in 1944, one of the darker acts of retribution during the Greek Civil War.[8] It was the closest distance from which I'd ever seen Michaloliakos, and he was stumpy and short. I watched him for a while: His face was slack, entirely expressionless, and he looked bored, as if this was all part of a routine, as if it was just a day job he had to trudge through until he could clock out and go home. He adjusted his glasses, lifted his hand, and checked his wristwatch.

That all changed when a speaker introduced him, and he ascended the stairs. Michaloliakos is a fiery orator, and his voice—it is croaky, has a sort of curmudgeon quality that, at least to me, feels like an assault on your ears—only underlines the anger that imbues his speeches. He rouses crowds, sends electric volts through his supporters, a fact that testifies to the depth of the cult of personality he cultivated within Golden Dawn throughout its nearly four-decade existence. In one 2012 speech that frequently appeared as B-roll footage in news segments and documentaries, Michaloliakos raised his hand in a fascist salute in front of some two thousand supporters. "We may sometimes raise our hand this way," he bellowed, "but these hands are clean, not dirty. They haven't stolen."[9]

That night ahead of the Macedonia rally, Michaloliakos was true to form. He swung his stubby arms, his face mangled. Everyone but Golden Dawn was guilty. Everyone but Golden Dawn had betrayed the nation. Everyone but Golden Dawn was part of the anti-Hellenic conspiracy. Exasperated, he paused occasionally, adjusted his glasses, and heaved—all that talk about the struggle for national liberation was exhausting, after all. During each break, the crowd interjected. "Anarchists and Bolsheviks, this land doesn't belong to you," they chanted in a singular shriek, thrusting their burning torches as high as they could in the twilit sky.[10] The torch light flashed across their faces, grimaced and tight lipped, as they glared back at their leader. And again: "Blood, honor, Golden Dawn."

Michaloliakos started up again. "Greece is not only the sell-out politicians," he said. "There are also people like us." (The crowd again chanted, this time: "Punks, politicians, traitors.") If the organizers of the Macedonia rally the next day didn't harbor any loyalties to political parties, no one had passed on the message to Golden Dawn. "Tomorrow there are no parties," he said.

"There is only Greece and Macedonia . . . It's only Greece and Macedonia—to overthrow the anti-Greek government and stop their anti-Greek plans from passing."[11]

DURING THE DAYS leading up to the rally, anti-fascists, squatters, and refugee solidarity activists were concerned. Everyone had seen what happened in Thessaloniki, had watched on the news as the flames consumed Libertatia. A few sensational media reports had alleged that armed fascist militias were gearing up for the protest, preparing to unleash a series of attacks on political opponents around the city. Dozens of squats dotted the map of Athens, and if far-right participants wanted to identify a target, they'd have plenty to choose from. Thousands of refugees and migrants lived in and around a dozen of those squats, making them particularly vulnerable.

I woke up that morning and walked down to Exarchia Square. A bone-rattling breeze swept through the place, and most of the cafés, restaurants, and shops were shuttered. I made the half-hour trek to Syntagma Square. Halfway there, I saw the Hellenic Police's riot vans blocking Akadimias Street, parked sideways. Police officers stopped anyone who tried to pass, checked their identification cards—a counterdemonstration was getting underway down the street, and they worried that anti-fascists may try to slip past them and seek out a confrontation. Arriving in Syntagma, the city's central square, I saw that the crowd was large, but it was a far cry from the million-plus patriots the organizers had promised. A police spokesperson later told local media that the demonstration hadn't topped one hundred forty thousand people, adding that many of them had been bused in from other cities, towns, and villages around the country.[12] MACEDONIA IS NOT

For Sale, declared a banner, a massive one stretching more than a dozen yards and held up by several dozen people.

On the podium, Mikis Theodorakis made the case for Greece's exclusive claim to the name *Macedonia*. "Macedonia is and will always be Greek," he said. The audience responded with roaring applause.[13] "It is not nationalism, but patriotism to defend the homeland and its people."

Theodorakis's participation in the rally had left many anti-fascists and leftists depressed. He was ninety-three years old, a renowned composer, and in recent years, he had adopted several uncharacteristically nationalist political stances. Born on the Greek island Chios in 1925, Theodorakis had for decades enjoyed prominence as an icon of resistance to injustice. Still a teenager, he traveled to Athens in 1943 and signed up for a reserve unit of the Greek People's Liberation Army (ELAS), the militant wing of the communist party, a group of battle-hardened rebels that waged a brutal fight against the Nazi occupation during World War II and against the nationalists during the country's civil war (1946–1949). During the Greek civil war , Theodorakis was captured and exiled to Icaria, an island in the Aegean Sea. Later, after being transferred to Makronisos, he survived brutal torture. He later became a fierce opponent of the military junta that ruled the country with an iron grip from 1967 to 1974. He provided the iconic soundtrack to Costa Gavras's Oscar-winning political thriller Z. During that time, the composer was exiled again for his vocal opposition to the regime of the colonels. Before being banished from the country, Theodorakis saw his music banned and spent a five-month stint in prison. Once in exile, he continued to advocate for democracy in Greece and was received by international anti-imperialist icons such as social-ist Yugoslav leader Josip Broz Tito and Egypt's Gamal Abdel Nasser, the Arab nationalist leader who represented to many a bulwark against Zionism and the occupation of Palestine as well as American hegemony in the Middle East.

More than seven decades after taking up arms against fascists, Theodorakis had drifted rightward, and his rhetoric hardly diverged from that of far-right nationalists who ardently opposed Macedonian self-determination. After the composer threw his weight behind the protests, a group of anarchists vandalized his home in the Acropolis area of Athens. The vandals doused the walls in red paint and left behind a message. YOUR STORY BEGINS IN THE MOUNTAINS, they wrote in spray paint, referring to the regions that provided a haven for communist guerillas during World War II and the Greek Civil War, AND ENDS IN THE NATIONALIST SWAMP OF SYNTAGMA.[14]

There in Syntagma, the onetime leftist hero shared a stage with Greek Orthodox clergy and virulent nationalists who called on Greece to conquer Istanbul and rebuild Constantinople, to assert Greek control over the historic Hagia Sofia, which was a church for a thousand years before the Ottoman Empire converted it into a mosque in 1453. Theodorakis wasn't the only self-described leftist betraying his principles. The Communist Party of Greece (KKE), although it did not participate in the rally, dipped its toes into the swamp. In a statement, the KKE had claimed that the "Greek people" were "justifiably concerned" by "developments" surrounding Greece's northern neighbor. The party attempted to frame the dispute as an "imperialist" plan orchestrated by NATO.[15]

Although the KKE formally denounced the "irredentist" claim that Greece had an exclusive right to the name, the party said: "The developments aren't exclusively about the Greece-FYROM [Former Yugoslav Republic of Macedonia] relations. They consist [of] part of the overall plans that are being promoted by NATO, the US, and the EU in order to strengthen their economic-political-military presence in the Western Balkans and the broader region."[16]

The rally marked an embarrassing failure for its organizers, but the danger was nonetheless present. Golden Dawn threw fliers out across town, leaving the leaflets strewn across the pavement in alleyways and streets. MACEDONIA IS ONLY GREEK, the leaflets read. GOLDEN DAWN. Anti-migrant graffiti appeared on the city's walls. Although protest organizers failed to put on a show of strength, the participants were nothing if not daring. All around the city, black-clad Greek nationalists tried to launch attacks.

AROUND 5:00 P.M., as the protest peaked in Syntagma Square, dozens of men appeared in front of Embros, a squatted theater around a mile from the square. Embros was one of the many self-organized, autonomous spaces in Athens, and they had just wrapped up a three-day theater exhibition. A lot of people were still hanging around inside, chatting about the exhibition, and the squatters worried that the space was an easy target for the fascists amassing outside. They called for help, and a few dozen anti-fascists showed up, denying the would-be attackers the opportunity to spill blood.[17]

I returned to Exarchia shortly after nightfall. There I found notes posted on the doors of apartment buildings, warning that fascists could attempt to invade the area. I walked around the narrow residential streets and reached the square. The normally crowded area sat empty save for a few migrants listening to a radio, huddled around small bonfires. Down one street, I saw a band of young anti-fascists, wearing gas masks and motorcycle helmets, mulling around with sticks and metal rods. The site looked like a scene from *The Road*, Cormac McCarthy's post-apocalyptic novel.

A fire here. A guy digging for garbage there. Another guy wielding a sledgehammer. MACEDONIA BELONGS TO ITS BEARS, said one poster plastered on a wall near the square.

Now and then the sound of a disparate Molotov cocktail filled the night sky, followed by a stun grenade, usually from some corner on the periphery of the neighborhood where riot police had posted in anticipation of clashes. Those were the only clashes, but they were mild compared to the near-weekly battles between anarchists and police in the neighborhood.

Along with a handful of photographers, I turned down Notara and headed to the squat. Outside a group mulled around, motorcycle helmets hung on the crook of their arms, holding baseball bats and flagpoles. The night was quiet save for the occasional *bang* of a stun grenade and the chatter in front of the squat. Not much going on, someone said.

A couple months later, I sat in the reception area of Notara, the squat for refugees and migrants in Exarchia, with Marcos, a pseudonymous solidarity activist and anarchist. He was in his early forties, wore a Star Wars T-shirt, sported a thick goatee, kept filters and tobacco in a fanny pack fastened around his waist, smoked cigarettes in rapid succession, and had chosen his dog's name as his nom de guerre. Crushing one cigarette into an ashtray and sparking another, he spoke for a while about Exarchia. Cops and fascists alike had long targeted the neighborhood, he said. They knew that Notara would likely be a target during the rally—black soot was still smeared across the side of the building, a reminder of the August 2016 arson attack. Everyone had prepared, practiced security measures, patrolled the neighborhood, and relayed anything suspicious they saw back to their comrades at the squat. Every able-bodied person had a role to play, he said. If police advanced toward the squat, or fascists appeared in the street outside, the solidarity activists would confront them while the refugees and migrants, many of them vulnerable due to a lack of residency documents, would retreat inside the building. "We had information that they had discussed . . . entering [Exarchia] on that day," Marcos explained.[18]

Notara adopted the strategy employed by the broader anti-fascist and anarchist movement in Exarchia. That is, they focused on defending their spaces rather than launching offensive attacks. "In Syntagma, you could not just go clash with them," he said. "If the protesters were all fascists, I think Molotov cocktails would have fallen like rain . . . but to name everyone a fascist is to devalue the word."

His comments flew in the face of the rhetoric of centrist liberals and nationalists, both of whom had often regurgitated the overwrought claim that anti-fascists did not engage in nuanced discussions about what exactly constitutes fascism and who constitutes a fascist. While small bands of insurrectionary anarchists clashed with police on the periphery of the neighborhood during the weekend of the protest, most activists focused on defending their spaces, squats, and strongholds. For that weekend, anti-fascist organizers avoided much of the infighting and intra-movement squabbling that often pops up during mass mobilizations. The protest concluded without any successful raids on Notara or Exarchia. "If we didn't [defend the squat], most likely we would have had serious problems in the area," Marcos said, "but I think the mobilization of all the people of the movement, people of solidarity, and comrades was what prevented the fascists from [carrying out a successful attack]."

AROUND FIFTEEN MINUTES walking from Notara was City Plaza, a squatted hotel that provided residence, at any given time, to between two hundred and four hundred refugees. Like Notara, solidarity activists there practiced self-defense in the lead-up to the Macedonia rally, implemented carefully planned security preparations.

Leftists and refugees had occupied the abandoned hotel nearly two years earlier; it sat in a neighborhood that housed an eclectic assortment of crisis-punished Greeks, long-established migrant communities, and newly arrived refugees. For two years, the hotel's owner had tried to get the municipality on her side, had tried to convince the police to evict the squatters, and had made her case to any reporter that sought her out for comment on the squat. Because activists at City Plaza regularly engaged with the media, and often organized pro-refugee rallies in the capital, they suspected the squat may fall in the far right's crosshairs during the Macedonia rally.

Nasim Lomani was one of the chief architects of the squat, had been there since its inception in April 2016. At thirty-six years old, with years of left-wing activism under his belt, the refugee crisis had led him to throw himself even deeper into organizing. After all, he had fled his native Afghanistan nearly two decades prior, arriving in Greece as a teenager and a refugee, penniless and not knowing the language. Nasim had never been attacked, but his name regularly cropped up on far-right and neo-fascist websites. Once in 2011, while living in the Platia Attiki, he'd had a close brush with fascists. Platia Attiki was infested with racist violence, and he'd noticed men following him on several occasions. One night that year, he spotted a couple of guys, a suspicious pair, following close behind as he walked home. Hoping to avoid a confrontation, he ducked into a gas station. He waited there for eight hours while the men, whom he was now certain had intended to attack him, stood around outside until sunrise. A week later, he packed up his bags and moved to Exarchia.

I had met Lomani several times since 2016. He was always willing to speak to reporters, and he could be found nearly every day sitting around at City Plaza. At night, he haunted a handful of bars in Exarchia. After the Macedonia rally, I phoned him and scheduled a time to talk.

When I arrived at City Plaza for my interview with Lomani, I found him in the reception area. He wore an orange hoodie, unzipped, over a black T-shirt that read: HUMANS WITHOUT BORDERS. A five o'clock shadow occupied the bottom half of his face, and he spoke with a gentle but gruff voice as he recollected what he described as "the weekend of nationalism."[19] A steady stream of residents passed each other on the stairs leading into the hotel. Children giggled and ran in circles near the reception desk. A man in a beanie and house slippers sat on a nearby bench, charging his phone in the corner of the foyer.

After hearing of the violence in Thessaloniki before the Athens rally, Lomani and others at City Plaza knew they needed to be prepared. They coordinated with other squats and activist networks, all of which worked together to support one another in the lead-up to and during the rally. "Of course, refugees, the LGBTQ community, activists, leftists, and anarchists are the first target of the fascists," he told me.[20]

For his part, Lomani couldn't imagine a large mob of violent racists bursting into the hotel, dragging people from their rooms. Rather, he worried about the possibility of a quick hit-and-run attack like the one that targeted Notara two years earlier. With a seven-story hotel full of families—around half of the residents were children—a fire at the entrance would be detrimental and potentially fatal.

When the weekend of the rally finally arrived, more than two hundred solidarity activists, among them Greeks and volunteers from across Europe and beyond, mobilized at City Plaza to help protect the squat. For twenty-four hours a day, shifts of dozens of activists and refugee residents alternated patrolling the building's perimeter and keeping watch from the balconies. When far-right-ists cruised by on motorcycles, or inched past in crowded cars, none dared to make a move on the heavily guarded space. "You could recognize people who were suspicious," Lomani said. "We were ready for any possibility or attack."

According to Lomani's estimation, the two-day flurry of organizing demonstrated not only effective community self-defense. It also sent messages to both the far right and the broader society. "It showed that this isn't only a building with some people living inside," he insisted. "It's also a center of struggle and mobilization. I think it was well done."

Inside the squat movement and the broader solidarity community, the experience served to strengthen mutual bonds and confidence. "It's not only about solidarity activists protecting other people. It's about participation, and it's a practical way of warning people of what's dangerous and what's happening, how they can protect themselves and how they can be part of the same struggle," Lomani continued. "It gave strength to people living here and let them know that they are not alone. It brought us all closer."

Beyond that, the counter-mobilization sent a resounding message: City Plaza, Embros, Notara, and the rest of the squat community would resist fascist violence. "It told them not to think about doing anything stupid," Lomani said. But the threat didn't disappear after that weekend. If, as Lomani insisted, the weekend served to demonstrate that the anti-fascist movement was still there and ready to fight back, he couldn't have known what lay in store in future Macedonia protests. The far-right elements buoying the rallies would be sure to assert their presence.

*

THOSE ORGANIZING THE anti-Macedonian rallies condemned the violence from time to time, but participants did little to oust the far-right agitators from their ranks. In the fall, Golden Dawn chief Nikolaos Michaloliakos took to the pages of the party's newspaper, *Empros*, to accuse the Syriza-led government of national treason. "True Greeks," he declared, would never accept a deal in which their northern neighbor's name includes a reference to Macedonia.

In November, when Golden Dawn threw its support behind high school students demonstrating against the proposed accord with Macedonia, education minister Costas Gavroglou warned that the neo-fascist outfit sought "to inject nationalist poison into schoolchildren."[21]

Christos Rigas, founder of the far-right LEPEN (Popular Greek Patriotic Union) movement, led his followers to an Athens mosque, where they paraded anti-Muslim banners, and chanted slogans calling for anti-fascists to be stabbed, and brawled with anarchists in the capital's city center. Rigas, a former Golden Dawn central committee member, had also deployed LEPEN supporters at anti-deal rallies in Athens and elsewhere. He was a large, lumbering man, someone who'd once been accused of a double murder and got off the hook.[22] His fledgling new nationalist outfit was small, but his reputation was vast; he was one of the few former Golden Dawn members who could speak out against the party without prompting a response.

When I met him at his souvlaki restaurant in April 2018, Rigas crushed a cigarette into an ashtray as he accused the leftist-led government of plotting to "create a fake state" at the expense of Greek sovereignty. Arguing that the negotiations fit into a US plan to counter Russian influence in the Balkans, Rigas grimaced. "Macedonia is one, and it's only Greek," he said. "It's about our history and our ancestors. Skopje will never be called Macedonia. We won't negotiate the name."

In June, police arrested four far-right men armed with knives, an electroshock weapon, and twenty glass bottles while traveling to a Macedonia protest in Thessaloniki.[23] That same month, then-Greek foreign minister Kotzias told a local radio station he had received more than eight hundred death threats in the first six months of the year. Among them were envelopes bearing bullets and a box of blood-soaked soil.[24]

In July, Golden Dawn parliamentarian Konstantinos Barbarousis took the podium in the parliament, his long brown hair falling to his shoulders and framing a bushy-bearded face. The unsnapped top button of his pristine white dress shirt revealed the top of his chest. "The dismemberment of Greece has begun," the thirty-seven-year-old lawmaker declared, calling on the Greek army to "abide by their oath" and arrest the prime minister, defense minister, and president to "prevent this treason."[25]

With outrage mounting, Golden Dawn begrudgingly expelled Barbarousis, who went into hiding after authorities revealed that they were investigating him for high treason. Police arrested him a few days later. After appearing in front of a magistrate court a week after his fiery tirade, Barbarousis posted $35,000 bail and was freed from detention. Authorities issued him a temporary travel ban and mandated him to check in with police three times a month.[26]

That same week, the far-right tabloid *Makeleio* published a paper bearing images of the prime minister, the foreign minister, and the president shot dead by a firing squad. "At eight meters, like Beloyiannis," the headline declared, referring to a Greek communist leader who was executed in 1952.

In September, when a fracas broke out between photographers and a protester during a Macedonia rally in Thessaloniki, a second demonstrator revealed a gun and threatened the photojournalists.[27]

*

ON JUNE 17, 2018, Nikolas Kokovlis arrived in Syntagma Square and scanned the crowd. Greek flags as far as he could see, stretching all the way to the twin stairwells leading up to the parliament. A freelance photographer, he was on assignment for a local newspaper. He snapped a photo, and then spotted turmoil ahead, up toward the front of the demonstration. He weaved through the swell of bodies, shot a few photos as gusts of wind swept through the demonstration and left the sea of flags trembling against the gray-carpeted afternoon skies. He noted the hostility in the crowd early on. "Rape Kammenos," a red-faced woman shouted, referring to the Greek defense minister. "Tsipras's mother is a whore," a group of men not far off shrieked of the left-wing prime minster.

Small beams of sun hacked through the low-hanging clouds, glinting off a cluster of riot shields. Rows of riot police perched on the stairwells, blocking protesters from advancing. Inside the broad, salmon-colored parliament, a neoclassical building that once housed Greek royalty, Greek lawmakers were debating an event taking place more than three hundred and fifty miles away on the shores of Prespa, a pair of lakes straddling Greek, Macedonian, and Albanian borders. There, Greek foreign minister Nikos Kotzias and his Macedonian counterpart, Nikola Dimitrov, were hashing out the details of a final name agreement, an accord that would formally end the conflict between the two countries and open up the path for Skopje's ascension to the European Union and NATO. That day, Kotzias and Dimitrov agreed that the former Yugoslavian country would change its name to the Republic of Northern Macedonia, a concession from both sides. In Brussels, European Union officials celebrated the development. A step toward stability at a time when populism and far-right nationalism held hostage much of Europe.

There under the shadow of the parliament, though, these concessions weren't popular. It was a muggy day, but the youngsters draped in black slid on their masks, geared up for whatever it was they were planning. Others waved Greek Orthodox Church flags. Some raised placards bearing the faces of saints. In the front row, Golden Dawn supporters cracked their knuckles, chanted against the Syriza-led government, which, they insisted, were a treacherous bunch that had sold the nation.

Kokovlis pushed forward through the columns of sweaty bodies, grimaced faces, and hastily scrawled placards. He noted the sharpening hostility, the violent slogans, but standing a full head above most protesters, he could not avoid being noticed. When he reached the front, the twenty-five-year-old photojournalist noticed the black-clad youth moving in quick dashes. He realized they were attacking the riot police guarding the Greek parliament. Chunks of concrete whirred over the protesters and bounced off the police officers' shields. Empty beer bottles shattered into puddles of shards at their feet. Kokovlis lowered his head, lifted his camera, and snapped a photo of the youngsters. Someone clawed at him, yanked his camera strap from behind, he later recalled in an interview. Thistles of pain shot down his neck. Spun around, he found himself blinking back at eight flag-bearing men, their faces covered, their eyes searing through masks. His heart hammering, Kokovlis eyed possible escape routes, but the men encircled him.

The mob screamed at Kokovlis, accusing him of intentionally photographing protesters' faces, and set upon him. Their flagpoles crashed into his torso, their boots collided with his thighs. Noticing his darker skin tone—Kokovlis is of mixed Greek and Portuguese ancestry—they shouted "half breed" as they pummeled him. Kokovlis wobbled but kept his balance. No one objected, no one intervened, and no one appeared to notice, he later told me.

The photographer burst free, but not before his attackers dashed off with his camera and bag, disappearing into the mass of demonstrators and endless rows of Greek flags. "They saw that my skin is darker and that I had a camera," he later told me, "and they asked if I was taking pictures of faces [because] they're afraid of people seeing what happens during these rallies."

The police eventually dispersed the protesters, and the Greek government deflected criticism from New Democracy, the main opposition party, and far-right outfits like Golden Dawn. But with lower voter turnout in Macedonia's September referendum casting uncertainty on the agreement's finale and a majority of Greeks polled opposed to the accord, Greece's once-ailing far right seized the moment to propel ultra-nationalist rhetoric back into the mainstream political discourse.[28]

In the weeks following the dismal referendum, junior coalition leader and ultra-nationalist defense minister Panos Kammenos decried the results as invalid, even though his own party was in a governing coalition with Syriza. Far-rightists attacked a left-wing lawmaker in Kalamata, and Greece gained a new (albeit short-lived) far-right party, the Force of Hellenism.[29] In mid-October, after a heated exchange in which Kammenos lambasted him over the accord and accused him of being backed by Jewish billionaire philanthropist George Soros, Kotzias, the Greek foreign minister, handed in his resignation.[30]

With vigilante attacks piling up, Kokovlis urged fellow reporters to remain steadfast. "I'm worried, but I won't stop doing my job," he concluded. "People need to know the truth . . . and we [journalists] are a threat to the fascists."

*

KOSTIS NTANTAMIS, A thirty-six-year-old freelance photojournalist, had seen the attacks on press workers like Nikolas Kokovlis,
and had, initially, avoided covering the protests. With a long po-
nytail and an earring, he worried that he could be marked as a
leftist or anarchist by far-right groups infiltrating the demonstrations, although he had worked as a journalist for nearly a decade.
But when he accepted an assignment to file photos for Sputnik,
a Russian media outlet, he headed to the protest on January
20, 2019. It was a Sunday, and tens of thousands of people had
amassed in front of the Greek Parliament in Syntagma Square,
and Ntantamis photographed the attendees for more than four
hours without incident.

Inside the parliament, Greek lawmakers debated a motion to
ratify the accord. The afternoon wore on and the protest took a
violent turn in the streets outside. Ntantamis rushed to a nearby
office to file photos and returned to the rally around 4:15 p.m. to
snap a few more photos before the day ended.

He spotted in the distance far-right protesters scuffling with
police officers from the riot squad. A fog of tear gas laid siege
to the area, and he tightened his gas mask and secured his helmet. Blue-and-white flags fluttered under the ashen sky. Stepping
into the mayhem, he elbowed his way forward, jostling for space
to snap a photo of masked youth stomping an officer who was
splayed out on the pavement in front of the stairs leading to the
parliament. Tear gas seeped into his mask, and he again pulled its
straps tighter. As he turned to leave, a man pulled down the scarf
covering his face and said, "Give me your camera."

"Sorry, man, but I'm doing my job, and I'm leaving now,"
Ntantamis replied, but within moments he realized a throng of
some seven men armed with sticks had encircled him. Flagpoles
and wooden poles thudded off his protective helmet, and one

attacker yanked him by his camera strap. Lefteris Partsalis, a thirty-two-year-old photographer and videographer for Xinhau and CNN Greece, had just finished recording the attack on the police officer when he spotted Ntantamis in trouble. "When I stepped out of the cloud of chemicals, I saw Kostis," he recalled, explaining that the masked attackers "were trying to hit him" in parts of his neck and throat unprotected by a mask and helmet.

Partsalis ran to his colleague and attempted to separate him from his attackers. Partsalis tried to reason with the men but eventually gave up and turned to leave. The men pursued Partsalis and Ntantamis, several of them catching Partsalis when he tripped and fell to the street. They whacked him with sticks, but he made it back to his feet. "He's secret police," a masked attacker screamed to the others.

"They were going after everybody with a camera," Partsalis later recalled.

One man ripped off his gas mask, while another took a handful of his camera strap and pulled on it. Unwilling to give up his camera, he clutched it by the body. One of the attackers plunged a screwdriver into his hand, leaving a deep hole in the flesh. Partsalis broke from the men and ran, sticks and stones whizzing past his head as he darted away. "If I'd have left moments earlier, I would have been safe," Partsalis said. "But if I hadn't started running, they would have never stopped hitting me."

At the same time, another mob pounced Ntantamis, knocked him to the street. He curled into a ball, attempting to protect his neck and torso from the blows. The assailants tore away his camera and snatched a backup camera from his backpack. As the strap broke, his helmet rolled away, and his mask was pulled off. He looked up as the crowd opened and braced himself as a man entered wielding a thick flagpole with both hands like a baseball bat. The first blow rattled the top of his skull, and the second slit another large gash on top of his head. Blood streamed down his face as the attackers ripped out fistfuls of his hair.

Suddenly the attackers stopped and moved on. Ntantamis rose to his feet, still in a daze, and adrenaline dulled the pain. A man tossed him a packet of Kleenex. "Take the whole thing," the man said. "You're going to need it, you fucking asshole."

Ntantamis darted from the area, beelined down the street until he found colleagues. "I didn't look back," he said, "because maybe I would've provoked them by just looking back at them." He took a seat on a curb and surveyed his stained clothes, wiped blood from his eyes with the tissues. He counted back from one hundred several times, trying to assess whether he was dizzy or had incurred a concussion. He was sure he had neither, but blood continued to flow from the pair of gouges on his skull. A medic came and treated the wounds, and an ambulance shuttled Ntantamis to a nearby hospital.

Sitting in the emergency ward and waiting to receive stitches, Ntantamis noticed a bald man with arms blanketed in far-right tattoos. "He had five or six doctors working on him because it was an emergency," he recalled, "but he was still staring at me angrily." It took thirteen stitches to seal the wounds on Ntantamis's head.

Back in Syntagma, riot police eventually pushed the far-right rioters from the square. As the tear gas settled, news of more attacks emerged. In the hospital, Ntantamis tried to quell his anger and fear as he learned that he was only one of several reporters attacked that day. Around an hour before the assault on Ntantamis, a gang of five protesters surrounded Thomas Jacobi, an Athens-based foreign correspondent and documentarian who coproduced *Golden Dawn: A Personal Affair*, a film that examined the rise of the neo-fascist party during the early years of Greece's economic crisis.[31] They screamed at Jacobi about the documentary he had worked on, and then the group pummeled him, punching him in the face and busting his nose.[32] Afterward, they forced him to delete photographs and video clips from his phone and smashed his audio recorder. The attackers scattered as a throng of riot police approached.

Later that evening, an Athens-based union for photojournalists issued a statement speculating that the attacks "may be premeditated," pointing to the reports that the black-hooded assailants had arrived equipped with photos of well-known reporters and photographers to target.

On January 25, five days after the violent rally, the parliament narrowly ratified the name accord, with more than 150 of 300 lawmakers voting in its favor.[33] By the end of the week, the police had arrested a handful of suspects. The name deal was official. But in the snaking streets of Athens and elsewhere, the anger still simmered, and some of the most radical elements of the far right were enjoying a fresh burst of energy.

When I spoke to him nearly three months later, Ntantamis had yet to return to work. Shaken but defiant, he said, "Of course, I'm not going to stop doing my job. When I was taking the beating, I knew that these were the types of photos and footage that need to be shown, to show what kind of people they are, what they do, and how they act."

He added, "These protests have given a lot of strength [to fascists], and I'm really afraid that another time of pogroms will come again. Average people are saying, 'OK, they are too strong, they're too violent,' so they don't oppose them. It's really dangerous because you don't know when or from where you're going to be hit, and they don't discriminate [between targets]."

CHAPTER NINE

"YOU CAN KILL EACH OTHER AFTER I LEAVE": THE FAR RIGHT LASHES OUT

On February 25, 2018, in Piraeus, the port city next to Athens, Eleftheria Tombatzoglou and five other volunteers showed up at the Favela Social Center at around 5:00 p.m., a little earlier than usual, opened their doors, and started preparing for a weekly meeting. Each Sunday, the activists at the social center welcomed their neighbors and planned the week's activities: dance lessons, history courses, photography classes, and book club meetups. Tombatzoglou was thirty-eight, a longtime lawyer and left-wing activist, and represented the family of slain rapper Pavlos Fyssas.

Activists had founded Favela nearly a year earlier, and the social center stood out in Piraeus, where the number of openly left-wing spaces paled in comparison to neighboring Athens. Right-wing and far-right parties had long been active in the port city, and Golden Dawn's local branch ranked among its most violent and most notorious in the country.

Tombatzoglou and the others set about organizing the room: They unstacked the chairs and arranged them around the table. Nothing appeared out of the ordinary until a thin man entered. He wore blue jeans, a black jacket, and a motorcycle helmet. The way he strolled in confidently, almost cheerfully, surprised Tombatzoglou. His helmet's mask hung open, a grin stretching across his face.[1] "It was like he was surprised he made it in so easily," she told me. Then another man—shorter, stockier, and dressed in all black—appeared in the doorway. All of a sudden, a wave of black-clad men poured into the building. They stormed toward Tombatzoglou and the others, slipping wooden poles and tire irons from beneath their coats. A moment passed before the anti-fascist activists realized what was happening, but it all sank in. "No way," Tombatzoglou said.

"You know what happens next," one replied.

The room froze in a brief instant that felt to Tombatzoglou like hours. Then the assailants lunged toward the activists. They smashed windows and tables, stomping on the furniture and pounding it with their weapons. A few lit road flares and waved them in the faces of the activists. A tire iron came down hard on Tombatzoglou, first on her shoulders and then on her skull. "In Piraeus?" the man beating her shouted. This was Golden Dawn territory, he said, and the party wouldn't tolerate left-wing organizing in their backyard. "Seriously?"

Her vision went blurry as the rod thudded on her head—once, twice, and then again and again. "Faggots," she heard. "Cunts."

After a few minutes, someone shouted, "Time's up."

Before anyone could gather their wits and fight back, the attackers barreled down the hallway and out the door, disappearing into the winding alleyways outside. "Blood, honor, Golden

Dawn," Tombatzoglou heard them chant. She placed her hand to her skull to assess the wounds. She pulled it away and saw her palm drenched in blood. More blood dripped down her hair, soaked the back of her shirt. She put her hand back on her head and applied pressure to the wound, but the blood kept flowing. Police and paramedics arrived, and the latter stapled her head, but it was no use. The gash kept spilling until doctors sewed eight stitches in her skull later that night at the hospital. Another activist received two stitches.

It looked like a storm had passed through Favela, the meeting room in shambles. Tables, windows, and chairs lay busted on the floor. The flares had left papers charred and destroyed. Backpacks were burned up, ruined. "I have read more than a hundred times the way they [Golden Dawn] do attacks," Tombatzoglou told me. "In a way, I was prepared. I know what these people are capable of doing, and I thought that sometime in my life I'd find myself in this situation."

It wasn't the first time that fascists targeted Favela, but that attack stood out as the worst. In April 2017, only a month after the social center opened shop, supporters of the far-right Autonomous Maeandrist Nationalists (AME) movement vandalized the building. PIRAEUS BELONGS TO THE NATIONALISTS, the spray-paint read. A swastika and crudely sprayed crosshairs were next to it. Four months later, in August 2017, the Golden Dawn splinter group Apella tossed a barrage of Molotov cocktails at the building. Police later tracked down five suspects they believed carried out the attack—officers from the counterterrorism unit found in their homes knives and flags bearing swastikas.[2] All that was scary enough, but nothing shocked Tombatzoglou like the raid on February 25. "I didn't ever expect them to do something like this because of the trial," she said.

Only two hours after the attack, Golden Dawn released

a press statement. The party had nothing to do with the incident, Michaloliakos said. That puzzled Tombatzoglou—the victims had been tending to their injuries in the hospital, and no
one had spoken to the press yet. Of course, she knew Golden
Dawn lurked behind the attack, but no one had accused them
of anything yet. When police officers did eventually round up a
group of suspects, they learned that two of the men were active
Golden Dawn members—and one of the attackers, who reportedly worked as Michaloliakos's driver, had been fingered in the
attack on Tombatzoglou's fellow civil prosecution lawyer Evgenia
Kouniaki in November 2017, an attack that took place in front of
an Athens courthouse in broad daylight and that left Kouniaki
with a busted nose. [3]

THREE MONTHS EARLIER, Kouniaki had exited a trolley near the
courthouse where a panel of judges inside listened to testimony in
the ongoing trial. Stepping onto the pavement, she spotted several
fliers scattered about: Golden Dawn pamphlets commemorating
two members whom anti-fascists allegedly killed in 2013, retalia-
tion for the murder of Pavlos Fyssas. She started toward the stairway leading to the court's entrance, but stopped short—looking
up, she saw a blur of black-clad men sprinting down the sidewalk,
chasing a man who was now heading toward the trolley. The man
leaped into the trolley, but his pursuers followed him. "Close the
doors," Kouniaki shouted up to the driver. It was too late. The men
were already in the train, hammering the man with wooden poles
and slugging him with their fists.

Kouniaki had worked on the legal support team for Egyptian
fishermen attacked by Golden Dawn in 2012, and she knew how
the party operated, had witnessed its attacks. She wasn't the type

to stand by with folded arms. Once during the rapid surge in violence in 2010, she rushed to Agios Panteleimonas to help a group of Afghan refugees after an assault that left them bloodied and bruised. She pulled out her notebook, asked the victims what happened, and jotted down the answers. Around fifty people, apparent Golden Dawn supporters, surrounded her. They hurled insults, threatened her. "There were a lot of attacks in Agios Panteleimonas in this period," she told me, "and normally when people [attacked] went to complain to the police, they were arrested."

Kouniaki urged the police to intervene and arrest the mob for inciting violence against her and throwing eggs at her, and a police officer slammed her against the wall. "You will not file any complaint," he told her. In the end, the far-right crowd claimed that the Afghans had attacked them first. The police detained the refugees for lacking residency documents. When news outlets caught wind of the attack, Kouniaki spent the subsequent weeks weathering death threats.

That day in November 2017, as the mob pounded a man on the trolley, Kouniaki tried to intervene again. She jumped back on the bus, screamed at the attackers. One turned her way and sent a fist crashing into her nose. Blood streamed down her face, onto her shirt. When they were satisfied with the beatings, the men walked off. As they passed a cluster of police officers stationed outside the courthouse, no one ran, no one sprinted, and no one was stopped.

Weeks passed before the police found suspects—twenty-five of them, all Golden Dawn supporters, she said. Kouniaki went down to the station to identify the man who hit her out of a lineup, but none matched his description. She recognized her attacker from Golden Dawn's Piraeus chapter, and he wasn't among the men pulled in for the lineup. When I met her in December 2017, her attacker still hadn't been brought in for questioning, not to her knowledge, although she'd found his name and shared it with the investigators working her case.

She spent more than a month thinking about the attack, and although not shocking, she found it worrisome. So confident were Golden Dawn's members that they could beat a civil prosecution lawyer suing the group—outside the very courthouse where sixty-nine of its members, including its leadership, stood accused of operating a criminal organization and overseeing years of lynch mobs in Greece. "I was shocked because the reality is that I didn't believe it could happen outside of the court where they are on trial," she told me.

I asked if she was fearful, and she said she wasn't. Kouniaki was confident that the court would convict Golden Dawn of most or all the charges, but she knew that a guilty verdict wouldn't guarantee justice. Only the maximum possible sentences would do that, and Greek courts had a long history of downplaying the severity of far-right extremism and violence. "They are not afraid of police," she told me. "The police opened the path and let them pass. You cannot see this with another political group. Secondly, they are panicking. It wasn't only me; other people were yelling at them. They feel pressure from people, so they got angry. I cannot explain everything really."

TWO MONTHS AFTER the attack on Favela, I met Tombatzoglou again one afternoon in April 2018 at a café in Athens. She had thought long and hard about what happened that day. All around Athens and Piraeus, far-right attacks were again surging. She wondered why Golden Dawn went to such lengths to deny their involvement in the attack—perhaps the internal conflicts in the party were sharpening—but she knew there were still more to come. "They cannot hold it back," she told me. "It's their nature. They cannot exist without violence. There is no point in being a member of this party without the violence."

MARCH 22, 2018. Athens, Greece. Around 9:00 a.m., Taher Alizadeh arrived at the office of the Afghan Community in Greece. At forty-three, he served as the president of the organization, a position he had taken over after Yonous Muhammadi's four-year leadership term. Alizadeh worked five days a week, showing up every morning and filling out paperwork, arranging asylum interviews for refugees, and organizing advocacy efforts for Afghans in Greece. The fifth-story office was located in Omonoia, not far from the square, and was surrounded by drab, gunmetal gray apartment blocks, office buildings, and parking garages. Crime had swelled in Omonoia throughout the economic crisis, but migrants, refugees, and working-class Greeks gravitated to the area for its cheap rent and central location in the capital. A five-minute walk to Exarchia, a ten-minute trot to Monastiraki, the tourist area overlooked by the Acropolis. Alizadeh checked in on the volunteers in the office. Another normal day. A handful of refugees sat around waiting for consultation on their asylum requests, but the volunteers had it under control. He hung around for a while, and then stepped out. He had a few errands for his other job, a home renovation business.

Back at the office, the volunteers decided to step out for a late lunch at around 1:00 p.m. As always, they locked the door: Tucked away in filing cabinets were thousands of documents pertaining to asylum cases, and robberies weren't uncommon in Omonoia.

A few minutes later, Alizadeh's cell phone rang. It was the maintenance man. "Do you know your office is on fire?" he asked.[4]

He panicked, scrolled through his phone to dial one of the volunteers on shift that day, but before he could press call, his phone rang again. It was an activist from an anti-fascist organization. Someone had phoned the daily newspaper *Ethnos* and taken credit for an attack on the Afghan Community in Greece. An article broke the news online. The caller had told an *Ethnos* reporter that he belonged to Crypteia, an obscure neo-Nazi group, and that the fire was a message to migrants: Leave Greece, or else. Alizadeh's mind raced. Was anyone hurt? Did anyone die?

He called several colleagues and finally got one on the line. He was relieved—no one had been present when the office went up in flames. Alizadeh and the others rushed back to the office and found the fire extinguished, but the damage was severe. Flames had swum through the single room, crawled up the walls. The door hung loose on its hinges, charred and blackened. Soot covered everything. Framed photos lay on the ground, their glass panes shattered. A desk in the corner was cracked in the middle, sagging to the floor and standing on two legs. Puddles of water. Charcoal patches of ash smeared across the walls. The flames had touched everything, had danced, zigzagged, and wrapped around furniture, leaving chairs, filing cabinets, and tables collapsed and mangled. Altogether, fixing the damage would cost the Afghan Community in Greece nearly ten thousand euros. The organization needed to replace electronics, computers, a printer, tables, a desk. Files and documents had been incinerated. All those asylum applications, all those residency forms, disappeared in the fire. "This makes our work much harder," Alizadeh later told me. "Some of those files hadn't been digitized yet, so they are completely lost."

✳

THE NEXT MORNING, reporters mulled about the destroyed office. A few snapped photos. Yonous Muhammadi stood there, his arms folded. He wore a blue sports coat, denim jeans, and boots. He surveyed the wreckage around him, took it all in, and shook his head solemnly. "Crypteia is a new name for us," he told me.[5]

A gust of wind entered through the broken window, sent shivers through a pair of flags—one Greek, another Afghan—on the conference table. The smell of souvlaki rose up from the street and mingled with the odor of burned furniture. Next to the busted door, propped up on a radiator, a sign welcomed visitors to the Afghan Community in Greece. Anti-racist activists and migrant community leaders packed into the office for a press conference. Alizadeh addressed the crowd. "If the law doesn't hold them accountable," he said of the attackers, "I'm worried this could happen again."

The room was full, and I stepped out into the hallway. There I found Naim Elghandour, a towering man with a bald head. He was sixty-four and served as president of the Muslim Association of Greece. Since migrating from Egypt to Greece decades earlier, he had witnessed attacks firsthand and saw his name pop up on far-right websites from time to time. He had his doubts about Crypteia, he told me. Two months earlier, a blocked number called his phone. He answered in Greek. "Hello?"

"We are the ones who kill refugees and Muslims, who burn mosques and who attacked Emir's home," the caller said, referring to an attack on an Afghan refugee's home two months earlier.

"If you were a man, you'd call me from a phone number that isn't blocked," Elghandour shouted.[6]

The next morning, Elghandour checked the news and learned that several migrant organizations and nonprofit watchdogs had received the same phone call: An unidentified man claiming to belong to Crypteia, promising to expel Muslims from the country.

The timing struck Elghandour as suspicious. Only a few days earlier, he testified against Golden Dawn at a courthouse in Athens.
There on the stand, he delivered an eight-hour testimony about the
party's wave of violence against Egyptian fishermen between 2010
and 2013. If they thought they'd deter him from speaking out, he
said, they were wrong. "If you are going to call me from a secret
number, then fuck you," he told me. "We've learned from everything that happened. Anyone who has belief in god isn't scared.
Every human has two important dates in their life: the date of his
birth and the date of his death. Their birthday is already known,
and the day they die is up to god."

What alarmed him, though, was the police inaction. Crypteia
had been claiming responsibility for attacks since the previous
October, but authorities hadn't arrested anyone yet. "The police
need to act because they know very well who these people are,"
he said, insinuating that Crypteia was actually a front group for
Golden Dawn. "They are an enemy of everyone, of humanity."[7]

Elghandour wasn't the only one at the Afghan Community
in Greece's office with doubts about Crypteia that day. Stepping
through the wreckage, I found Petros Constantinou, a city
councilor and director of the anti-fascist union KEERFA.
Constantinou knew Golden Dawn's modus operandi well; he'd
been on the frontline of more anti-fascist rallies than he could
count, and he'd fought Golden Dawn members in the streets.
Golden Dawn was lashing out because the trial had left it isolated
and vulnerable, he told me. "They want to show that they are [still
here]," he said.[8] He stepped over the legs of a chair, broken and
singed. A day earlier, when the attack happened, the court heard
evidence that suggested high-ranking Golden Dawn members
communicated second-by-second in the moments leading up to
Pavlos Fyssas's murder. "So, they wanted to distract the attention
of everybody on this day."

When police detained several members of another neo-Nazi group, Combat 18 Hellas, earlier that March, they learned that the arrestees had belonged to both groups, Golden Dawn and C18 Hellas. When the police belatedly cracked down on the group, C18 Hellas had already carried out more than thirty attacks on squats, left-wing social centers, Jewish memorials and cemeteries, and advocacy groups that work with refugees and migrants. From what he could tell, Golden Dawn allowed its hardcore members to operate separate organizations, Constantinou said. Whoever claimed to be in Crypteia would also be linked to Golden Dawn, he guessed.

THE WEEK AFTER the firebombing, on March 30, 2018, a few dozen activists gathered in front of the office block where the Afghan Community in Athens sat. Passersby stopped and snapped quick photos, while a handful of latecomers arrived every few minutes. Mahdi Husseini, an eighteen-year-old Afghan refugee who had been attacked by far-rightists while still a minor in November 2017, strolled up with a bundle of yellow flags bearing KEERFA's logo.[9] A police officer pulled up on a motorbike and stopped. She lifted the dust-specked face mask on her helmet, underneath which long locks of blonde hair rested on her shoulders. When she motioned to Mahdi, he turned to her and they exchanged words. He walked away from her grinning broadly, flashing a quick wink and concealing a middle finger he raised as if to say "fuck you" to the officer.

Shop owners stood on the sullied pavement outside their stores. A homeless man swaddled himself in a sleeping bag, half buried under a cluster of murky blankets in front of a boarded-up corner store. He raised his head briefly, assessed the scene without enthusiasm, and let his face fall back onto the crumbled knapsack he used as a pillow.

Yonous Muhammadi strolled up on his bicycle just in time to deliver the final speech. He wore slacks and a windbreaker and spoke succinctly. In the crowd, demonstrators nodded each time Muhammadi made a point. Behind him, a drunken man holding a haggard broom cawed unsolicited advice at a motorist backing out of a tight parking spot. "Back, back, back," he clamored, his face emaciated and hushed. Muhammadi wrapped up his speech, and the crowd broke up into small circles before shaking hands and preparing to part ways. The intoxicated man crossed the street and turned back abruptly. "I've been sweeping these streets for twenty years," he howled in the direction of the activists. "We are not racists or Golden Dawn. We're just Greeks."

Another onlooker, a tall, stern-faced man cloaked in a time-worn leather jacket, joined him. "They have to become Greek," he barked, directing an accusative finger at the protesters and ashing his cigarette with his other hand. "We are not going to become Afghans or Pakistanis or Somalis."

A hardnosed police officer slogged around, periodically checking his wristwatch. Raza, an Afghan activist, traded insults with the angry onlookers before turning to appeal to the police officer. "Make them stop," he pleaded. The officer, his face tired and colorless, failed to register much interest. Shade engulfed the street as the sun sagged beyond the horizon of tattered apartment blocks. Rogue rays of sunlight, the last of the day, chopped through the shadows. "As far as I'm concerned, you can kill each other after I leave," he replied with a shrug. "I don't care."

*

BEFORE LATE 2017, no one had heard of Crypteia. Then on November 2, a group of men appeared outside a home where a refugee family lived in Dafni, a suburb of Athens. Inside the apartment with his family was an eleven-year-old Afghan boy named Emir. In late October, Emir had been chosen to carry a Greek flag during his school's annual Oxi Day parade, which commemorates Greek resistance to invading Italian fascist forces in 1940.[10] Public uproar prompted the school to change course and prevented Emir from carrying the flag. Well past dark that night, the men hurled stones and bottles at Emir's home. His mother screamed out for help. Her children broke down in tears. The window shattered and glass fanned out across a bedroom in their flat. A beer bottle flew through the open window. More stones followed. She panicked. "I didn't know what to do," she later told local reporters.[11]

When the attackers stole off into the night, the family found a haunting note left outside their flat. Go BACK To YOUR VILLAGE, it read. LEAVE.[12]

Someone claiming to speak on Crypteia's behalf phoned a Greek news outlet later that night. "We will fight until the last immigrant leaves," he said, "and to that end, we will use force and violence, mercilessly."[13]

MANY CONTEMPORARY SCHOLARS maintain that in ancient Sparta, Crypteia referred to a band of state-sanctioned guerrilla soldiers who patrolled the lands and carried out clandestine military operations. As one historian notes, they waged "a form of guerrilla warfare against the helot [slave] population," and the "elite guerrilla soldiers [were] used to keep the helots in line, and perhaps even played a role in the larger Spartan military in special operations."[14] When the subjugated helot population grew restive,

Crypteia operated as "lightly armed soldiers sent to fight the helots using unconventional tactics."

In present-day Greece, Crypteia operated as a vigilante group, highly secretive and largely unknown to experts and observers. By the time the group took credit for torching the Afghan Community in Greece's office, it had claimed several attacks on migrants and anarchist squats. In the months that followed, the group continued to escalate its attacks. The group claimed responsibility for a beating that targeted a migrant on May 13, 2018, then said its members "assisted" in a violent assault against Pakistani workers less than two weeks later. "We are stepping up our attacks until the last illegal immigrant leaves the country," a caller told the *Iefimerida* newspaper.[15] Two weeks later, on June 7, Crypteia members reportedly set fire to a migrant workers camp in Nea Manolada, burning their belongings and, in some cases, the money they had stored in their shacks. On June 25, in the Athenian neighborhood of Petralona, more than thirty far-rightists surrounded Pikpa, a social center and squat run by anarchists, and hurled a Molotov cocktail into the building.[16] "Our struggle continues after the arson in Manolada," the group told *Iefimerida*. "We will not leave any anti-racists standing. Our attacks on anti-racist squads will continue."

CHAPTER TEN

"THERE ARE ALSO ANIMALS": MORE ATTACKS, MORE DEATH

I t was May 19, 2018, in Thessaloniki, and a crowd of angry faces surrounded Yiannis Boutaris. As the mayor of the country's second-largest city, he was accustomed to the occasional heckling, but this felt like more. The crowd gradually contracted around him, tightening. A few muttered insults, curse words. Boos erupted from pockets behind the front row. "Leave," someone screamed. At seventy-six years old, he didn't imagine anyone would put their hands on him, but these were angry people. He felt claustrophobic; his muscles tensed. He coached himself: "Stay calm," he heard himself say. "I heard voices from here and there, and these voices came little-by-little closer," he told me. The jeers escalated to a steady roar of screaming, shouting. A breeze rippled through the Greek flags above the mass of heads and red faces. Boutaris realized he was surrounded.

A former winemaker and recovering alcoholic who hadn't "even smelled whiskey for the last twenty-seven years," Boutaris first became mayor in 2011. He introduced a new stripe of politics to the northern coastal city, a type of social liberalism in a region of the country where nationalism ran rampant. He didn't look the part of a politician, either. He wore a silver stud in his left ear, tattoos on his arms, hands, and fingers. He championed LGBTQ rights, celebrated Pride parades in the city. He called for a greater appreciation of the city's Ottoman and Jewish histories. He initiated plans for a Holocaust museum, and did his best to attract tourists from Turkey, Israel, and the Balkans, including the Republic of Macedonia, whose name had long been a source of contention for the Greek far right. And the far right took notice—Boutaris was a constant target.

There in his city, protests against the Macedonia name deal had become routine in recent months, and hundreds of thousands of demonstrators swarmed the street on January 21 to oppose the Macedonia name deal. "There is only one Macedonia, and it is Greek," they shouted. Others passed out fliers decrying Boutaris as "a slave of the Jews." Some attacked anarchist squats, setting one ablaze. By the time the squares and streets emptied, the local Holocaust monument had been defaced: spray-painted on it was Golden Dawn's logo.

Boutaris received an endless stream of hate mail and death threats. He ignored most of them, but he couldn't ignore the fact that far-right sentiment was cropping up at a greater frequency than he could remember in the past. "You are a fucking Jew," one letter said. "You are a fucking Turk," another said.

He didn't let that deter him from attending the annual commemoration that day in May. Each year, hundreds—sometimes thousands—gathered there to commemorate the ethnic cleansing of Black Sea Greeks, a campaign of violence in Turkey that killed hundreds of thousands of ethnic Greeks. Each year since becoming mayor, Boutaris attended a swath of commemorative events in the city, and although he was two weeks fresh from a heart operation, he didn't want this year to be any different. That morning, he dressed in a navy-blue suit—tieless, but donning a commemorative yellow badge on his lapel—and spent the day shuttling from one memorial to another. Last on the day's program was a flag-lowering ceremony at Thessaloniki's White Tower, once used as a fort to defend the city's harbor from invaders. Today, the tower sits toward the end of the three-mile promenade tracing the Thessaloniki's coastline and offers a panoramic view.

Along with his driver, bodyguard, and Kalypso Goula, the president of the local city council, Boutaris exited the small black sedan that carried him to the tower. More than a thousand people crowded outside the tower. As he approached, Boutaris spotted Panagiotis Psomiadis, a right-wing hardliner and Thessaloniki's former regional governor. Until his resignation from the party in 2014, Psomiadis had been a loyal member of New Democracy, but he was also known for his extremism: He'd praised Greece's military junta and defended Golden Dawn in the past, and he railed against immigration. Psomiadis cursed at Boutaris, but the mayor brushed it off, continued toward the tower. He stopped as the shouts started rippling through the crowd. The moment lingered, pregnant with tension. Someone in the back shouted, "Let's go."

Within seconds, frantic young men encircled him, shoved him, spat on him. Bottles flew his way. A punch landed on his face, then another. His small entourage grabbed him, gripping his rawboned arms and trying to guide him back to their car. The mob broke into a frenzy. Someone punched Goula. The attackers chased them. Some sprinted from the back to catch up and swung their fists at the mayor. A tall, limber young man wore a black, athletic fit Everlast shirt. He bounced on his toes like a mixed martial arts fighter, and then unleashed a salvo of kicks against Boutaris's sternum. Boutaris struggled to keep his balance, but he tumbled to the ground. Several people joined in the beating, many kicking him in his flanks and chest. His bodyguard dragged him back to his feet. Goula pried open the passenger-side door long enough for the bodyguard to squeeze the mayor into the vehicle. Fists and feet pounded the sedan as the engine roared to life. The rear window burst into a scatter of jagged shards as the driver floored it. Goula stayed behind: The mob's anger had disappeared, and in its place, deafening applause.

THE MOB HAD targeted Boutaris, many speculated, because of comments he'd made about the Macedonia name dispute, but he had so long been the focus of far-right ire that it could have been any number of issues. Macedonia was a stand-in, but it was a potent one. All around the country, nationalist opponents of the name accord were escalating violence against whomever they viewed as betraying the nation. Ministers were targeted with threats, and politicians were accosted and sometimes beaten.

ONLY BY LUCK, Boutaris escaped the attack with minor injuries. Police officers insisted that he see a doctor, however, and there in the hospital, he spotted one of his attackers in the corner, a nurse bandaging him from cuts caused by the shattered windshield. Boutaris tried to meet his eyes, but the man kept his gaze toward the ground.

In the days that followed, local police rounded up several suspects, including a forty-four-year-old police officer who had been off-duty that day. Across the spectrum, political parties issued strong condemnations of the violence, as did the Pontic organizations that had organized the commemorations in Thessaloniki that day. Syriza described the incident as a "fascist assault," and the center-left Movement for Change (an alliance that included PASOK) said it was "embarrassing" and "unacceptable." New Democracy condemned the attack, but Prime Minister Aléxis Tsipras called the right-wing opposition party out for laying out a "carpet for the far right," referring to New Democracy's opportunistic position on the Macedonia name accord.

Official condemnations aside, plenty reveled in the moment. One ultra-nationalist official in Kavala, a city in Greece's north, took to Facebook and said that Boutaris "got what he deserved."[1] Down south, in a village called Argos, New Democracy member and local mayor Dimitris Kambosos rushed to label Boutaris a "traitor" for his comments on the Macedonia issue.[2] A few weeks later, Kambosos showed his anti-Semitism when he concluded a long rant by complaining that Boutaris "can say what he wants because he wears the kippah."[3] (New Democracy expelled Kambosos.)

Few compared to Golden Dawn, however, whose glee hit a fever pitch in the wake of the attack. In a press release, the party accused Boutaris of "tarnishing" the commemoration's sanctity, and another statement celebrated the "popular rage" of the attackers who left the mayor battered and bruised. Party chief Nikolaos Michaloliakos's daughter, Ourania, complimented the assailants on Twitter. "Bravo to each and every one who carried out his duty in Thessaloniki today," she wrote.[4] "Respect."

I MET BOUTARIS in his office at city hall two months after the May attack. After we introduced ourselves, he lit a filter-free cigarette and took a seat. Souvenirs adorned the walls of his office, and a clutter of papers and folders sat atop his desk. Each time he took a puff of his cigarette, a black-and-gray lizard tattooed on his hand wriggled some. He thought hard between each of my questions, taking time to consider his words carefully. He knew that any slip of tongue could be exploited by his right-wing opponents. "I am considered a traitor because 'I love Turks,' 'I love Jews,' 'I love gays,' 'I love refugees,'" he told me. "This is totally foolish, so I don't pay much attention anyway."

After the attack, he noticed more and more people driving past his home, screaming, and cursing up at him. He dismissed them with a casual wave of his hand. "If I am a traitor, I ask them: What did you do for your country apart from saying 'Alexander the Great'?" he said. "Alexander the Great died more than two thousand years ago. Did you create jobs? Did you support the market [through] tourism?"

He planned to run for mayor again, but a few months onward, he would abandon that idea and retire from politics. I asked what the attack meant to him, if it signaled something more worrisome than an isolated event. Boutaris thought for a while, sparked another cigarette. The most disturbing part of the violence, the thing he couldn't shake, was the memory of a man holding his baby as he chased the mayor, shouting.

After he was attacked, people passing by his house screamed and cursed at him. "Nationalists are always violent," he said. "They don't hear anything else other than what they believe."

ON JUNE 15, 2018, in Menidi, not far from Athens, it was the final morning of Ramadan, the holy month for Muslims, and Shahzad Ahmed woke up at 4:30 a.m. He was happy, excited to swing by the mosque for morning prayers. He had a grueling eight-hour shift at the meat factory where he worked after that, but that evening, a group of Pakistani workers would gather at his place and celebrate the end of Ramadan, a conclusion to the month-long fast, with a big meal. He was thirty-four, and he somehow looked younger than his age, an impressive feat given the backbreaking work he did. He slipped into a crisp white *thobe* and slathered a palmful of gel on his short, coal-black hair. He checked the time, checked himself in the mirror one last time. Satisfied with his appearance, he stepped out and readied himself to leave.

Nearly four thousand miles away in Ahmed's native Sialkot, his wife and two-year-old daughter were already awake. Ahmed spoke to his wife every day, updating her of the most inconsequential details of daily life in Greece: conversations he had at the factory, results of cricket games with his friends and coworkers, and what he ate for dinner. He never kept secrets from her. And as every day, his wife rang him on Facebook messenger shortly before 5:00 a.m. on Eid. They wished each other a happy holiday, but Ahmed, already running late, rushed her off the line and promised to call her back in the afternoon.

In Menidi, the downtrodden Athenian suburb where he lived and worked, Ahmed had celebrated sundown for twenty-nine days. Because most of the workers were pulling in less than thirty euros ($33.94) a day, they pooled their money and scrapped together small Ramadan feasts: lamb, chicken, potatoes, rice, lentils, sweets. They all cherished Ramadan, but a month of fasting during daylight had left them exhausted and ready to return to their routines. After the Eid celebration, life would return to normal, he would be able to eat whenever he wanted, he would have more energy at work.

Charcoal clouds streaked the purple sky, and the predawn breeze made the morning far more tolerable than the feverish afternoon temperatures brought on by the early summer heat-wave. In the murky fog of those hours overlapping late night and early morning, his rickety motorbike kicked up dust along the pothole-pocked road leading to the main street, whizzing past hillocks of garbage and unlit convenience stores still hours away from opening. He thought about his wife, pressed on the brake, felt guilty for rushing her off the line earlier, and brought the bike to a trembling halt at the first intersection.

A group of men, fellow migrant workers, whooshed past him, dashing away on foot from the black Smart car parked nearby. He scanned the intersection for an explanation. Nothing. Then some-one lunged in his direction. "Fucking Pakistani," a voice snarled. Ahmed's heart hammered, and before he could plead, he turned to see a fist hurtling in his direction. Five knuckles smashed into his temple like a car crash. He scrambled to keep his balance, but his attackers crowded him. He couldn't get a good look at them un-til he tumbled to the rough pavement. Two limber, young Greeks hunched over him. "Get out of our country, you Pakistani jerk-off," one shouted.

"Leave Greece, asshole," the other chimed in.

Another blow collided with his eye, and then a pair of brass knuckles crashed into his jaw. He threw up his arms like a goal-keeper blocking a penalty shot, but it was no use. He stopped scram-bling, letting his body go limp as kicks continued. All was quiet save for the sound of each punt thudding dully against his ribcage.

The ambush was over in a matter of minutes. Ahmed, sprawled on his back, peered upward through blurry eyes as the rising sun splashed yellow across the sky. He heard the car doors opened and slammed shut, and the engine rumbled to life. He rolled to his side, delirious and aching everywhere. He felt wounds on his face and arms, and sharp, painful gushes felt like small jolts of electricity in his flanks. His *thobe*, pristine and white just a few minutes earlier, was saturated with sticky blood. He fumbled for his telephone as if operating on autopilot. He typed in the license plate number just before the vehicle screeched away, hightailing through the intersection and gradually shrinking into the distance.

JAVED ASLAM, PRESIDENT of the Pakistani Community in Greece, was just stepping out of the mosque after morning prayers when his phone rang. "Mr. Javed Aslam?" asked a frenzied voice on the other end. "Is that you?

"Yes," he replied. "This is Javed Aslam."

Shahzad Ahmed launched into a full-throated account of the assault, struggling to keep the details in order. Aslam hung up and hailed a taxi. When he arrived in Menidi, he found Shahzad Ahmed "bloody from head to toe," he later told me. Aslam quickly started doling out tasks for the workers who'd gathered outside Ahmed's shack, a squat, one-story building with two rooms and four occupants. "This is my way," he told me. "If they are busy, they are less likely to be frightened and worried."

Aslam accompanied Ahmed to the police station to file a complaint. Police investigators used the license plate number to locate and arrest the assailants within a couple days. Tracking down attackers was a welcome effort but didn't seem to be enough, didn't seem to grapple with the root cause of the violence, Aslam thought. "They are trying to increase [the attacks]," he insisted, "but the public is more helpful [now]."

ASLAM AND AHMED said six others were attacked in the area that same week. Those workers, who were undocumented, were too afraid to file police reports, several people in Menidi told me. When we met at his shack a couple weeks after the attack, Ahmed looked nervous, casting furtive glances at the doorway every now and then.

Fifteen years prior, his family gathered the funds needed to send him to Greece. His father had passed away, and they took out loans to finance the journey. "I thought life in Europe was beautiful, and that we could work here without problems," he said.

His roommate, Mohammed Ishaq, had come to Greece from the same village, Sialkot. He was thirty-six, barrel-chested, and had callused hands. Since the attack, they'd been considering leaving it all behind in Greece. "These are very alarming conditions for us," said Mohammed Ishaq, sitting next to Ahmed. "It makes us think of going somewhere else, to a quieter country."

Everyone had relatives back home who depended on their income to survive. "When someone attacks us, they are not hurting one person," Ishaq added. "They are hurting five, six, seven people for each [attack]."

For his part, Ahmed was still struggling to return to life as usual. He had trouble concentrating on his work. For weeks after the attack, he felt pain in his eye and face, a dull, throbbing ache. He had to take more breaks at work—the chronic headaches were too painful to push through, and nothing seemed to help. "After the attack, I don't go outside anymore," he told me. "They beat me on the face, so that other people could see the damage they do to us."

Worse still was the pain somewhere deep down in his sternum, a feeling that he had betrayed his wife. Since he was left bloodied and beaten, he'd thought often of whether he should tell her. Knowing his wife would demand he come home, playing out in his mind their hypothetical arguments, and already feeling the pinch of a lower salary in Pakistan, he ultimately decided against it. Each morning when she called him on Facebook Messenger, he placed a band aid over the camera on his phone. It was broken, he told her, because he'd dropped it at work. "I knew she'd want me to come back home," he admitted. His face hung, a shattered blood vessel reddened his eye, and he slumped down in his chair. His hands were clasped loosely on the table, fidgeting. "And I didn't want to make her cry."

He'd managed to survive Golden Dawn's rise without a single attack. Sure, sometimes people made racist comments, but no one had ever laid a hand on him, he said. During his initial years in Greece, he had encouraged friends back home to come to the country, to search out work opportunities. Sitting there, he paused for a moment. "If someone in Pakistan asked me about coming here now, I'd tell them not to," he said. "There are some really good people, but there are also animals."

THAT SUMMER, IN the nearby suburb Sepolia, fifty-two-year-old Thanasis Nasiopolos and fifty-six-year-old Thymios Christodoulou looked forward to the annual end-of-the-year celebration at the local school their children attended. They were both members of the parents' association at the school, and they helped organize the party on June 9, 2018. Worried by the anti-migrant violence again on the rise in the area, they brainstormed ways to offer support to local Pakistanis. Moreover, not many parents had volunteered to help out during the festivities. While planning the party, Nasiopolos and Christodoulou reached out to the Pakistani Community of Greece and offered to hire Pakistani workers to man the food tables. The Pakistani Community of Greece found four migrant workers who were glad to volunteer without compensation, but Nasiopolos and Christodoulou insisted on paying.

"We do the party every year," Christodoulou told me. "We said we'd pay them for their services because work should be paid for."

The pair expected some tension ahead of the party: For more than a year, another two parents, both Golden Dawn supporters whose children also attended the school, had been railing against Nasiopolos and Christodoulou's support for a Pakistani Sunday school put on for children of the migrant workers in the area. The anti-migrant parents tried to get Nasiopolos kicked off the party planning committee but ultimately failed. "Why did you offer to pay these four immigrants, and why would you call them to come here?" one asked, angry that his child would be around foreigners.

When the day of the party came, Nasiopolos and Christodoulou manned a food table and cooked souvlaki for the attendees and the Pakistani workers assisted. The two parents arrived. "You guys are ridiculous," one said. They left but returned fifteen minutes later.

"I've never spoken to you in this way," Christodoulou replied. "Why do you talk to me like this?"

"Let's go inside and I'll explain the problem to you."

"Why do we need to go inside?" Nasiopolos interjected. "Explain it to me here."

That's when things escalated. The first man, who wore a sharp ring, struck Nasiopolos above the eyebrow, and blood ran down his face. The two assailants began shoving and slugging both Nasiopolos and Christodoulou, who attempted to fight back. A fist to the face crushed Christodoulou's nose. The attackers threw his son to the pavement and knocked over a woman standing nearby. By the end of the assault, a crowd had formed around them. Children were crying. "I'll fuck your white ass," one of the men screamed at Christodoulou and Nasiopolos when the scuffle finally ended.

In the days that followed, neither Christodoulo's nor Nasiopolos's children wanted to go to school. Frightened and up-set, they wanted to stay home. The parents filed a legal complaint against their attackers for assault and racist violence. All around Athens, in Sepolia and other suburbs spilling out from the capi-tal, far-right violence was rearing its ugly head once again. Asked why he thought Greece was enduring another surge in attacks, Nasiopolos speculated that Golden Dawn was lashing out owing to the crushing weight of the ongoing trial.

"We are sure that something bad is happening again," he told me. Above his eyebrow was a deep scar from the gash of the first blow more than a month earlier. "When you have a dog backed into a corner, it will try to bite you."

IN PERISTERI, GREECE, on June 19, 2018, four days after Shahzad Ahmed was attacked, hundreds of anti-fascists—social-ists, anarchists, and migrant labor unions—trickled into the main square. Peristeri was a crisis-hit suburb of greater Athens that was home to parallel communities of working-class Greeks and migrant laborers. Anti-fascists from KEERFA had arrived early, passing out anti-racist and socialist fliers for an hour before the rally was slated to start. A large sculpture of a boxer stood in the square's grassy center, and sporadic gusts of wind provided mo-ments of respite from the late afternoon sun. The Clash blasted on the loudspeakers, echoed throughout the square: "Should I Stay, or Should I Go?"

By 7:30 p.m., when the protest was meant to start, a few hun-dred people had assembled. A young activist with rectangular-rimmed glasses and a "no pasaran" T-shirt distributed left-wing newspapers into the open windows of cars passing by. An unlit cigarette dangled from his lips for several minutes, until a queue of vehicles had passed, and he remembered to spark it. Blocks of demonstrators set out on a march, with a contingent of Pakistani workers at the lead. CLOSE THE OFFICES OF THE NEO-NAZIS, declared red-and-black placards bobbing above the procession. NEVER AGAIN FASCISM, read yellow-and-black signs bearing a fist crashing through a swastika. "No racist attacks," an activist said through a loudspeaker. "Open borders for the workers."

Behind the workers was a block of KEERFA activists, and behind them a string of groups: Trotskyists; communists of various ideological bents; the anti-fascist Organization of Militant Antifascism (ORMA) collective; and the fedayeen, a group of anti-fascist and anarchist soccer fans for the local Atromitos Football Club. While all the groups had a long track record of confronting the far right in the streets, the fedayeen, whose name was a loan from the Arabic word for militant groups that risk their lives in revolutionary struggle, were notorious for brawling with their political adversaries. In the back, a large banner ominously summed up the day's shared sentiment: HANG THE FASCISTS.

As the march twisted through the narrow streets, onlookers watched from their balconies above and in front of shops and kiosks. At each major intersection, police officers scrambled to redirect traffic. By the time they reached Sepolia, the neighboring borough, the sun sagged behind the horizon of rooftops, casting splashes of fading light onto the oil-blotted pavement. In front of a supermarket, shoppers stood by waiting for the march to pass. A young man stepped out and unlocked his bicycle from a lamppost. "Fucking Pakistanis," he muttered within earshot of several fedayeen. They turned to him. "What did you say?" one demanded. "Are you a fascist?"

He replied, "I'm neutral."

A youngster's foot crashed into the man's bicycle. Another shoved him back, leaving him struggling for his balance. He pushed back and protested the steady stream of insults flung in his direction. Then, a powerful blow smashed into his temple. His eyes were closed before he hit the ground. His body lay limp on the pavement, a crimson puddle of blood pooling beneath his head. A cluster of observers stood nearby, many of them with mouths agape. A police officer, standing some ten feet away, surveyed the scene and simply turned away. He was outmanned and wouldn't be putting himself on the line. "Smash the fascists," the fedayeen recited together as they made their exit, disappearing into a subway entrance.

Far-right violence, of course, sharpened tendencies for violence among parts of the left and among some anarchists. In a country where neo-Nazis had run roughshod over whomever they pleased for years, it was no surprise that many felt the only way to fight back meant balling their fists.

CHAPTER ELEVEN

"DIDN'T YOU GET ENOUGH LAST NIGHT?": NEW GOVERNMENT, SAME ENEMIES

In May 2019, Syriza suffered a sound defeat at the hands of New Democracy in European Parliament elections. Soon after, Prime Minister Aléxis Tsipras called for legislative elections in Greece. In the European Parliament vote, New Democracy had secured around 33 percent of the vote to Syriza's 23 percent, a result that prompted New Democracy leader Kyriakos Mitsotakis to declare that "the Greek people have withdrawn their confidence in this government."[1]

The European election results appeared to predict Syriza's downfall, while also suggesting that several smaller parties would remain in the Greek parliament: the centrist Movement for Change (KINAL, which included PASOK) pulled in 7.18 percent, the Communist Party of Greece reeled in 5.75 percent, and Golden Dawn secured some 4.85 percent. Newer small parties also gained representation in the European Parliament: just more than 4 percent voted for the ultra-nationalist, pro-Russian Greek Solution, and around 3.15 percent cast their lot for MeRA25, the left-wing breakaway party led by former finance minister Yanis Varoufakis.

On July 7, 2019, Greeks headed to the polling stations to decide who would govern the country next. New Democracy, which had partly made migration a centerpiece of its electoral campaign, was expected to repeat the successes it had during the European elections. But the right-wing party performed even better, gaining nearly 40 percent of the vote and an absolute majority in the Hellenic Parliament. Syriza came in second, locking up nearly a third of all votes, but the defeat was resounding.

"Today, with our head held high we accept the people's verdict," Tsipras said, accepting defeat.[2] "To bring Greece to where it is today, we had to take difficult decisions [with] a heavy political cost."

Yet, Golden Dawn's performance proved one of the most surprising. Although the party had appeared on course to enter the parliament yet again, it failed to get enough votes to surpass the 3 percent minimum threshold required for parliamentary representation: only 2.93 percent of Greeks backed the neo-Nazi outfit at the ballot box, meaning the party had lost around 35 percent of its voters from the European Elections, pollster Costas Panagopoulos told Reuters at the time. "Golden Dawn was born from the rage that people felt," Panagopoulos argued. "This rage no longer exists. The people who were very angry in 2012 or in 2015, feel uncertain rather than angry now and see no reason to vote for it."

That explanation was debatable. After all, New Democracy's electoral platform had included promises to tighten borders, ramp up deportations, and crack down on left-wing campus groups—all positions that arguably overlapped with the policy wishes of those on the far right. More telling still, Greek Solution, who would enter the new parliament with 3.7 percent of the vote and ten seats, had vowed to advocate draconian far-right changes, including introducing the death penalty and fully sealing off the country's borders.

Whether Greek voters who had once cast their lot with Golden Dawn had truly abandoned their rage or not, the neo-Nazi party struck a recalcitrant note. Speaking after his party crashed out of the parliament, Michaloliakos promised to rebuild Golden Dawn's bases in a statement on television that night. "Golden Dawn is not over, they had better understand this," he warned. "We will continue our fight for nationalism. We'll return to where we grew strong, on the streets, on the squares."

GOLDEN DAWN MAY have been out, but the freshly minted New Democracy government presented a laundry list of new challenges for Greek anti-fascists and refugee solidarity activists. Since the refugee crisis erupted in 2015, left-wing activists and anarchists had channeled much of their energy into building an alternative to the status quo: squatted residences for asylum seekers, community-run health clinics and soup kitchens, and protecting Exarchia as a hub for solidarity and anti-fascist resistance.

Golden Dawn's website disappeared from the internet, and its offices around the country were shuttering and accumulating dust, but the New Democracy–led government had given police free rein to crack down on anarchists and leftists. New Democracy had drummed up the fear of crime and anarchy in Exarchia as part of its electoral campaign, and new mayor Kostas Bakoyannis, whose father had been gunned down in 1989 by the revolutionary organization 17 November, a small Marxist urban guerilla outfit, had promised to squash the autonomous hub. In April 2019, the

month before mayoral elections, Bakoyannis had addressed a pid-
dling crowd of rally goers on the outskirts of Exarchia, promising
to "clean up" the neighborhood and accusing Syriza of turning a
blind eye to crime. "Shit on your father's grave," someone shouted
from afar. Later that night, dozens of masked anarchists clashed
with riot police in and around the neighborhood. They hurled
Molotov cocktails, stones, and bottles, and the riot police fired
tear gas and flash bangs in the anarchists' direction.

Tensions simmered throughout the summer, and the new
government boasted of plans for the enclave: scrubbing the
graffiti from the walls, planting and pruning trees; repairing
the battle-worn sidewalks; building a new metro station in the
central square; and most worrisome of all, evicting the squats.[3]
Altogether, the government bragged, upwards of ten million euros
would be allocated to what the newspaper *Kathimerini* described
as an "ambitious makeover." When the streets of Athens cleared
out in August—the time of the year most Greeks pack their bags
for vacation—riot police forces launched a series of raids targeting squats in Exarchia. A day after Bakoyannis was sworn into
office on August 25, 2019, helicopters buzzed above Exarchia as
riot police officers geared up with shields and helmets and tear
gas, then raided and cleared four squats, arresting more than a
hundred migrants and refugees.[4] The crackdown on squats had
started under Syriza's watch, but New Democracy was dead set on
completing it and turning the neighborhood into a tourist-friendly,
cash-accumulating bohemian enclave.

A few days later, police set their sights on their most ambitious
target to date: Vox, a theater that had been squatted and turned
into a café and anarchist hangout, a place that activists involved
with the Rubicon (*Rouvikonas*) collective were known to frequent. Once inside Vox, police officers fired tear gas and stun grenades, injuring several and engaging in clashes with activists who

attempted to defend the space.[5] "As a result of the attack, people were injured, some seriously and needed stitches," a Rubicon supporter wrote on Facebook. "Riot police threw teargas into the Vox as they retreated." Two days later, thousands of marchers spilled into Exarchia's streets. NO PASARAN, their banners read. DEFEND SQUATS AND HOODS, others said.

Arash Hampay, an Iranian refugee with asylum in Greece, tried to keep track of where evicted refugees and migrants ended up. Many went to the already overcrowded hot spots and camps, he said, but some ended up sleeping in the streets. As an activist, he had been involved in refugee demonstrations and organizing on Lesbos Island, where the notoriously decrepit Moria camp was now housing upwards of ten thousand asylum seekers. Since relocating to Athens, however, he had been working with residents of camps and squats around the city. Then one day in early September, he found himself personally targeted by a member of the new government. He took to Twitter to mock the far-rightists celebrating the renewed efforts to target refugees and migrants. "Hey fascists, I'm OK in my new country," he wrote. "You can't choose my movement, I will continue to change my new city['s] face and atmosphere. Our city has to be clean of fascism."

Theo Giannaros, who worked with New Democracy's working group on health, responded to Hampay.[6] "You are gonna be kicked back to where you came from, you monkey!" When Hampay posted screenshots of Giannaros's comment and tagged new prime minister Kyriakos Mitsotakis, Giannaros buckled down. "Monkey is the one who calls Greek citizens fascists! As a country, we have shown how we feel about refugees [...] by supporting them! But the moment people like you call us fascists, the joke is over! Sorry!"

Hampay had never called Giannaros—let alone all Greeks—fascists, but the right-wing politician's response may have been an indicator of how he viewed himself and the new government. "I've never seen any behavior like this from politicians," Hampay told me. "A member of the government on Twitter has very clearly called me a monkey . . . I didn't call all Greek people fascists, but maybe he feels that he is a fascist. I love Greek people, of course." He added, "It's very racist and very stupid."

A day after the exchange, the government canned Giannaros, but the threat remained. As arrivals to Greek islands swelled— more and more refugees were making the journey from Turkey across the Aegean—the New Democracy government sought to create a climate of fear for refugees.

In the weeks that followed, Hampay's Our Home initiative, which worked with homeless refugees, faced fresh challenges. Each time they set up a soup kitchen for asylum seekers sleeping rough, police arrived and started demanding people's papers. On one occasion, Hampay told me, police officers detained seventy people and released them a few hours later.

THE OCCUPIERS REMAINED in Vox, despite the police attacks and the eviction of so many squats in the neighborhood. On September 9, however, the Greek daily newspaper *Kathimerini* revealed harrowing news for the anti-authoritarian movement. Officials had green-lighted an eviction, even though a government social security body, which owned the squatted theater, had been reluctant to drive the activists from the building.[7]

After lagging at the tail end of the summer, protests and direct action started to pick up speed again by early fall. On November 2, 2019, around a hundred anarchists and leftists poured into Exarchia Square. Earlier in the day, riot police had raided and cleared out a squat in the neighborhood. Heavily geared officers stayed on the periphery of the neighborhood, not engaging with the gathering in the square. The standoff wouldn't last long. Five days later, someone strapped a Molotov to a police motorcycle, sending three officers to the hospital. MAT, the riot police force, responded immediately. Tear gas filled the square, and officers sought to round people up. They tried to enter a café on the square, hoping to arrest a suspect, but the patrons inside locked the doors and pressed against them to keep them from being pried open. Not to be bested without retaliating, riot police poured into the square and swarmed the streets surrounding it. They pushed aside a burning dumpster. A column of officers rushed up to a banner that bore the anti-fascist slogan No Pasaran and tore it down, grunting and celebrating as it broke free and hit the ground. As the officers retreated, they ripped posters off the walls of cafés and apartment blocks.

Two days later, anarchists, leftists, and others, now around a thousand strong, assembled in Monastiraki, a downtown area popular with tourists and overlooked by the Acropolis. Red-and-black anarcho-syndicalist flags fluttered above the mass of people marching through the streets. Refugees and Greeks locked arms and moved forward. The front row carried a No Pasaran banner, much like the one that had been taken down in the square only two days earlier. "Cops, TV, neo-Nazis," they chanted. "All the scum are working together."

Riot police watched on as the march advanced through the winding streets, eventually reaching Syntagma Square, across from the Hellenic Parliament. The marchers continued down Akadamias Street, and the rally ended without any clashes.

*

WHEN GREEK POLICE stormed a pair of cinemas screening *The Joker* in October 2019 and arrested nineteen minors—including four who were viewing the film with their parents—the incident made national and international headlines.[8] Student activists and critics were up in arms. In 2016, Greece had lowered the voting age to seventeen, but a seventeen-year-old still could not attend a K-17-rated film screening. They demanded an answer: Why should the newly elected right-wing government dictate which films young people watch?

The new minister of culture, Lina Mendoni, insisted that her department's employees and the police were justified in ensuring that cinema staff checked identification cards and admitted only those eighteen and older. Under mounting pressure, however, Mendoni apologized. "I admit that I am bothered by the repression of underage children and their families," she said.

In Greece's fragile, politically charged landscape, the uproar fueled a broader public conversation about the country's new government. For the government, the incident was little more than enforcing the law. Many young people, however, understood raiding a movie theater as a microcosm of a broader attempt to police popular culture.

While New Democracy secured nearly 40 percent of the vote in the election, among young voters the conservative outfit failed to win broad backing. Less than a third of youth voters aged between seventeen and twenty-four cast their ballots for New Democracy, while more than half voted for left-wing and center-left parties—including 38 percent for Syriza. Greece might have been fresh from a nearly decade-long financial crisis, but more than a third of young people remained unemployed. With unrest brewing and the government cracking down on leftists, anarchists, and refugees, students were drawing the first battle lines against a government most of them rejected.

For months, tensions had been rising as students took to the streets to rail against the government's plans to implement a makeover of the higher education system, privatization, and financial reforms that unions said would help boost profits for big businesses while eroding workers' rights. When municipal workers launched a strike in late October, students rallied in solidarity with the striking employees until their protest ended with tear gas and police clashing with demonstrators.

So, when the Athens University of Economics and Business (AUEB) announced a weeklong closure after police raids, it was little surprise that students responded with outrage. The police insisted they had retrieved materials intended to be used in attacks on their officers: motorcycle helmets, face masks, fire extinguishers, and beer bottles, along with anarchist pamphlets and protest literature. Hundreds of students showed up on campus the following Monday, occupying the courtyard and demanding a campus free of police.

Carrying shields and batons, wearing face protectors and helmets, columns of riot police flooded the courtyard. They clubbed the students, launched a volley of tear gas canisters, and hurled firecrackers at the crowd inside the campus's gates. Some students covered their faces with cloth, some bolted up the stairs leading to the university's main entrance, and others shoved the officers back as they struggled to evade arrest. Ioanna Rizou, a twenty-two-year-old law student and leftist activist, tried to enter the campus, but police officers blocked her. Stuck on the street outside with others unable to break the police cordon, she watched on in horror as the violence unfolded. The sharp smell of tear gas stung her nostrils and burned her eyes. Medical workers tended to injured demonstrators, but police officers burst into the ambulances and dragged some out. "We were in shock," she said. "I am still in shock from all the violence."

The incident marked the first of its kind since New Democracy pushed through parliament a measure to abolish campus sanctuary in August, which forbade police from entering universities. In November 2019, the clashes at AUEB came less than a week before the commemoration of the 1973 student uprising. "That is a problem for our struggle in the universities," Rizou said, "because we will not be able to organize our fight anymore; because now police will enter our universities without any permission from the administration."

Rizou stood at the front of some three thousand students ready to march across the city from Akadimias Street in downtown Athens. "It's not only students in the universities. There has been a series of violence from the police toward young people," she said. "It is about what's happening to the whole youth movement in Greece. We are not going to take any of that. We are going to fight for our rights to be free in our schools and in our streets and in everything."

Behind her, row after row of demonstrators perched red flags on their shoulders. Those in the front hoisted up a banner demanding bread and justice. The students locked arms, motorcycle helmets handy in case riot police confronted their march. "Teboneras lives on," chanted the swell, referring to Nikos Teboneras, a left-wing professor killed during a fight with members of the New Democracy party's youth wing in 1991.[9]

Giorgos Papanikolaou, a twenty-five-year-old student at the Polytechnic University, insisted that the timing of the AUEB raid encouraged more students to join the upheaval. Standing in front of the march, he accused the New Democracy government of attempting to impose a "police state in every aspect of our lives," recalling the broken arms and bloodied faces he'd seen a few days earlier at AUEB. "The new government is trying to hit first the young people," Papanikolaou said. "It's not just that they entered the university. They beat us."

As the demonstrators marched through Athens, sending taxi drivers and other motorists turning down side roads and paralyzing several busy streets, their chants drowned out the steel shutters creaking shut in front of shops. The march weaved around Syntagma Square and halted in front of the parliament. The protesters held their red flags to the sky. "When the stars shine again," they sang together, reciting a World War II–era communist folk song. "When it's February again, I can grab my rifle for my beautiful homeland and to leave mothers without sons and women without husbands."

Coming to an end on Akadimias Street, the march concluded without clashes with riot police. With the Polytechnic Uprising anniversary only three days away, students were gearing up to take the lead, Papanikalaou said. "It's not just an anniversary," he said. "You can say it's a permanent struggle. Every year for these three days, people are demonstrating against their government because the police are the same as the government. That's why they want just to be an anniversary, just like a museum, but we haven't let them [do that]."

The following evening, dozens of black-clad anarchists set out from the Polytechnic University to rally in support of the AUEB students. Black flags raised to the sky, the block descended on the square in Exarchia. Police had been redeployed to the restive neighborhood since New Democracy's electoral victory. Columns of riot police posted up on nearby Tositsa Street, but the march passed without incident.

AHEAD OF THE annual Polytechnic Uprising anniversary on November 17, 2019, the Hellenic Police deployed more than five thousand officers throughout the capital to prevent clashes like the ones that had erupted in previous years, when Molotov cocktails, stones, and flowerpots rained down riot police.[10] Athens mayor Kostas Bakoyannis, who took over the mayoral post after local elections in May, urged demonstrators to remain peaceful. "On this anniversary, let's send out the right message," he wrote on Facebook.[11] "A shared message about memory. We should not obscure the essence which is the struggle of youth for democracy. On this anniversary, let's show respect toward the city."

When the anniversary arrived, a long queue stretched from the gates of the Polytechnic University down the street. They waited their turn to place wreaths at the foot of the original gate toppled in 1973. Meanwhile, police helicopters buzzed above. Drones recorded video of small caches of Molotov cocktails and gas masks stockpiled on apartment building rooftops in Exarchia. Across town, tens of thousands assembled in Klafthmonos Square. In the front stood the aging men and women who survived the junta's prisons. Along with others, seventy-seven-year-old Evangelos Kouris held up a banner against fascism. On April 21, 1967, the first day of the dictatorship, security forces arrested him as he walked down Bouboulinas Street in downtown Athens. After the junta collapsed in 1974, he served as a lawyer for the families of several killed during the Polytechnic student uprising. "If we stop marching each year, this democratic right [to protest] could disappear," he told me.

From Klafthmonos Square, the demonstrators—numbering twenty thousand according to police, although participants insisted the number was far higher—marched past a stretch of riot police geared up and lining the road next to Syntagma Square, overlooked by the Greek parliament. "Bread, education, freedom," demonstrators chanted, demanding that campus asylum be reinstated. They continued to the US embassy, where they paused to sing chants against American foreign policy and backing for the military junta that once ruled the country.

Shortly after 8:00 p.m. in Exarchia, riot police blocked off several roads leading to the square. Shields raised, holding tear gas canisters, dozens of heavily armed riot police officers posted on Stournari Street waited for a pretext to move in. A mass of black-clad demonstrators appeared a hundred yards down the road. Someone set ablaze a mound of trash in the middle of the street. The green light of laser pointers glinted off the officers' riot shields. Then came the sound of a beer bottle crashing down on the pavement. A flare, fired by demonstrators, lit up the street. When the first Molotov cocktail hit, the riot police erupted in a sprint toward the demonstrators.

The security forces chased the demonstrators, pushing through the square and pursuing them down a pedestrian street lined with restaurants. Tear gas filled the area, while riot police shoved passersby and continued their hunt. Around the corner, a Molotov cocktail exploded on a street hugging the square. A flowerpot, hurled from a balcony or rooftop, crashed down moments later. Nearby, an observer standing on their balcony filmed riot police catching demonstrators. One riot police officer dragged a man by the hood of his sweatshirt and pulled him across the asphalt. Three encircled another demonstrator. One kicked the man; another slammed him on the ground. A few feet away, an officer stomped down on another demonstrator's leg. A few minutes' walk away, a police officer clubbed a twenty-year-old girl in the head, sending blood rushing down her face.

The rioting paled in comparison to previous years, but the number of arrests was astounding. Throughout the day, police arrested at least twenty-eight people and detained another thirteen in Athens alone. In Thessaloniki, where Molotov cocktails exploded in the city center, fourteen were arrested and detained. In

Patras, Greece's third largest city, police swept up another ten, and on the island of Crete seven wound up in police custody. Less than an hour after unrest erupted, riot police sat on the curb and ate sandwiches, congratulating each other for a job well done. "The police authorities took all appropriate measures to safeguard and protect the events," the department said later in a statement.

The next morning, though, they came back for more. Police raided an apartment on Stournari Street and arrested two, publishing photos of gas masks and materials the department said were meant to be used in attacks on riot squads. Later in the day, a phalanx of riot police confronted a group of people standing outside the courthouse, quietly waiting for the release of those arrested the night before. Officers clubbed the crowd, taunting them. "Didn't you get enough last night?" one said.

Following the massive police operations that weekend, New Democracy officials were elated. "Yesterday, doing something un-thinkable for many while the anti-government block was on its way, we stepped in and gathered their bases in Exarchia Square," Konstantinos Bogdanos, a journalist-turned-parliamentarian, told the *Good Morning Greece* television program. "We held Exarchia Square."

Fresh from controversy after referring to migrants as "dust" and Exarchia-based activists as "garbage" months earlier, Stavros Balaskas, vice president of the police union, jumped into the fray. "We are doing our job, we are cleaning Exarchia and yesterday we had a peaceful event," he also told *Good Morning Greece*.[12]

ON DECEMBER 6, 2019, eleven years had passed since a police officer gunned down fifteen-year-old Alexis Grigoropoulos in Exarchia, and a few hundred demonstrators gathered in downtown

Athens, preparing to march through the city. In the front row, black everywhere. Young women and men wore black masks and black jackets, and raised black flags. A few had fire extinguishers on hand, while others lugged chunks of concrete they'd broken off the sidewalk curb. Down the street, hundreds of riot police waited, shields lifted, gaits steady, prepared. A drone fluttered in the sky above, and the brisk December air was pregnant with tension. With anarchists and leftists still reeling from months of escalated police violence and the mass arrests that marred the November 17 commemoration of the Polytechnic student uprising, it remained uncertain whether confrontations would break out. But riot police officers, following them on sidewalks of each side of the street, hemmed the marchers in.

When the march started, the demonstrators gradually made their way down toward Omonoia Square, and then turned and started toward Syntagma, the main square overlooked by the Hellenic Parliament. As the march advanced, storefronts shuttered and café employees whisked tables and chairs inside in a hurry. "Cops, TV, neo-Nazis," they chanted, "all the scum are working together."

In front of the parliament, riot police stood at attention. On the rooftops of office buildings and ritzy hotels overlooking the strip of street, police officers watched on. The march made it full circle, reappearing at the same point it started. As participants set off together toward Exarchia, riot police followed closely behind, at one point almost chasing them. A row of demonstrators in the back walked backward and kept facing the police officers to ward off a potential ambush from behind. In the tight corridors of narrow neighborhood streets on the outskirts of Exarchia, it appeared for a moment that violence could erupt. In the end, however, the riot police stopped their advance at an intersection that serves as a gateway to Exarchia, the demonstrators disappearing down the pedestrian streets chopping through the dense rows of apartment blocks. It was still early afternoon, though. Another demonstration was planned for 6:00 p.m. The Ministry of Citizens Protection had failed to make good on their threat to evict the remaining squats—the deadline had passed a day earlier—and security forces were gearing up for potential riots in the beleaguered neighborhood. More than four thousand officers from a swath of units—riot squads, motorcycle cops, and plainclothes, to name a few—had been deployed throughout the city.

BY NIGHTFALL, MUCH of Exarchia had cleared out, and few cars remained parked along the streets in the neighborhood. Shortly before 6:00 p.m., the crowd began gathering in front of the University of Athens on Panepistimiou Street. Upwards of six thousand demonstrators marched, this time with the riot police keeping a safe distance ahead of the rally. In the front row stood activists with the No Pasaran collective. NEVER FORGET ALEXIS, someone had spray-painted on a nearby wall. KILL COPS.

The march followed the same route it had earlier in the day, but tension and anger were more palpable than a few hours prior. "Cops, pigs, murderers," they shouted.

Unlike earlier, though, most of the march's participants continued their long walk until they reached Exarchia. In the square, youngsters in black masks got to work ripping stones off a statue. A mound of garbage went up in flames, and someone tossed a Molotov cocktail on it. It hissed for a few moments and then exploded in a loud bang that prompted many to cover their ears.

A few hundred yards away on Tositsa Street, a mass of riot police swelled as more and more joined their ranks. Large trucks carrying water cannons parked on the street. When a staccato of

Molotov cocktails exploded around a bend, the youth geared up. One tore a payphone stall out of the pavement, hurled it in the middle of the street. Stones took flight above and crashed down at the feet of the riot police around fifty yards down the street. Young anarchists screamed at journalists to get out of the way. When a contingent of police officers tore off toward the square, the rioters scattered. The riot police seized one young man, dragging him on the street. One officer swung a fire extinguisher at his shins until another intervened and stopped him. They trampled another demonstrator, dragged him to his feet, and carted him off.

This scene played on repeat for much of the night, with riot police storming the square, rounding up a handful of demonstrators, beating them, clubbing them, and disappearing down the road with the arrestees. Tear gas drenched the square and much of the surrounding area, flash bangs exploded on the streets and sidewalks, and water cannons soaked mounds of flaming rubbish.

In one instance, a swarm of riot police stormed down Metaxa Street and into the square as anarchists posted on rooftops hurled flowerpots and stones down on the street, barely missing their mark. Each time police officers trampled a demonstrator to the ground, a gaggle of photojournalists encircled them, jostling for position. Some officers shoved and threatened the reporters, barking orders. "Get off the street," one yelled at a photographer posted up a few yards away.

By the time the confrontations dissipated, police had detained and arrested at least sixty people in Exarchia alone. In Patras and Thessaloniki, dozens more were detained and arrested. Before the sun came up the following morning, at least twenty-two banks and businesses around Athens had been vandalized, ostensibly retribution for the heavy-handed police attacks on Exarchia just hours earlier.

CHAPTER TWELVE

"WE'RE DYING LITTLE BY LITTLE HERE": A NEW STAGE OF THE REFUGEE CRISIS

In February 2020, I traveled to Chios again, the Greek island in the northern Aegean Sea and one of the country's main landing points for refugee boats. The flight from Athens took around a half hour, but the mainland was a world away for refugees and migrants on the island. When I returned there for the first time in almost four years, more than five thousand asylum seekers were confined to it. Across the five Aegean islands hosting refugee camps—Chios, Kos, Leros, Lesbos, and Samos—more than thirty-six thousand asylum seekers were bottlenecked there, living in camps with a combined capacity of less than six thousand. Although the New Democracy government had made a big fuss about overhauling the country's migration system in the last seven months, there was a crucial—and devastating—hangover from the Syriza era: The asylum seekers could not leave them until their applications were processed. Despite Syriza's claims to support refugees and migrants, the party had consistently treated arrivals as a crisis, a move that highlighted its shift from the radical left to one that was more aptly placed on the center left.

On a Saturday afternoon, I hopped in the middle row of seats in a van bound for Vial, the only camp left on Chios. Dipethe and Souda had been shuttered, and everyone had been relocated to Vial. Behind the wheel sat Antonis Vorrias, the humanitarian worker that weathered death threats for his solidarity activism back in 2016. Now fifty-one, he spent his weeks divvied up between visiting Vial and organizing aid for asylum seekers: gathering donations of winter coats and other clothes; finding housing outside the camp for vulnerable individuals; and helping to find solutions for asylum seekers with unique problems, such as specific health ailments.

In the front seat, someone put on a dance song I knew only from cafés. The van whipped around bends, navigating the narrow, crater-stricken road to Chalkio, the village that hosted Vial. We passed petrol stations and staggeringly large farm homes built with old stones, olive tree groves, and traditional Greek restaurants. Nadir Zitaway sat in the middle row with me. He'd lived in Vial for two months, but a year earlier, the government sent him and his wife to live in an apartment in Thessaloniki, on the mainland. When he left the camp, around two thousand asylum seekers lived there; now that number was inching up toward five thousand.

Vorrias turned off the pavement road onto a dirt path leading to Vial. In the fields, a group of women wearing *jilbabs* and *hijabs* tried to string up a clothesline on which to hang their laundry. WELCOME TO EUROPE, read a banner on a small storage shack a few hundred yards before the entrance to the camp. Locals had pinned it up, a sarcastic gesture. CHIOS NOT FOR SALE. A cluster of riot police muddled around Vial's front gate—they were there twenty-four hours a day, a constant reminder of what awaited asylum seekers if they decided to protest.

We parked and stepped out into the cold afternoon. Tubes of pale sunlight oozed through heavy gray clouds. Wind swept through the camp and scattered garbage across the olive tree orchard encircling Vial. I walked into a wall of stench—burning logs, burning paper, burning garbage. Chalkio was home to less than a thousand people, while Vial held more than 4,700. Of the total number of asylum seekers at the camp, well more than half lived in the shantytown mushrooming in the grove.

Many of the olive trees loomed like limbless scarecrows, stripped bare for firewood. Over the winter months, temperatures had dipped below freezing a handful of times, but even when they didn't, bone-rattling cold was a daily reality. We weaved between the shacks and tents. Soiled diapers. Small mountains of garbage. Piles of human shit. It looked like a storm had carried the battered leftovers of humanity through the field.

We finished our trek at the far end of the field, back behind row after row of shacks extending like an appendage from Vial's rear side. We entered a small, cordoned area with two shanties and a pair of gardens, craters dug out in the earth and filled with small plants and flowers. The jerry-built shacks weren't the same— no two structures in the field hemming in Vial were the same. We found thirty-year-old Saber al-Kolak near the shack he shared with two others. A Palestinian from the besieged and war-ravaged Gaza Strip, he survived three Israeli wars on the coastal enclave he called home for the first three decades of his life.

Saber received us warmly, explained that he never wanted to leave Gaza. His work was good—he managed a hookah café and spent his free time either with his wife and two children or performing. He was a skilled break dancer, and he enjoyed putting on shows for people and kids in his neighborhood: fire-breathing, firewalking, and all the circus acts you could imagine. But opportunities were scarce and decreasing by the day. He couldn't make ends meet on his shrinking wages, and he knew that eventually— everyone knew—another war would arrive one day. Here in the camp, children loved him. They assembled in a huddle outside his tent each day, begged him to perform something. "The kids love Ali Baba," he joked of Antonis, "but I'm more powerful than him here."

One of his roommates, twenty-four-year-old Mohammed al-Shareef, had been a musician back in Gaza. He pulled out a set of ramshackle drums and children poured into the area. A cloud formed above and the weather grew colder. Wind crashed through the camp. Some wore sandals, and few wore winter coats. Mohammed banged away. Little feet danced; little hands clapped.

AROUND DUSK, I walked the perimeter of the camp. The sky brooded dark and purple as the sun sagged behind the curtain of mountains on the horizon. I was with the photographer Nick Paleologos, who asked a man if he could snap a photo of children without their faces, and the man shot him a thumbs-up. Before he was able to take the picture, a swarm of men appeared in front of us. They were worried that their faces may have appeared in the background, thought Greek asylum authorities would punish them if they showed up in the press. No one wanted to do an interview, but everyone had complaints. The nights were cold, the water and electricity absent, and the camp staff indifferent, if not hostile. "No pictures please," said a man from Syria. "We don't want them to send us back to Syria."

Another Syrian said he felt guilty that so many camp residents had chopped down olive trees, but what could they do? "It's a shame to cut down these trees, I know they belong to someone," he said. He pointed toward his son, a small kid of no more than five or six. "But isn't it worse to let this child freeze to death?"

He wasn't exaggerating. Children and adults alike had died of exposure in the camps. Others had suffocated or burned alive when their makeshift heaters went haywire. In November 2019, a few months earlier, a nine-month-old Congolese baby died of severe dehydration in Moria, the camp-turned-ghetto on Lesbos Island.[1]

After an hour, most of the men dispersed back to their shacks. But one lingered, a pensive look on his face. He turned to me. "We're dying little by little here," he said.

NADIR ZITAWAY AND his wife, Eli, lived in Vial for two months in 2018. The government transferred the couple to Thessaloniki, but he couldn't find work there. When I first met him in February 2020, he had returned to the island for a brief trip— he was searching for a job. The 270 euros in financial assistance they received each didn't last more than two weeks. Worse still, they shared an apartment with another family—a deeply religious and conservative Syrian man, his wife, and their child. Progressive and not abiding by any religion, Nadir had been at odds with the man from the first day they found themselves living under the same roof.

Back in Chios for the first time since leaving the year before, he hoped to find a job that could pay enough to cover rent and put food on the table for his wife and his newborn daughter. He brought his university degree in marketing with him when he left

Syria, but now he was looking for odd jobs painting homes, something he'd done during his last stint living on the island.

Born into a family displaced to Syria by the 1948 war that led to the creation of Israel, the thirty-year-old Palestinian had lived his entire life stateless. When the civil war broke out in Syria in 2011, his family tried to outlast it without leaving, splitting time between a house in Umm Walad, near Daraa in the country's southeast, and their farm home on the outskirts of the small town. One day toward the tail end of December 2012, he walked from the farm to their home in town, gathered some family valuables, such as his mother's jewelry, and filled a sack with food to take back to his parents. The street was busy—pedestrians were everywhere—when Syrian government helicopters filled the skies. He counted at least eight before the barrel bombs started raining down. Buildings collapsed around him. Craters were blown into the street. People tore off running. A barrel hit earth not far from him, and shrapnel flew in every direction. "I remember two things: the lights and voices," Nadir told me. He woke up in a makeshift clinic, one of the many like it operating in the parts of Syria the government had lost control of during the uprising. His head was foggy, and he'd sustained nerve damage in his left hand, on which he'd lost his ring finger.

By the end of 2013, more than a million and a half Syrians had become refugees, scattered across the map of the Middle East and beyond. But Nadir remained, unable to leave behind his parents. Then one day in 2014, he looked up to again see helicopters buzzing above, barrel bombs plunging down on Umm Walad, not far from his neighborhood. He thought his parents were home, and he rushed there to make sure they were alright. When he arrived, he found a heap of ruptured concrete and maimed steel where the house had stood just minutes earlier. He dug through the rubble. Nothing. He ran to the clinics where the bodies were piling up. Nothing. He scoured the list of the dead. Nothing. Had his parents escaped? Had they died elsewhere? Four more years of war crawled by, and he knew nothing of their fates. In late 2018, he and Eli packed their bags and set off for Europe.

They waited in Turkey for two months—a smuggler had robbed him, and he didn't have the cash to pay another one. Eventually he met a Syrian man who let them make the passage to Chios on credit. There in Vial, they slept in a structure pieced together with tarps, ropes, and scrap wood. When his wife missed her period, they went to the medical staff in the camp, but the pregnancy test came back negative. Then she missed another, and they tried again. Still negative. He nonetheless thought she may be pregnant, but he also worried that the missed periods could've signified some deeper health concern. Because the medical staff was notorious for doling out nothing more than ibuprofen to the sickest among the asylum seekers in Vial, they were suspicious. They tried again with a nonprofit medical association working in the camp, and they finally learned that Eli was pregnant.

Expecting a child and still indebted to the smuggler, Nadir searched for work. He eventually landed a gig doing day labor and saved up enough to rent an apartment. Vial was no place for a pregnant woman, and he worked long days to make sure Eli didn't have to live there in the camp any longer. The government then sent them to Thessaloniki, where she gave birth to a healthy baby girl—a small miracle, he told me, because she had two miscarriages in Syria during the war. Miracles aside, one thing left him shocked and saddened: When his daughter was born, a nurse filled out the requisite paperwork. Under nationality, the nurse wrote REFUGEE. They could apply for the girl to have Greek nationality after five years, but Nadir couldn't shake the feeling that displacement was an ancestral curse.

WE MET AT Antonis Vorrias's home, where Nadir and Eli were staying for a few days. The couple had met Vorrias while they were living in Vial, and he was constantly opening his home for people in need.

One evening Nadir, Nick, and I shared a taxi to Vial, around twenty minutes' away. We followed Nadir through the camp. He knew his way around, but he was slightly thrown off—its population had more than doubled since he and Eli left the island. He stepped over piles of shit, kicked aside water bottles full of urine. When people hacking down olive trees shot suspicious looks our way, Nadir would offer, "I'm a refugee, too, and these guys are with me."

The moon rose high over the camp, looming over the wall of mountains in the distance. When we left to head back to Antonis's, small bonfires flashed in the field like oversized fireflies. Plumes of smoke danced from the makeshift fireplaces asylum seekers had cobbled together in their shanties.

NEARLY A YEAR had passed since the European Commission declared that the refugee crisis was over, but there on Chios, there in Greece, the catastrophe was present as ever.[2] A resurgent wave of refugee boats in late 2019 had pushed the number of new arrivals that year past sixty thousand, the highest annual tally since the European Union and Turkey reached their deal in March 2016.

Before the EU-Turkey deal, solidarity overshadowed hostility in Greece. Nearly four years later, though, the way squats had fanned out around Athens, the way so many Greeks flocked to the islands to help, was now giving way to a new wave of frustration.

By the time 2020 arrived, more than 112,000 asylum seekers were in the country, and the closed borders meant one of two things for any individual: they were there to stay, or they would be thrown into the often lengthy deportation process. During its first seven months in office, the New Democracy government had continued Syriza's disastrous policy of confining refugees and migrants to five Aegean islands—including Chios—while their asylum applications were processed. But processing asylum applications crawled at a tortoise's pace, and the Greek government was facing a backlog of tens of thousands.

On Chios, Kos, Lesbos, Leros, and Samos islands, local communities grew frustrated. The boats were still arriving, and they outpaced transfers from the islands to the mainland. All throughout the fall of 2019, local communities on the islands and mainland revolted as anti-refugee bigotry ballooned.

During the post-midnight hours of October 23, 2019, eight buses carried around four hundred refugees heading northward to Nea Vrasna, a seaside village near Thessaloniki. The refugees had left the overcrowded camps on Samos Island, and they were meant to resettle in a hotel-turned-refugee-accommodation in the northern Greek village.[3] As the buses pulled into the outskirts of the village, though, they were brought to a quick halt. Barricades bisected the path, and a mob of angry locals manned them. A dumpster had been set ablaze, large tractor tires spread across the road.[4]

Earlier in the day, far-right groups had reportedly driven around town bellowing through loudspeakers. They had urged the townspeople to mobilize against the refugee relocation scheme.[5] By the time the refugee buses bypassed the barricades after 3:00 a.m., it was no use. The hotel owners, under pressure from locals, reneged on their agreement. The protest continued until 6:00 a.m., and when the buses finally drove off in defeat, rerouting the refugees to Chalkida, the demonstrators erupted in applause.[6]

The spectacle was grim, but it was one that would be repeated all around Greece throughout the following weeks. A week later on Leros Island, where the hotspots were already teeming with misery, mayor Michalis Kolias rallied a mob of locals to block refugees from disembarking on its shores.[7] The following day on Kos, another Aegean island, mayor Theodosis Nikitaras gathered a crowd of residents to prevent a boat with seventy-five refugees from unloading its passengers.[8] All around the country, demagogues trafficked in hate speech and fear, rallying their followers to focus their anger on refugees and migrants that had fled war and economic catastrophe rather than the European Union policies that had turned Greece into a holding pen for displaced humans.

In Skydra, situated in Greece's West Macedonia region, a local priest urged a town council meeting to take up arms against "illegal migrants." "The Koran is fascist," he said, claiming that Muslims sought to convert the local Christian population to Islam. "We must think of everything," the priest continued. "He who is hungry will steal. And when he comes into the neighbor's field to steal, he who steals will go and beat him. But the point is . . . is the one who beat the thief to blame? We can't accept people next to us but because we can't take care of them."[9] (Only three years earlier, Skydra residents had hurled pig heads at an abandoned military camp for fear of it being transformed into a refugee camp.[10])

When an attendee suggested that the townspeople "take out rifles" to confront the refugees, whom he described as potential rapists and thieves, the priest agreed.

On November 10, 2019, nationalists assembled in Diavata, a village on the outskirts of Thessaloniki. They had this message to send to refugees: They may have fled war and economic devastation, but they were not welcome in Greece. Spearheaded by the far-right United Macedonians group, the organizers boasted of a "new and unique protest" against refugee transfers from the crowded Aegean Islands to mainland communities.[11] Overnight before the rally, far-right locals attempted to storm the camp, sparking clashes with asylum seekers residing inside. Channeling an Islamophobic idea that had become common in North America in the last decade, they promised attendees a bottomless supply of pork, beer, and local wine, ostensibly believing that adhering to different diet regimens and consuming alcohol would somehow deter refugees and migrants from seeking safety for themselves and their families. Racism and far-right sentiment were not new to Diavata. During the refugee crisis's high point following the 2015 surge in arrivals, locals participated in violent demonstrations. Later, when refugee children were slated to start attending local Greek schools, several villagers kept their children home in protest, using padlocks to seal the gates to the schools. "This situation cannot continue," Dimitris Ziambazis, leader of United Macedonians, told a reporter.[12] "Our homes and communities are turning into ghettos, and we will not stand for it."

Around that same time, unknown assailants sawed away at an electricity line providing power to a refugee camp in Veria, another village in northern Greece. The perpetrators toppled the power line, and local media speculated that the incident was carried out with intent to cut off the electricity supply to the camp.[13]

Back on the islands, the situation spiraled further out of control. On December 17, East Samos mayor Georgios Stantzos showed up in Pythagoras Square in Vathy, where a handful of asylum seekers were mulling around.[14] He'd heard that they were planning on occupying the square, and he later claimed that five cars had been vandalized in the area, pinning the blame on the asylum seekers. Stantzos yelled at them, then lunged toward several and shoved them. "Leave, you fuckers," he shouted.

He shoved another woman, who replied and said she was a

tourist. "You filth," he said. "Get out of here." A local journalist with the Samos24 news site stood by and filmed the assault on his phone. The mayor approached him. "You didn't film me saying 'fuckers,' right?"

SAMA ASKED ME not to use her real name. There was too much at risk, she told me when we met in Chios in February 2020, both for herself in Greece and for her family back in Syria. At twenty-nine, she had a mischievous smile, liked to teach the humanitarian activists curse words in Arabic, and had endured a long sequence of deception, illness, and heartache before she traveled to Europe.

Born to an Arab father and Kurdish mother, she grew up fantasizing about visiting Greece. In high school, she imagined what the country was like, looked at photos of its historic ruins, and read about it in books. When she arrived on November 19, 2019, the sight she gazed upon at Vial did not line up with her childhood daydreams. Children everywhere were crying. Tents spread out in the olive groves around the camp. She had come alone, and her heart sank when she absorbed her new reality.

Sama never planned on leaving Syria. Along with her husband and two daughters, aged one and five, she survived the first eight years of the war without thinking once about filling her suitcases and taking off. In October 2019, she traveled to Damascus and had surgery for a cancerous brain tumor. Laid up in a hospital bed and recovering for three weeks, she didn't know that the Turkish military and Turkey-backed militias—hardline jihadist groups—had reached her hometown, Qamishli. Her parents visited her in the hospital, but they didn't tell her what was happening back home. A few days before the surgery, she had visited her childhood home in Douma, an area near Damascus, and found it destroyed by an airstrike, but she felt grateful for the relative stability in her neighborhood in Qamishli.

When she finally checked out of the hospital and went home, though, she found her home in Qamishli demolished. A Turkish airstrike had hit it. Her two daughters had died, her father told her, and her husband had split—he couldn't stay married to a woman with cancer, he'd said. She felt like she had nothing left to live for, and her father saw it as an opportunity to leave the blood-stricken country and seek out better medical care in Europe. Go, he told her, and she went. On a fake passport, she crossed through Iraqi Kurdistan and flew from Erbil to Tehran, Iran. From there, she hopped another flight to Turkey. The journey wasn't easy as a single woman, and the smugglers tried to take advantage of her. For three days, she and dozens of refugees—most of them Syrians—sat together on the shores of Izmir and waited for the signal to depart. One day the smugglers tried to get her to walk off into the woods with them, she told me. She had heard tales of smugglers raping women, robbing them, even killing them. She refused, and after prodding her for hours, they eventually gave up. She looked around her and wondered how all these desperate people, all these fellow countrymen, could have sat with folded arms and said nothing when the men tried to lure her into a situation that, no doubt, would have ended badly.

Hours before sunrise on the fourth day, the smugglers appeared on the shore again. The coast was clear, they said, and the Turkish coast guard was nowhere in sight. She boarded the dinghy with the others and reached Oinousses, a small idyllic island next to Chios, around 6:00 a.m. From there, Greek authorities transferred the boat's passengers to Chios.

In Vial, she spent the first few days sleeping in a tent outside, and when the harassment she endured was too much, she approached the camp staff and requested a caravan inside. But the caravans were all occupied. She approached the medical staff and informed them that she had recently had surgery for cancer, but again, there was nothing they could do. They didn't have the medicines she required, and she was on her own. "Vial is psychological torture," she told me. "I was a woman alone. How am I supposed to protect myself?"

She was still mourning her daughters when, one day, she spotted a crew from the International Red Cross in the camp. Was there any way they could obtain the list of the dead from Qamishli? They promised to do what they could, but they couldn't guarantee anything. A few days later, a Red Cross worker informed her that her daughters' names weren't present in any log of the deceased. "At that point, I felt ninety-nine percent sure they were still alive," she said.

She phoned everyone she could think of, and she eventually tracked down her estranged husband's new phone number. He finally picked up, and she heard her daughters in the background. They were still alive—her father had lied, thinking it was the only way to convince her to get the treatment she required in Europe. Her head swirled. She had lost everything, and now she hadn't.

Meanwhile in Vial, she grew frightened and desperate, and she knew that one day she wouldn't be able to fend off the men harassing her. That was when someone working in the camp pulled her aside and said he had an idea. There was a local solidarity activist who might be willing to put her up.

She moved in with a local humanitarian that same day, happy to escape Vial but now wondering how she could return to Syria and be reunited with her children, even if her husband had no intention of taking her back. She could apply for voluntary return to Turkey, but she'd heard rumors that refugees deported to the country were forced to spend months, even years, behind bars before they could go back to Syria. She decided to press forward with her asylum request in Greece, despite the lengthy backlog of applications slowing down waiting times. And with the Greek government planning to relocate asylum seekers to closed detention centers, her plans to leave the country she grew up fantasizing about faced an obstacle. How could she be there for her children if she was stuck in a holding cell on a Greek island? "Do you know any other way to get back?" she asked me.

SITTING IN THE shack belonging to Saber al-Kolak and two others, I watched as the men stuffed plastic bags and water bottles into an oil drum they had rigged as a fireplace. They said they didn't feel right about chopping down the olive trees, knowing someone's livelihood depended on them, and they only did so when all other options had been exhausted. There was already tension with villagers in Chalkio, who had protested outside the camp in November, and no one thought it wise to exacerbate the situation without good cause.

The shack was a puzzle of garbage and tossed-out materials. Saber, Mohammed, and Omar al-Daloo, their other roommate, had purchased a damaged wicker lawn chair and some other odd supplies from a Roma encampment near Vial. They had hunted down old pipes and parts of various appliances—a window frame filled with a sheet of wood and equipped with a lock was the front door; marking off their sleeping area—they shared a single mattress, old and weatherworn—was a wall of chicken wire with a refrigerator's static condenser fastened to it as a swinging door.

Everyone in the tent had run out of money. For two months, they bought food at a grocery store, trying to avoid eating the meals they were given each day by the army. When there was chicken, it arrived still bloody. When there were hardboiled eggs, they arrived frozen. When there were potatoes, they arrived un-dercooked. When there was bread—there was always bread—it arrived with mold on it. Earlier that evening, I had walked out past a garbage can on the edge of the field. There, I saw a pile of unopened, prepackaged meals on the ground. "Once I got chicken that still had a feather in it," a man told me. Sometimes, the expi-ration date stamped on the meals was two weeks past.

"We knew there would be difficult conditions before we came here," Omar told me, "but we couldn't imagine this."

Saber added, "We didn't know we'd be living like this, in tents."

He placed a heat-blackened kettle atop the fireplace and dropped a few bags of Lipton inside it. Later, while he sipped from a plastic cup, he picked up his phone and scrolled through photos of meals he used to make in Gaza: pizza, pastries with za'atar, pies and other sweets. He was smiling.

ON FEBRUARY 13, 2020, I walked through the capital's Syntagma Square toward the Ministry of Interior, where three mayors from North Aegean islands, the right-wing regional governor Kostas Moutzouris, and islanders had called for a protest against the government's plans to build closed detention centers on five is-lands hosting refugees.[15] As I neared the ministry, a motorbike swerved onto the sidewalk and a man hopped off the back. Ilias Kasidiaris, Golden Dawn's spokesperson. Next to him, I noticed, stood Giorgos Germenis, a squat, baldheaded former Golden Dawn parliamentarian.

Around four hundred people gathered in the street. It wasn't much of a protest. The mayors took turns standing in front of news cameras, making their case in polite terms.[16] They focused on the hardship islanders endured as a result of the refugee buildup. Only two days earlier, the mayors and the regional governor had severed dialogue with the government in Athens after it was revealed that permanent, closed detention centers would be built on the five islands.

The protest in Athens drew political parties from across the spectrum. The far-right LEPEN movement was there, the ultra-nationalist Greek Solution, a few members of New Democracy at odds with the government's new migration overhaul. Worse still, seemingly leftist and progressive outfits showed up. A few rogue Syriza parliamentarians, supporters of the Greek Communist Party (KKE). The communists took issue with Golden Dawn's presence and shouted through a bullhorn, "Golden Dawn out now." But when Kasidiaris and the others hit the road, the communists stayed at the protest and held up their placards and banners, surrounded by people equally as opposed to refugees and migrants as the neo-Nazis that had just been booted from the demonstration.

I found the North Aegean regional governor, Kostas Moutzouris, standing at the edge of the protest, giving quick quotes to journalists. Moutzouris had far-right views, had railed against refugees for months as their presence swelled on Greek islands. He'd rejected their designation as refugees and insisted that they were "economic migrants," and he'd hobnobbed with far-right protesters that had been stirring up trouble on the islands, but now he put on a kinder face for the press. "We nearly had violence between the inhabitants and the immigrants, but we avoided it—we interfered and avoided it—but this may happen again anytime," he told me. "But the point is, that for the moment being, there is a kind of violence between the local people and the government . . . because the government is acting one-sided, in a way, taking decisions by itself only. It doesn't discuss with us; we don't have consensus, we don't have brainstorming, we don't have a decision taken together."

Later, I spotted Chios mayor Stamatis Karmantzis. He'd served in the military and had been active in politics for more than three decades. In 2014, Chios residents elected him to the Hellenic Parliament as a member of New Democracy. Two years later, the party ousted him after he penned a post on social media endorsing the slogan that "the only good Turk is a dead Turk"[17]. In 2019, voters picked him as the island's mayor. Karmantzis took to his Facebook nearly every day to incite fear and hatred of the asylum seekers on Chios. I asked if he would answer a few questions, and he dismissed me with the wave of a hand. "I'm a man of action, not words," he said. "I don't give quotes ever. You can go talk to all the other mayors. They like to talk."

"In that case," I said, "I'll quote you on that."

He looked unnerved, and I went back into the rally to find more people to speak with.

Later, Chios mayor Karmantzis reappeared behind me, tapping my shoulder. He'd rethought his position and was willing to speak for a moment. A few months earlier, he'd shared a Facebook post suggesting that refugees and migrants were part of a nefarious plot to replace Greece's population—whether he knew it or not, a nod to the white nationalist "Great Replacement Theory"—but true to form, he adopted a friendlier lexicon while speaking to me. Other European Union member states that hadn't taken in their share of refugees needed to step up, he told me, "because our islands are the eastern border of Europe." Those whose asylum requests were rejected need to be sent "back to their countries of origin."

"The situation here is out of control," Karmantzis continued. "It is not right that the islands can absorb this amount of displaced people; it's not possible."

*

AROUND 9:30 P.M. on March 3, 2020, in the northeastern Evros region of Greece, CNN Greece journalist Kostas Pliakos hopped in his rental car and started the drive from Didymoteicho to Feres, a forty-mile trek down the border. Based in Athens, the twenty-year veteran reporter had traveled to northeastern Greece to cover the latest phase in the refugee crisis. Less than a week earlier, the Turkish government ordered border guards to stand down. With nearly four million refugees and migrants in the country, Turkey was bracing for another wave of displaced Syrians as its armed forces and proxies in neighboring Syria were bogged down in Idlib, the site of a brutal military escalation with the Syrian regime. Thousands heeded the Turkish government's call and amassed on the Greek border. As clashes erupted along the border, Greece dubbed the buildup on its frontier an "invasion."

It was Pliakos's first time reporting in Evros, the regional unit that abuts the country's border with Turkey. After covering the tear gas and water cannons on the northern strip of the border, he decided to head south, where rumors purported that armed vigilantes had taken border security into their own hands. Around halfway to Feres, Pliakos spotted three men on the side of the road and pulled over. He introduced himself and asked where they were from. Syria, they told him. As he chatted with them, a pickup pulled up and skidded to an abrupt stop. When two men and a woman hopped out, Pliakos noticed one was carrying a rifle. Pliakos asked what they were doing there, and they said they lived in nearby villages and patrolled the fields for refugees and migrants. Then two more pickups pulled up, and more armed men appeared in front of him.

Understanding that they stood face-to-face with vigilantes, the Syrians took off in a sprint, Pliakos told me. One man fired the rifle into the air, the sharp crack of the gunshot rippling out in the night. Two of the Syrians escaped, but the vigilantes caught the third, tossed him to the ground, and wailed on him with fists and boots. Standing some ten meters off, Pliakos watched the violence unfold until one of the vigilantes accused him of filming the attack on his phone. He admitted that he was a reporter, but he insisted that he wasn't filming anything. It was no use: The men snatched his telephone and hurled it onto the pavement.

Even as he watched his phone shatter into pieces, Pliakos assumed he was safe—until the first fist slammed into his face. The reporter tried to defend himself, he explained, but he eventually tumbled to the ground. As the three or four men punched him, kicked him, and struck his body with a wooden stick, no cars passed. "You fucking journalist," one shouted. "We are trying to defend our communities and you do this stuff here."

By the time the beating ended, Pliakos had a black eye and his arms and legs were covered with bruises and scrapes. Two days before Pliakos was assaulted, a mob set upon a German journalist, Michael Trammer, at the Thermi port on Lesbos Island's northern shore.[18] They knocked him to the ground, slugged and stomped him, and threw his equipment into the sea. Throughout the week leading up to that incident, similar groups on Lesbos beat freelance reporters, busted up their cars, and told them to leave the island. Pliakos suspected that police "turn a blind eye" to the type of violence fanning out around Greece. Although attacks on press are not new in Greece, the recent uptick has left him stunned. "I don't remember in my career so much hate against journalists," he said.

THE DAY AFTER Pliakos was attacked, I stood atop railway tracks on a hilltop overlooking the Kastanies border crossing. A few dozen reporters had gathered there to get a clear view of the violence unfurling around five hundred yards away, blocked by the military and police from getting closer. Some scribbled in their notepads, a few did live broadcasts on camera, and others jostled for the best spot to snap photos. There, we watched the clashes unfurl a few hundred meters away, a cat-and-mouse game that started in the morning and groaned on well into the afternoon. The border crossing was closed for civilian traffic, but every now and then an olive truck full of soldiers would bounce down the crater-pocked road and enter the restricted military area. Gray clouds formed above like balled-up fists in the skies. Rows of police and soldiers occasionally inched closer to the border fence, an ominous barrier adorned with curls of concertina wire.

On the other side, refugees and migrants gripped the chain links, chanting "freedom" and trying to signal to the journalists that watched from afar. Greek riot police fired tear gas over the fence, streaks of chemical smoke briefly scarring the air and then dissolving. Every now and then, a tear gas canister would land on the Greek side, either returned by a protester or fired by Turkish police. A police vehicle lurched forward, showering the protesters with powerful streams of water. A helicopter buzzed above, and what sounded like a burst of gunfire echoed in the fields.

An employee of Greek prime minister Kyriakos Mitsotakis's press office mulled around among the reporters. Worried because we were standing on active railroad tracks, he eventually led us to another spot around a hundred meters behind the last police line. The spokesperson occasionally complained about "fake news." Someone asked him about the gunfire, and he claimed the sounds we heard were merely tear gas canisters, even as photos of apparent gunshot victims on the other side of the fence were cropping up all over the internet. He wasn't taking press inquiries and wouldn't comment on the record, but he remained present to push the eight-month-old Greek government's official narrative. He insisted that the people rallying on the other side of the barrier were not actual refugees. "Look how they are calm now that journalists are here," he said. "That's because they want you to think they are refugees."

A chief concern on both the Greek and Turkish sides was controlling the narrative. The night before, on March 3, prime minister Mitsotakis said Greece was facing an "asymmetrical threat" as the final country on the EU's southeastern periphery. "This is no longer a refugee problem," he told a press conference. He was touring the border region with European Council president Charles Michel, European Commission head Ursula von der Leyen, and European Parliament head David Sassoli. "This is a blatant attempt by Turkey to use desperate people to promote its geopolitical agenda and to divert attention from the horrible situation in Syria."[19]

The following day in Ankara, Turkish president Recep Tayyip Erdoğan met European Council president Michel—a rendezvous Erdoğan's spokesperson claimed ended with "no concrete proposition" to de-escalate the tensions on the border.[20] That same day, interior minister Süleyman Soylu told CNN Turk that Turkey was preparing a case against Greece for the European Court of Human Rights over the shootings on the border, which Greek officials dismissed as "fake news."[21]

As a regional unit, Evros spills across some 1,635 square miles, includes five municipalities, and is home to an estimated one hundred fifty thousand people. A largely flat patch of land, Evros touches Greece's borders with Bulgaria and Turkey, the latter of which mostly follows the Evros River down to the delta, delivering its rough waters into the Aegean Sea. If you drove down any of the roads abutting Greece's land border with Turkey for long enough, you would spot refugees and migrants trudging across patches of open field, lugging knapsacks and weighed down by the mud accumulating on their shoes like anchors. In the predawn hours, before the sun fully ascended, they appeared like apparitions on the hilltops, shrouded in the morning fog that afforded them less visibility. When a rickety police van or bulky army vehicle lurked past, the asylum seekers tore off for the trees or dove into the bushes, hoping to go unnoticed.

After the clashes in Kastanies died down that day in early March, I drove with colleagues to Pythio, a decaying village crawling up a hillside on the border. Sitting just a few miles from the Evros River, which separates Greek from Turkish territory, the village is home to a few hundred people who live between the ruins of a pre-Byzantine castle, a scatter of shops that are rarely open, and a handful of cafés shedding their paint and bearing faded signs.

There, we found Antonis Polisakis playing cards in a coffee shop. A pair of men sat in the corner smoking cigarettes, while an action movie played on a television fixed to the wall. Polisakis farmed cotton and sunflower on land that huddles up to the borderline. At fifty-one, he had lived his entire life in Pythio, a village he said struggled to keep its youth from leaving elsewhere in search of work and opportunities. Locals recently elected Polisakis president of the village, a largely symbolic, part-time job he managed between farming and passing hours in the café. According to Polisakis, farmers in the village often went out into their fields with carbines to patrol for refugees and migrants. A few nights earlier, he had opened Facebook and found a post that said around four hundred refugees and migrants had entered the village. Police had arrested about half of the asylum seekers, but the rest had escaped. If the Greek government was committed to reducing arrivals, he argued, "they would let the hunters and farmers protect their own lands . . . but they don't even let them access their own lands [parts near the border]." He argued that the village couldn't support a refugee population, and that Europe should "open the borders and let them pass through."

*

ON THE MORNING of March 5, 2020, Greek officials said that the refugee buildup was moving farther south down the border, toward Ipsala—the same area where Turkish authorities said Greek security forces shot and killed a Syrian man called Ahmed Abu Emad a few days earlier. Greek government spokesperson Stelios Petsas had dismissed those reports as "fake news" and Turkish propaganda, but videos captured that day in the same area appeared to show Greek soldiers firing live ammunition across the border.

We headed south. Army vehicles drifted to the shoulder and let us pass, gun-carrying soldiers crammed in the open-face cargo area. A little more than a mile before the exit to Soufli, a town situated in the Evros Valley and once famous for its silk production, we whizzed past an army truck parked on the side of the highway. Two soldiers stood staring out into a vast field.

We pulled over and walked to the edge of the hill overlooking the field. Several hundred meters out, walking along the rows of trees on the perimeter of the field were around three dozen refugees and migrants. A police vehicle rolled down the farm road on one side of the field, an army truck shivering down the other side. As the vehicles got closer, most of the asylum seekers took a seat on the dirt and waited to be detained, but a handful broke away running through the field. Carrying a rifle, a soldier followed them in a sprint. As we watched, a soldier approached us on the shoulder of the highway. "You know you can't be here," he said.

We packed up, continued south to Tycheró, a

four-thousand-person town located a few miles from the border. The Greek side of the Kastanies border crossing had been closed for days, and the Turkish side of the Kipoi crossing had been closed on and off throughout the previous twenty-four hours. In an empty lot between a souvlaki restaurant and a few homes, volunteers from the Greek Red Cross sat in a tent and stared at their cell phones. With the army and police deployed in massive numbers along the border, they had no asylum seekers to treat.

Dressed in fatigues, the soldiers popped into the restaurant every few minutes, grabbing bags of takeaway before heading back to the restricted access area near the border. Around lunchtime, local firefighter Christos Zak and Ioannas Zapartas, who bred sheep on his family land, posted up at a table and kicked back several beers. Both were forty-eight and had lived in Tycheró for their entire lives. As far as Zapartas saw it, the recent buildup was a political game played by Greece and Turkey. "They are humans, too," he told me of the refugees, "but they [Turkey] told them the borders are open. They were blackmailed."

Although Zak said no one wanted to see the asylum seekers harmed, he had nonetheless succumbed to the anti-refugee fear of the moment. He had recently started patrolling the narrow streets that weave through Tycheró on his motorbike, carrying a large stick. "Before all this erupted, you could see people passing by and nobody would do anything," Zak told me, "but now people call the police when they see [refugees]."

CHAPTER THIRTEEN

"PAVLOS LIVES ON": IN THE COURTROOM, IN THE STREET

B y late 2019, the Golden Dawn trial was reaching a crucial point. The party's leaders, having boycotted most of the hearings throughout the last four and a half years, were taking the stand, doing their best to dismiss the accusations facing them. Confronted with his own descriptions of migrants as "subhuman," "trash," and "scum," high-ranking party member and former parliamentarian Ilias Panagiotaros told the courtroom that he had only been referring to migrants who committed crimes.[1] (He also begrudgingly admitted that, according to his estimation, 99.9 percent of migrants were criminals.) The violence, he claimed, had been the work of local chapters, which prompted the party's central leadership to punish the culprits.

Earlier that month, another former Golden Dawn

parliamentarian, Nikos Michos, also sought to shield the leadership from legal retribution, claiming that party chief Michaloliakos had never instructed his followers to carry out attacks or other crimes. During his testimony, however, he admitted that Golden Dawn jackboots raided a home in Perama in June 2012 and attacked sleeping Egyptian fishermen with wooden clubs.[2] Michos revealed that Michaloliakos was made aware of Pavlos Fyssas's murder only hours after the rapper bled out in the street, unwittingly contradicting the leader's long-held claim that he had not known of the slaying until the following day.

With even more gruesome details of Golden Dawn's activities emerging each week during the trial, and the alleged perpetrators scrambling to deflect accusations that they were responsible for the bloodshed, Dimitris Psarras's investigative journalism and expertise became more important and relevant than ever. Thanasis Kampagiannis, who represented Egyptian fishermen in the civil suit portion of the Golden Dawn trial, told me that Psarras and his colleagues covered the neo-Nazi party for so long and so thoroughly that their reportage helped lay the foundations for understanding the "ideological structure of the organization and also their criminal actions."

Now out of the parliament and shedding its once loyal supporters, Golden Dawn had shut down and boarded up the offices where it plotted its political future. The party's once lively headquarters, a slate-gray five-story office building on Mesogeion Avenue, sat quiet and abandoned. The massive banner depicting Michaloliakos's bespectacled face no longer hung from the building's windows, and torch-wielding party supporters no longer assembled for boisterous rallies in the street out front.

Across town, another former party office bore few signs that Golden Dawn had ever occupied it. Near the office, pro-Golden Dawn graffiti remained on a retaining wall—WE WANT OUR

COUNTRY BACK, it declared—but the party's red-and-black flags, bearing its swastika-like emblem, no longer flew from the balcony overlooking the impoverished borough in central Athens.

WHEN PARTY LEADER Nikolaos Michaloliakos was slated to testify on November 6, hundreds of anti-fascists and leftists filled the walkway in front of the courthouse. HANG THE FASCISTS, a banner read. Riot police stood in columns above the stairway leading to the entrance, regulating who could pass into the courthouse and who couldn't.

Inside, a row of riot police sat in a line dividing the courtroom into two sections: Golden Dawn supporters and opponents of the neo-Nazi party. Magda Fyssa arrived wearing all black and with a pendant bearing her slain son's face attached to her necklace. Photographers crouched in front of her. *Click, click, click.* She held up a booklet containing information about her son's murder. "Six Years," it read, blood spattered around the words. Attendees trickled in, and the room was nearly quiet until Michaloliakos arrived, flanked on both sides by police officers. "Rise up," a Golden Dawn member shouted, and around a hundred party supporters stood at attention. "You dog," someone screamed from across the room, but others in the anti-fascist crowd urged everyone to stay quiet.

Eight justices and court officials sat on an elevated podium overlooking the table where Michaloliakos took a seat, where he would be grilled. The last of sixty-nine defendants to testify, he came prepared to deny everything. For more than three hours, he echoed earlier claims by defendants seeking to push the blame off on local chapters and individuals. Golden Dawn's leadership, he claimed, had never sanctioned or encouraged violence. He claimed he was a "nationalist" but not a "Nazi."[3] His words, he argued, had never prompted anyone to carry out an attack. Migrants had to "return to their homelands," he insisted, but denied that Golden Dawn had ever caused harm to any of them. When questioned about his presence at a neo-Nazi metal concert caught on video in 2005, he denied that it was him. "Anyone who knows me will tell you I don't like heavy metal," he said.

The testimony dragged on, rife with heated questions from the justices and shameless denials by Michaloliakos. "There are some slogans and phrases that have been mentioned in conversation at your offices," the judge said of the party's often violent chants. "You have personally said something about strike teams," she added, referring to the organized battalions Golden Dawn operated to terrorize migrants and political opponents in the past.

"There were no strike teams," he insisted. "I said that before, and I wrote about it."

Michaloliakos insisted that the type of speech he and his acolytes deployed "do not condone acts of violence. I have never suggested to anyone to act specifically in a violent manner. Speaking of which, there are lyrics in the La Marseillaise, the national anthem of France, the phrase about the bayonets saying 'the blood of our enemies will flow at the edges of the pavements.'"

Summing it all up, the neo-Nazi leader said he and his comrades were on trial as part of a left-wing conspiracy concocted to persecute nationalists. "I want to plead innocent to the charges against me. They are the result of a political conspiracy and targeting [of me] for twenty-five years," he said.

When his testimony came to an end, Michaloliakos stood to leave the courtroom. His supporters erupted. "Blood, honor, Golden Dawn," they chanted. One threw his arm up in the same Nazi salute several of the defendants had denied using throughout the trial.

On the other side of the courtroom, the anti-fascists and

leftists attempted to outshout the Golden Dawn supporters. "Pavlos lives on," they screamed. "Smash the Nazis."

Outside, I found the Pakistani Community of Greece's president, Javed Aslam, standing alongside Khadam Hussein Luqman. "We are still waiting for justice," he told me. "Of course, he lied the whole time. What else could he do? Admit that he's responsible for the killing of Khadam's son or Magda's son?"

On January 19, 2020, hundreds of people, most of them apparent Golden Dawn supporters, gathered in Syntagma Square. Half a year had passed since Golden Dawn crashed out of the parliament, since party chief Michaloliakos had vowed that the party would regroup and rebuild its presence in the streets, and things were on the up again for the party. A month earlier, in December, the lead prosecutor, Adamantia Economou, had issued a startling recommendation to the court trying dozens of party members for operating a criminal organization: Drop the charges against Michaloliakos and other high-ranking Golden Dawn officials. Altogether, the years of violence, the militia-like training, the blood spilled in the streets, and the murders constituted "isolated acts for which the leadership was not responsible," Economou said.[4] "A political party's ideology is irrelevant from the point of view of criminal law; what we're investigating are criminal acts."

Magda Fyssa was outraged. Before leaving the courtroom that day, December 18, she confronted Economou. "Today, on the 18th, Pavlos Fyssas has been dead for seventy-five months," she said. "You chose today to stab him again?"

Just over a month later, on January 19, documentary journalist and *Deutsche Welle* correspondent Thomas Jacobi, was in Syntagma Square to cover the far-right protest. Had the mob gathered there waited one more day, it would have been a year to the day since he was last attacked by fascists during a nationalist rally in Athens.[5]

It was an overcast day with gunmetal gray clouds spreading across a drab sky. The rally had been called, at least according to the Facebook images advertising the event, by the "Greek people."

I parked down the road, far enough not to be followed back to my car in case I caught anyone's eye, and arrived shortly after the attackers had, yet again, set upon Jacobi. By the time I stepped into Syntagma Square, the rally was well underway. Around five hundred people had amassed—all of them Greek, as advertised, but almost all of them appearing to belong to Golden Dawn. Banners insisted that Greece was an Orthodox Christian country, while others demanded: STOP ISLAM. Yet another read: CLOSE THE BORDERS. REFUGEES NOT WELCOME.

The young men had encircled Jacobi, much like during the attack a year earlier, and beat him until he hit the ground. While on the pavement, he fielded more punches and kicks. Unlike last time, his attackers—because they wore masks, no one could say if they were the same ones that mobbed him in the past—didn't make off with his recording equipment. After breaking free with a bloodied face and busted nose, he told a group of reporters in the square that he wouldn't be backing down anytime soon. He'd already worked on one documentary about Golden Dawn, and he told reporters he fully intended to continue moving forward with another one. He told press he considered himself lucky because the attackers "didn't pull any knives."[6] He added, "I thought that with so many police present I could do my job. I was wrong, but I will not hide and not be scared."

Most of the Greek reporters and photographers had positioned themselves far from the demonstrators, taking notes and zooming in on shots from the other side of the square. I circled the rally first, passing through the outdoor seating in front of a McDonald's. There sat a group of rawboned shaved heads donning T-shirts with logos of Blood and Honour Hellas, the Golden Dawn–linked white power music scene in Greece. For a moment, I stood by and watched them bite into their burgers, tried to gauge their ages: probably in their late teens, I surmised. Then I waded into the rally. Leaflets were scattered across the street, which was blocked by the stage from which the speakers addressed the crowd. GREECE BELONGS TO GREEKS, the fliers insisted. I jotted down a few notes and snapped a couple photos with my phone, mostly the banners and shots from behind the crowd, hoping not to prompt unwanted attention. When I noticed a group of young men slipping their balaclavas over their faces and hoisting their flagpoles—their weapons—onto their shoulders, I took a few steps back, trying to create distance. I wasn't sure if I was being paranoid or prudent, but then I caught a glimpse of a young man, his face uncovered, watching me from a few feet away. Better safe than sprawled out on the pavement, I thought, and signaled to him. He was caught off guard. "Hey," I started. "Can you tell me what that banner says? I'm just passing through, and I don't read much Greek."

"Yes," he said. "It says, 'Close the borders.'"

"Thanks. Is this a protest for the islands?" I asked, referring to the recent uptick in refugee boats washing up on the shores of several Aegean Islands.

"It's all of Greece," he replied. "The refugees are attacking all of Greece."

When he then sauntered off and was absorbed into the crowd, I saw that the masked group had not yet left their position. They were clapping and chanting as a speaker onstage insisted that Greece would never become a "Muslim country," but they were also casting furtive glances my way. I walked off, circled the protest a few times, and then joined the handful of reporters waiting on the steps at the far end of the square. I watched for a while, took a few notes. The reporters told me that former Golden Dawn legislator Ilias Kasidiaris had been standing nearby, watching with folded arms, when Jacobi was attacked. Then a pair of Pakistani men, both speaking in Punjabi, each carrying a suitcase, descended the stairway, and a police officer standing at the bottom stopped them and advised them to walk around the rally. Good advice, I thought, but I wondered why police officers—so long implicitly involved in Golden Dawn's violent ascent—would offer it. Only a few minutes earlier, I'd heard one of the speakers rail against the presence of Pakistanis in the country.

Before I left, I checked the news on my phone. Government spokesman Stelios Petsas had already condemned the attack and vowed to investigate and prosecute the perpetrators. That type of violence marked an assault on "freedom of expression, pluralism, and democracy," Petsas said. The Union of Foreign Correspondents, which represents Greek and international reporters working for foreign press, called on the government to "take immediate action to identify the perpetrator." In a statement, Reporters Without Borders, the press freedom watchdog, said that "attacks by far-right activists against the media are too often ignored," insisting that the assailants "must be brought to justice."[7]

When I got home, I checked Golden Dawn's website to see if the party had issued a press release. Predictably, the statement claimed that "professional anti-fascists" had staged the attack on Jacobi.[8] These impostors hoped to "tarnish" Greece and abandon its people to "illegal immigration." Otherwise, the rally was a success, a "gathering of Greeks" who wanted nothing more than to "close the borders."

JUST OVER A month later, I drove to Amygdaleza, a migrant detention center on the outskirts of the Greek capital. I parked in a muddy lot across the street and approached the entrance with a fellow reporter and Arash Hampay, an Iranian who had become a refugee rights advocate after receiving asylum in Greece.

Seven miles from central Athens, Amygdaleza sits on a slope in Acharnes, a working-class suburb overlooked by the snow-capped peaks of Mount Parnitha. In April 2012, at the height of Greece's crippling economic crisis, the government opened Amygdaleza as the country's first migrant detention center.[9] Locals initially protested the center, but at a time when factories in the area were laying off thousands, the government insisted that the facility would create jobs, buoy the local economy, and enable authorities to clamp down on crime and undocumented migration. Throughout the years that followed, hunger strikes, protests against the overcrowded living conditions, and suicide attempts were a constant reality inside the facility's walls. Rights groups, migrant advocates, and activists have consistently called for its closure.

We joined a queue of a few dozen people in front of the sprawling compound. A gust of wind swept past the entrance, carrying errant items of rubbish. A woman sat on a curb, on her lap was a crying child swaddled in blankets. A man shouted into the receiver of his phone, cursing in Arabic. Many of them held bags filled with clothes and canned foods. Most of the people waiting there were refugees and migrant workers themselves, hoping to visit less fortunate loved ones inside. A few nervously puffed cigarettes. Everyone clutched their residency documents.

Behind the latched steel gate stood a Greek police officer, tall, slack-faced, and in his early forties. Posted atop a nearby watch tower, another police officer gripped a rifle and periodically peered down at the small crowd through sunglasses. Menacing coils of barbwire crowned the chain-link fences and cadaver gray walls surrounding the detention center. Every twenty minutes or so, a paddy wagon—navy blue, rickety, and weatherworn—hauled up to the other side of the gate. A group of visitors spilled out of its rear door, and the next batch of visitors piled in.

The police officer manning the gate took his time inspecting everyone's documents and passports before allowing them to enter for a visit. In front of me, a Pakistani migrant worker in his mid-twenties spoke neither Greek nor English, and he struggled to communicate with the officer. He handed over a sheaf of papers and the police officer shot him a shifty look. The top sheet appeared to be an email from the migration ministry: a document the migrant worker believed confirmed his legal status in the country. Original documents only, the police officer barked. The Pakistani man fumbled through his papers, tried to offer an explanation in clipped sentence, but the police officer grew impatient. "My friend, I am a policeman," he said. He shoved the papers back into the visitor's chest and dismissed him with a quick wave of his hand. "Go."

My turn came and I handed over my US passport. A puzzled expression spread across his face, but he waved me through when he found my entry stamp. He did not ask if I was a journalist, how I knew someone inside Amygdaleza, or why I was there. I slid onto the frigid steel bench in the back of the police van, joining a handful of men who entered before me, some chattering in Punjabi. When the van reached capacity—nine passengers, everyone's hands folded in their laps and knees touching one another's—the officer appeared at the back door. "Numbers?" he said, referring to the identification numbers of the detainees we were visiting. He jotted the numbers in his notepad, stared hard at the page for a moment, and then slammed the door with a thud. The engine grumbled and we set off. I peeked through little holes spangling the metal casing fastened to the back window: egg-white administrative buildings, cracked cement walls, and rolls of concertina wire whizzed past.

The van shivered over potholes and we bounced into each other. The driver braked to a stop, the back door swung open, and we all climbed out onto the gravel walkway. We formed a line outside a container, inside which we would visit the detainees. Beyond a chain-link fence a trio of men cast glances our way. They listened to a radio blasting rap music. "They're crazy," a guard said. She was in her mid-twenties and had a tight smile framed by tufts of brown hair that spilled from beneath her police cap.

"Yeah, well," said another guard, a man with a black balaclava pulled halfway up his face. "Arabs."

I couldn't tell what language the men were speaking, but I knew it was not Arabic. I assumed the police officer was using *Arabs* as a blanket term for everyone locked away in Amygdaleza. He rubbed the chill from his hands and turned to me. "Inside," he ordered.

In the container, two hard-faced guards barked commands as we entered. Visitors slid their bags across the chest-high inspection table, and the guards, scowling, rifled through them. They sniffed inside packets of cigarettes, ostensibly looking for drugs— they found none. They did find objectionable items, however: certain liquids and oils, which they shoved back across the table. "Not allowed," they said.

Along with the other visitors, we sidled up in front of four small holes in a glass panel that separated us from the detainees. Hussein, who asked me to use a pseudonym, appeared at the doorway opposite the panel. He waited until an officer motioned for him to approach the glass. He wore a tired gray sweatshirt with the hood pulled up on his head, and a smattering of teenage acne flecked his cheeks. He was tall enough that he had to bend down to speak through the holes in the glass panel. He told us that six days earlier, police officers stopped him in Exarchia. When he couldn't produce his residency documents, the officers carted him

off to a nearby police station. He found himself in Amygdaleza
later that night, sharing a container with five Afghans.

We asked how conditions were inside.

"Terrible," he said.

Cockroaches skittered across the floor and along the walls all
day and night, he explained. Next to us a visitor and a detainee
spoke in Arabic, both of their faces near the glass. The visitor
said the cops had inspected each individual cigarette the visitor
brought for his friend. Together they laughed the sort of pitiful
chuckle you let out when you pity someone for being dim.

Hussein went on, telling us about life in Amygdaleza—"It
is very bad," he said—but the roar of simultaneous conversations
between visitors and detainees left us straining to hear his words
through the small punctures in the glass. Every few moments,
the guards yelled at someone about using their cell phones, which
visitors are barred from using inside the facility. Down the row
of visitors, one man lifted his cell phone up to the glass, maybe to
show his friend on the other side a photo. "That's it," a guard said.
"Close your phone." He paused a moment, and then his face glazed
red. He threw his arms in a sudden fit, waving visitors out of the
container. "It's over. Finished."

THE NEXT DAY, a disturbing video emerged on social media: A detainee reportedly setting ablaze his container to protest the squalid
living conditions in Amygdaleza. I messaged Hussein on the encrypted chat app WhatsApp but received no reply. I called and
texted with no luck. A week grumbled past. Whether his phone
was dead, broken, or confiscated, I could not say. Whether he had
been deported, shipped back to an island, or moved to another
mainland facility, it was impossible to know with any certainty.

I contacted another detainee in Amygdaleza, a Syrian refugee called Noah. Along with his brother Muhammad, he fled Idlib under barrel bombs and airstrikes. The brothers were detained upon arrival on Kos Island in August 2019. Authorities eventually transferred them to Amygdaleza. After three months there, neither had a lawyer nor knew what to expect. They wore the same shirts and pants they wore when they arrived half a year earlier, Noah told me on WhatsApp. "In Greece, there is no such thing as law," he added.

I asked about the cockroaches Hussein had mentioned, whether Noah's container had similar infestations.

"Yes," he said, matter-of-factly.

"Is it true the food arrives moldy?" I asked, recalling a complaint I'd heard in several camps on the islands and the mainland.

"Not always . . . just sometimes," said Noah. "But the food is not good or healthy."

"It's undercooked?"

"Correct," he said. He waited a few moments to send another message, and then: "And the bathrooms are not clean."

"Are the toilets broken?" I asked. (During the dozens of times I visited refugee camps in Greece throughout the previous four and a half years, I had never seen a facility where at least some of the toilets hadn't fallen into disrepair.)

"See for yourself." He sent me photos of the bathrooms, layers of filth accumulated on the toilets and showers. He sent a short video clip, just thirteen seconds, of him walking through the container in which he slept. He was one of eighteen people in the container, he said, and the video revealed several bunk beds and a few mattresses on the floor. Blankets were strung up on clotheslines, marking off patches of personal space in the container.

The pressure of surviving in overcrowded spaces, the indignities the guards heaped upon the detainees each day, and the lack of clarity about their futures led a group of Syrians and Palestinians in Amygdaleza to plan a hunger strike. (If the hunger strike did happen, news of it never made it outside the detention center.) "They treat us like animals," Noah said.

And then, on February 26, 2020, Greek authorities recorded the country's first case of COVID-19, the coronavirus that went on to kill millions around the world.[10] After hearing the news of the virus, Noah told me that he worried the pandemic would eventually lash its way into the Greek refugee camps and detention centers. A few days later, he went dark. I called and texted, but like with Hussein, Noah's phone went straight to voicemail.

SEVERAL WEEKS PASSED before I heard back from Hussein and Noah. Greek authorities had transferred Hussein to a closed detention center inside the Moria camp on Lesbos Island, and Noah and his brother were shipped back to the refugee camp on Kos Island.

Two weeks into March, however, a new kind of threat emerged. As COVID-19 cases fanned out across the country and around the world, the Greek government announced a partial shutdown that started on March 14.[11] Gyms, restaurants, bars, and cafés shuttered, and authorities barred large gatherings, such as concerts and festivals. Over the weeks that followed, the lockdown was extended to include additional restrictions on travel and movement. The government also required everyone moving around in public to carry a passport or identification card, a rule that left undocumented people with few options. In the camps, refugees now faced new restrictions on movement, but the social distancing promoted by the Greek government and watchdogs was not an option.[12]

As the coronavirus tally soared, human rights organizations, aid agencies, and advocacy groups called on the Greek government to remove asylum seekers from the packed camps and relocate them to safer and more sanitary facilities. Those calls went unanswered, and the Greek government instead placed tighter restrictions on asylum seekers in the camps. Unable to travel to the Greek islands, I reached out to Mohsen, a thirty-eight-year-old Iranian marooned in the Moria camp. He told me that the camp had few doctors and scarce supplies, and that the food was unsanitary. "There are a lot of people in the [fields]," he said of the overcrowding.[13] "They don't have anything to keep them warm [or] clean, and there's no electricity."

In late March, a United Nations refugee agency (UNHCR) spokesperson, Boris Cheshirkov, told me that it was only a matter of time before the coronavirus hit the country's refugee population. "So far there have been no cases of the novel coronavirus among refugees and asylum seekers in Greece," he said. "But thousands of refugees and asylum seekers in Greece—including many who are older and vulnerable—are in locations where health services are overstretched."

At the time, more than 35,000 asylum seekers were living on five Aegean islands in camps designed to accommodate an estimated 4,500 people. "UNHCR has repeatedly alerted about the need to urgently improve living conditions [in the camps]," Cheshirkov added. "Hygiene and sanitation, and access to health services are priority areas, but the overcrowding has been a serious concern for months."

A week after I spoke with Cheshirkov, on March 31, 2020, the Greek government confirmed the first COVID-19 case in one of the country's refugee camps. In Ritsona, a camp located an hour's drive north of Athens, a woman had tested positive. Within a few days, the number of confirmed cases in the camp climbed to twenty.[14] Three weeks later, 150 residents of a refugee facility in Kranidi tested positive for COVID-19.[15] (How many refugees and migrants would eventually catch the coronavirus is impossible to know, but when vaccines finally became available, the government wasn't shy in revealing that residents of the crowded camps were not among their top priorities.[16])

All around Athens, on daily trips to the pharmacy or the grocery store that month, I would pass checkpoints manned by Greek police officers. The officers would check pedestrians' documents as they navigated the city, and more often than not, they would target migrants and refugees for stops. With the New Democracy government quietly working to implement migration policies that aligned with Europe's most virulently far-right movements, it was not hard to imagine a future in which migrants and other newcomers faced long-term limitations on movement. Meanwhile, the government doubled down on its plans to evict squats in Athens and beyond, a blow to both anti-fascists and refugee solidarity movements.[17] Squats were cleared. Refugees were rounded up. Anti-fascists and anarchists fought back as best as they could, but the lockdown kept many inside and years of pressure had no doubt left them in a difficult position.[18]

By early May 2020, the Greek government began reopening the country to everyone except those in the refugee camps.[19] The daily tally of new coronavirus cases had slumped, and the reopening was slated to take place in phases. In the camps, however, Greek authorities were tightening the restrictions on asylum seekers. In September, a fire broke out at the Moria camp on Lesbos, tearing through the olive groves where many refugees lived in tents outside the camp.[20] The camp, often described as "hell on earth," was almost entirely destroyed, and the government later announced that it would never be rebuilt.[21] Eventually, by the end of 2021, the government erected a handful of closed refugee centers—effectively jails—that would go in the place of the shuttered open camps.[22] The number of refugees and migrants reaching Greek shores would plummet.[23] Greek authorities would ramp up pushbacks and violence aimed at preventing refugees from reaching the country in the first place.[24] Meanwhile, seizing the opportunity to exploit pandemic-related restrictions, the government would use COVID-19 as a pretext to clamp down on protests—with tear gas and water cannons.[25]

The last time I heard from Noah, in spring 2020, he was still in a camp on Kos Island. He had little hope left. The coronavirus would likely continue ravaging the refugee community long after Greece's lockdown eventually ended, and I asked him how conditions were there. "It's very bad here," he said. "Very bad."

His response was short. What else was left to say?

ON OCTOBER 7, 2020, seven months into the global coronavirus pandemic, tens of thousands of people gathered outside the courthouse in central Athens. Inside, the judges would deliver a verdict on whether Golden Dawn had operated a criminal organization. More than five years after the trial first started, lead judge Maria Lepenioti said that seven of the party's eighteen former parliamentarians, including Michaloliakos, had overseen the gang, while the remaining former legislators were found guilty of participating in its criminal activities.[26]

When the announcement came over the loudspeakers outside, the gathered crowd broke out in applause and celebration. Four decades after Michaloliakos published the first issue of an obscure, pro-junta magazine called *Chrysi Avgi*, thirty-five years after he founded Golden Dawn as an association, twenty-seven years after the outfit gained official recognition as a political party, and seven years after supporters stabbed to death Shahzad Luqman and Pavlos Fyssas, Greece's most prominent, postwar neo-Nazi outfit was now declared a criminal organization. But as is the case with most political struggles in Greece, the history stretched back yet further—to the civil war that devasted the country between 1946 and 1949, to the German occupation of 1941 to 1944. Was it not a victory in an everlasting battle against the forces of fascism?

It wasn't long that day before clashes erupted between leftists and anarchists, on the one hand, and riot police, on the other. Molotov cocktails flew, stones rained down. Riot police attacked demonstrators with tear gas and water cannons. "Freedom for the people," some chanted.[27] "Death to fascism."

Videos and photographs from outside the courthouse showed masses of people rallying in celebration, riot police taking cover from anti-fascists, and crowds of people in gas masks and bala-clavas, others coughing and rubbing their eyes. But the most en-during image, shot outside the court's entrance, depicts Magda Fyssa whose son's murder at the hands of a party supporter had prompted Golden Dawn members' arrest. It shows her with her face mask dangling from one ear, her mouth wide, arms out-stretched, a look of disbelief across her face. "Pavlos did it!" she screamed. "My son."

Later, the court would sentence the party leadership to thir-teen years in prison.[28] Golden Dawn's lawyers would appeal the convictions. Splinter parties and other far-right outfits would step up to siphon the votes the neo-Nazis had once depended on. Anti-migrant violence would move into the state's official institutions, and attacks on leftists would mostly go on to be perpetrated by the police. But for that moment, outside the courthouse in central Athens, it was a celebration and a confrontation with the police who had once enabled the lynch mobs.

CHAPTER FOURTEEN

"MASKED MEN": ANTI-MIGRANT HATE AS POLICY

For Ali Muhammadi, the border was a buffer zone between Turkey and Greece. The way he told it, the border was sometimes a baton, a clenched fist, a stick a soldier swung in the woods, a warning shot fired into the sky. More than once, but not every time, the Greek border guards beat him and others after they traversed the Evros River, which traces most of the land boundary between the two countries. The border was also a routine, a journey he attempted so many times over several months in 2022 that he struggled to put a precise number on it. If he had to guess, his best bet would have been fifteen times, but he couldn't be sure. "Maybe twenty times," he told me when we met in Athens in November 2022.

Because of the coronavirus pandemic and travel restrictions, I had spent the previous two years back in Texas. Throughout that period, the Greek government had put in place strict border policies, and reports of illegal expulsions had mounted. When I returned to Greece in late 2022, Ali was the first person I met who had crossed from Turkey into Greece, and I was eager to speak with him about the impact that the new hardline migration policies had on people making the crossing.

Each time Ali crossed, Greek border guards confiscated his phone along with all the photos on it, he recalled, and sometimes took his food. Now and then, they forced the refugees to strip and walk back to the Turkish side. I asked him why he thought the authorities made them disrobe. "In our minds, they were belittling us and punishing us in order to [encourage us] to not come again," he said. "Of course, it doesn't work."

Before ever making it to the Greek-Turkish border, Ali's trek had been long and tiresome. He was studying art at a university in Kabul when the United States withdrew its troops in August 2021, ending a two-decade occupation and paving the path for the Taliban to overrun what remained of the country. He fled when the capital fell, first back to his village in the Ghazni province and later to Pakistan. From Pakistan, he crossed to Iran. From Iran, he recounted, he and others walked for days through the mountains until they reached Turkey. There, he passed around a year of his life living in a refugee camp in Edirne, less than five miles from the European Union's southeastern frontier.

Some of Ali's early crossings into Greece offered hope. On one occasion, he made it all the way to Thessaloniki, but Greek police caught him and shipped him more than 250 miles back to the Turkish border. On several trips, after the Greeks pushed him and others back into Turkey, Turkish authorities then made them turn around and walk right back to the Greek side.

After some failed crossings, he'd returned to the camp in Edirne and heard stories of those who drowned in the river.

During other crossings, people got separated from the group, lost their way, and disappeared. In one case, a friend of his, someone he'd grown up with in his village, went missing. More than a year had passed since his disappearance, and no one had heard from him, according to Ali.

Still, Ali kept trying. At twenty-two years old, he had a wide smile. He was tall and lean, with a soft face that made him look like a teenager. His family came from the Hazara community, an ethnic minority that mostly follows the Shia branch of Islam. In Afghanistan, sectarian armed groups have targeted Hazaras time and again.

Greece had turned its land border with Turkey into an especially dangerous and intensely surveilled crossing point for refugees and migrants.[1] Hundreds of border guard officers were deployed to the region, surveillance technology was everywhere, and much of the area is designated a closed military zone. In August 2022, officials announced plans to seal off the country with fencing that stretches the border's entire length. Around that time, Greek migration minister Notis Mitarachi boasted that "constant patrolling in the Aegean and the fence in Evros force the traffickers to find other routes."[2]

Fence or not, some got lucky—Ali counted himself among those. On his last trip, he explained, Greek police found him and five others who'd made it into the country. One of the officers recognized him from a previous crossing attempt. The other five were whisked back across the border, but he was allowed to apply for asylum. They sent Ali to a refugee camp, the first of several where he spent time. In November, he received asylum. Back in Turkey, more than forty-four thousand Afghans had been deported to their home country throughout the first eight months of 2022, a 150 percent spike when compared with the same period in 2021.[3] When I asked about the five others he'd crossed with on that last trip, he shook his head and said, "They're back in Afghanistan."

At the end of our first meeting in Athens that November, Ali lifted his phone and scrolled through photos he'd taken on the last trip across the border, the successful crossing: snapshots of friends beaten black and blue, a young man's shoulder welted from the blows. Even once he'd made it to Greece, Ali didn't plan to stay long. Even after receiving asylum, he hoped to push onward to Germany or elsewhere in Europe. Greece, he added, "is not a country where I can achieve my dreams."

THE BETTER PART of a decade had passed since the first sharp surge in refugees and migrants arriving in Greece. Throughout nearly eight years, hundreds of thousands of people had continued to board frail dinghies and cross the Aegean Sea. Few were ignorant of the risks—the news of fatal crashes, people drowning at sea, had become so common that it hardly merited a slot on the front page of many newspapers any longer. But people continued to leave. Closed borders hadn't stopped anyone—whether at sea or on land, they only made the journey deadlier.

Since then, new facilities had swept refugees and migrants from much of the public's view, while expanded border patrols at sea and on land cut down the number of new arrivals. In 2021, authorities said, 9,157 refugees and migrants reached the country, a 31 percent slump when compared with the previous year.[4] Meanwhile, rights groups and monitors said Greece had turned pushbacks—measures like the ones Ali Muhammadi described, in which refugees and migrants are kicked out without being allowed to apply for asylum—into routine policy. In effect, pushbacks are extrajudicial deportations, and depending on the circumstances during which they occur, they often take place in violation of international and European Union law.[5]

In July 2022, Forensic Architecture, the research group based at Goldsmiths, University of London, published a study examining "drift-backs," or pushbacks at sea, during which authorities force refugee boats out of their territorial waters. That study found that drift-backs had been used as a "systematic, calculated practice."[6] Forensic Architecture's research documented 1,018 drift-backs throughout a two-year period starting on February 28, 2020. Of that total, Frontex had been "directly involved" in at least 122 instances, the study said, and in twenty-six cases, the Hellenic Coast Guard threw people "directly into the sea." In December 2022, the Border Violence Monitoring Network (BVMN), a coalition of nonprofits and associations, released the *Black Book of Pushbacks*, an updated version of a dossier first published in 2020.[7] Commissioned by The Left political group in the European Parliament, the updated *Black Book* spans more than three thousand pages and paints a picture of what many refugees and migrants face on Europe's borders: beatings, threats, and summary expulsions.

Hope Barker, who researched pushbacks in Greece for the *Black Book*, said BVMN had started documenting reports of pushbacks in 2019. At that time, pushbacks "seemed random," she told me, but when the pandemic hit, pushbacks "began happening from deep in the mainland and into the interior." Cities like Thessaloniki had once been considered a safe distance from the border, but from early 2020 onward, that was no longer the case—authorities would detain someone hundreds of miles from the border and forcibly return them nonetheless. "It's totally normal now," she said. "It's happening on a daily basis, I would say."

While taking testimonies of pushbacks, Barker and other BVMN researchers learned of grim violence: the report mentions "masked men," "prolonged beatings," "forced un-dressings," "shaving of heads," and "the use of electric discharge weapons." Add to that the risk of drowning or dying from hypothermia. Refugees and migrants also faced legal risks: between 2015 and 2019, more than seven thousand people faced arrest for alleged human smuggling in Greece.[8] Oftentimes, refugees and migrants themselves ended up locked away and hit with smuggling-related charges. In May 2021, a Greek court sentenced a Somali asylum seeker to 142 years in prison for human smuggling, despite other passengers on the boat testifying that the man had saved their lives by taking the steering wheel when the boat began to capsize.[9] (The maximum time he could have actually spent behind bars, according to Greek law, capped at twenty years.[10] But in January 2023, an appeals court reduced his sentence to eight years and ordered his release.)

Humanitarians, researchers, and journalists weren't spared the government's crackdown, either. Hope Barker had lived in Thessaloniki for four and a half years, but her work led to "smear campaigns, arbitrary police checks, and fears of surveillance." Accused in Greek media of spreading false information, helping people cross the border, and acting as a supposed "Turkish spy," she left the country. With national elections scheduled to take place in Greece in 2023, Barker feared the clampdown on documenting pushbacks and other human rights research was "only going to intensify."

For its part, the New Democracy–led government continued to celebrate its migration clampdown as a success, but officials still denied allegations of human rights abuses. In late December 2022, the migration minister, Notis Mitarachi, appeared on the state broadcaster and dismissed reports of pushbacks.[11] Rather, he claimed, the accusations were part of an "organized attack" by nonprofits, some left-wing European politicians, and lobbyists—the same stripe of conspiracy theories far-right groups around

Europe and the United States had peddled for years. Describing migration and smuggling as a "big factory" worth hundreds of millions in profits, the minister said critics of Greece's border policies wanted "Europe to reopen its borders and let millions of people pass through." Under Greek prime minister Kyriakos Mitsotakis, he vowed, "this is not going to happen."

Alexandros Georgoulis, a lawyer on the island of Chios, had represented many asylum seekers and other displaced people in recent years. When I met him at his office in January 2023, he argued that neither the previous Syriza-led governing coalition nor the current one had handled the refugee issue in a way that respected human rights. "They're trying to prevent people from attempting these journeys in the first place," he told me. He said the New Democracy leadership wanted to send a message to people considering boarding a boat to Greece: "If you come, you either will be drowned, or you will be pushed back, or you will be arrested as a smuggler and spend decades in prison."

GOLDEN DAWN WAS out of parliament and banned, with many of its leading members in prison cells. In the lead-up to the May 2023 national elections, a court banned former Golden Dawn parliamentarian Ilias Kasidiaris's new party, National Party—Greeks (which he initially named Greeks for the Fatherland), from running in the elections. Kasidiaris was still sitting in prison, and he had stepped down from the party with the hopes of getting around the ban.[12] The move didn't work, and Kasidiaris insisted he would run anyway, claiming that "more than half a million Greeks" supported the far-right outfit.

Trumped-up numbers or not, Kasidiaris did enjoy something like support, and some of it came from the online video platform

YouTube. With more than one hundred thirty-five thousand followers, Kasidiaris pumped out videos from behind bars, racking
up millions of views. In March 2023 alone, his channel gained an
extra six thousand followers and more than a million new video
views. The message in his videos was standard far-right fare: he
claimed Greece was under invasion by refugees and migrants and
accused the New Democracy government of allowing the demographic annihilation of the country. According to the Global
Project Against Hate and Extremism, many of the videos enjoyed
ad revenue, despite YouTube's policies against extremist content.[13]
Citing estimates by Social Blade, the Global Project said that
"most, if not all," of the videos were monetized, and Kasidiaris
could be earning up to $76,800 per year off them. It is also no-
table that while the accounts of Golden Dawn have long been
suspended on other social media platforms, such as Facebook,
YouTube remained a holdout for more than a decade.

But the Greek far right hadn't limited its activities to social
media. One day in late April 2023, a group of masked individuals,
who claimed to belong to Golden Dawn, stormed a municipal
gallery in the Thessaloniki suburb of Kalamaria to protest an art
exhibition featuring work by North Macedonian painter Sergej
Andreevski.[14] A video on YouTube, posted on the Golden Dawn
Youth Front's channel, said the group had "banned" Andreevski's
exhibition for "casting doubt on the Greekness of our homeland."
In the video, one man addressed the artist, "You have no right to
be here." Of course, Andreevski not only had a right to be there—
the municipality had invited him. The local mayor dismissed the
far-right intruders as "irredentist hotheads" who wanted to exploit
nationalist sentiment ahead of the upcoming vote.

Meanwhile, the Supreme Court also barred Patriotic Force
for Change, another far-right party, from participating in elections. Known by its abbreviation Patrida, it had been founded

by Konstantinos Bogdanos, a former journalist and onetime New Democracy legislator. New Democracy had expelled Bogdanos in October 2021, after he claimed communists represented the biggest threat the country faced.[15] A month before his expulsion, he had reshared a Twitter post listing the names of migrant children at a kindergarten.[16]

The vigilante pogroms that had once taken place in the heart of the Greek capital had stopped, though smaller instances of racist violence, often aimed at refugees and migrants, still occurred. But for those people who had fled their countries in search of safety, the situation was more dangerous than ever. The chances that they would be mobbed in the streets may have reduced, but what difference did that make if the people who now controlled the coast guard and the border security forces harbored a far-right vision of mass deportations, deadlier borders, and a state-stamped policy of violence toward those who need protection most?

FOR YONOUS MUHAMMADI, the border was a gang of Greek nationalists armed with flagpoles and sticks, patrolling the park where he slept several nights when he first arrived in Athens twenty-one years earlier. When I visited Yonous at his office in late 2022, he recalled the most frightening years of fascist violence, years we had discussed time and again. People who had been attacked had at one time called him on a near daily basis. But since New Democracy's July 2019 election, he told me, "Everything has changed." In his view, the right-wing government had tried to make the lives of refugees and migrants "hell in order to send a message . . . to not come, and for those who are here to leave Greece."

Although the Greek Forum of Refugees received calls for help every day, Yonous worried about how much he could do. Yonous, like others, said he had recently learned that authorities had wire-tapped his phone for a brief period. "What can I say to [refugees] other than just go to the authorities and the police?" he said. "I know that the authorities will deport them, but on the other hand, I know that they are following my phone."

With his hands tied, Yonous worried about how dangerous crossing the border was becoming. More and more of those who turned up in his office knew little of how to access help, needed somewhere to stay, and asked for medicine for health ailments and injuries they sustained along the way. Some ended up in cramped apartments manned by traffickers, thirty to forty people to a place and running up a tab of five euros a night, he explained. More worrisome yet, the Greek Forum of Refugees was receiving a growing number of requests for help from people who couldn't locate loved ones who went missing. "So many people are lost on this journey," he said.

FOR SOME WHO tried to cross the land boundary between Turkey and Greece, the border was a bullet. Take, for instance, Muhammad Gulzar, the Pakistani migrant who had previously spent several years working in Greece and briefly returned to his home country to get married. On March 4, 2020, as he tried to make it back to Greece, he was shot dead on the Turkish side of the land border.

Two months later, a coalition of researchers and investigative journalists from Bellingcat, Lighthouse Reports, and Forensic Architecture released a report that pieced together witness testimony, videos, photos, and satellite imagery, among other clues.[17] Although the investigation couldn't say definitively who had fired the bullet that killed Gulzar, it concluded that "Greek security forces likely used live rounds . . . against refugees and migrants trying to break through the Turkish-Greek border fence" that day. Stelios Petsas, then a spokesperson for the Greek government, insisted that border forces hadn't fired any live rounds, claiming the reports were "fake news." Whether Greek security forces fired that bullet or not, there's no denying that the crossing often proves deadly. Between 2015 and 2021, the United Nations tallied at least 1,761 people who died or disappeared en route to Greece.[18] The real number, though, remained unknown: some small dinghies may sink without authorities ever knowing of the lost lives, and because the land border with Turkey remains a closed military zone, there's no way to determine how many people have perished there.

But even as crossings continue and bodies pile up on Europe's external borders, on the fringes of countries like Greece, the money kept flowing. In late November 2022, European Commission vice president Margaritis Schinas announced another 1.9 billion euros (more than $2 billion) in funds to support Greece on migration, describing the paycheck as "the first step" toward a new Europe-wide pact.[19] The Commission had already bankrolled Greece to the tune of between two and three billion euros. Under the umbrella of "migration management," those funds went toward uses including building border infrastructure, paying personnel, and equipment used to police the borderlands.[20] "Within this framework, Greece has received the strongest assistance from Europe," Schinas said at the time.

Eva Cossé, a Greece-based researcher at Human Rights Watch, said that Europe could have taken concrete action, including suspending Frontex collaboration with Greek authorities "as a bargaining chip" to pressure Athens "to end the abuses." In the meantime, she told me, "At the EU level, there is a lack of accountability, a lack of pushing Greece to end pushbacks."

*

ON A GRAY, windswept day in late November 2022, I found Javed Aslam, the president of the Pakistani Community of Greece association, in his office in central Athens. He sat behind his desk in the same office where I'd first met him more than five years earlier, anti-racist posters tacked to the jaundicing white walls around him. I told him I wanted to know how Pakistani migrant workers had fared in the two years since the court had convicted Golden Dawn as a criminal organization.

Attacks had decreased, Aslam explained, but they had not stopped altogether. He adjusted his glasses, pulled out a notebook, and flipped through pages of handwritten notes scrawled in Punjabi. He ticked off a list of violent incidents—beatings, stabbings, and even an airsoft gun shooting. "They want to tell us . . . 'We are [still] here and we can do whatever we like,'" he told me. "These [attackers] are not only Golden Dawn. They have new names with the same ideas."

One of those attacks took place in late October 2021, a couple weeks after the one-year anniversary of Golden Dawn's conviction. Around fifteen black-clad youth had mobbed three Pakistanis in the Kaminia area of Piraeus. A shaky phone video of the incident shows the attackers banging on the window of the home where the Pakistanis stayed and hurling stones. Two of the migrant workers managed to escape, but one was caught. "They also hit me with a beer bottle," he later told Ta Nea, a Greek news outlet.[21] "An ambulance came and took me . . . to the hospital, and I had seven stitches. I was covered in blood."

Six months later, in May 2022, a car of men pulled up aside a Pakistani man—identified only as Z.S. in Greek news reports—who had stepped out of his house to grab a coffee in Kokkinos Milos, an area in Athens.[22] "Pakistanis, Muslims, leave, we will fuck you," the men in the car threatened, according to the *Efimerida ton Syntakton* newspaper.

"Why are you talking to me like that?" Z.S. asked.

The men exited the car, surrounded Z.S., beat him, and stabbed him before fleeing. It marked the third attack in a week's time, the newspaper added. Only a few days earlier, a taxi driver had reportedly shot a Pakistani migrant with an airsoft gun, leaving him with three stitches on the side of his head.[23] Elsewhere, a battalion of far-rightists had beaten three Pakistani cell phone repairmen who had just finished prayers at a mosque near Omonoia Square in the city center.[24]

Aslam explained that he had celebrated Golden Dawn's conviction as a "day of victory," but he had no illusions that migrant workers' fight against fascism was over. Add to that the other problems Pakistani workers faced in a country now overseen by one of the most virulently anti-migration governments in Europe. Since New Democracy had come into power again in 2019, he told me, life had grown more difficult for migrant workers. More and more migrants had landed in the government's deportation machine, and detention centers like Amygdaleza had filled up with Pakistani workers. Every day he received phone calls about migrant workers who had been arrested, others from Greek farm owners who needed laborers. In the last six months, he said, he had witnessed "a very tough time" for workers, and in police stations and detention centers, dozens of people slept in small rooms cramped against one another. "Thousands of workers are inside detention centers."

FOR AYMAN, WHO asked me not to use his real name, the border was a police van, a dinghy across the river, coast guard ships in the Aegean. The border started at birth, surrounded him in a refugee camp in the Gaza Strip, and followed him to Europe. Born into a family displaced during Israel's 1948 establishment—known to Palestinians as the Nakba, or catastrophe—he came to Chios as a refugee twice over.

Before he ever boarded a dinghy to set off for a Greek island, he had already joined others trying to pass the Greek-Turkish land border three times in late 2019, he told me. Each time, Greek authorities pushed them back. During one attempt, they evaded border guards, passed the river, and walked for three days. Their food nearly ran out, and when their water supplies went dry, they drank from wells in gardens. They nearly reached Komotini, a Greek city located around a hundred miles from Edirne, but masked Greek authorities caught them. From there, Ayman and the other refugees were bused back to the border, held at an army building, and later forced to board an inflatable raft to cross back to Turkey at night. "It was terrible," he said. "I will never forget it."

Later, they moved to Izmir and tried their luck by sea. Along with others, Ayman took a boat bound for a Greek island. Either Frontex or the Greek coast guard pushed them back at least five times, he remembered. But eventually, their boat landed on Chios in late November 2019, where he wound up in the island's decrepit Vial refugee camp. More than three years later, he still felt a flash of fear when he thought of the pushbacks. The experience left many with psychological scars, he said. "Sometimes, we cannot explain what happened to us," he added. "It's too difficult."

One morning only a few days into 2023, not long after I met Ayman, the Port of Chios was busy. An Italian coast guard ship trawled into the harbor, part of the Frontex, the EU's external border agency, deployment to the Eastern Aegean Sea. The ship anchored across the water from a Greek coast guard boat. Pale shafts of sunlight sliced through the clouds, and the waves winked.

Along the promenade tracing the shoreline, restaurants and cafés began filling with customers.

The last time I'd visited Chios, in February 2020, refugees and migrants had often gathered in the town square, smoking cigarettes and chatting, passing time away from the camp. But three years into Greece's heightened clampdown on migration, many of those who made it to the island had been largely pushed out of sight, and the number of arrivals had plummeted.

That afternoon, I met Stamatis Karmantzis, the island's mayor, at his office. The last time I had seen him, in early 2020, he had been at the forefront of a push to prevent the government from building permanent camps on Chios and other islands. Sitting behind his desk now, he said the situation had improved but that Chios still needed a closed refugee facility like the ones elsewhere. The Greek government had proposed a site in Tholos, about a twenty-minute drive from the island's eponymous capital, but local resistance had stalled its construction. Karmantzis said the camp would be a better fit in a more remote, less populated area further north.

The mayor was glad that numbers had dropped but knew that people would not stop trying to make the journey. "New Democracy has done far better on the migration issue than any other government—we have to say it as it is," he told me. Later, he added of Turkey, "Our neighbor isn't a good neighbor, and they will continue using [migration] to put pressure on us." Because the islands sit on Europe's southeastern flank, he added, the borders needed to be further fortified. Locals carried a heavy burden as the first stop for many who reached Europe. "We have to guard Thermopylae," he said, alluding to the Battle of Thermopylae in 480 BC, a key battle during the Second Persian Invasion of Greece. His comparison echoed the increasingly nativist rhetoric many conservative Greek politicians had ramped up in recent years.

*

THE NEXT AFTERNOON, Vasilis Vigas manned the wheel of his single-cab pickup in Chalkio, a village located some four miles from the town of Chios. As president of the village since 2019, he offered to drive us to Vial, to show us around the fields outside the camp. I sat in the truck's bed, olive trees speeding past on either side. A rush of wind washed through the village, and the mountaintops knuckled along the horizon.

I thought back to nearly three years earlier, when makeshift shanties and scrapped-together tents spanned out across the fields around Vial. But when Vasilis pulled up to the camp, the fields were now empty, shin-high grass had retaken tracts of land once worn bald by foot traffic, and many of the olive trees had started to grow back, albeit gradually. A group of children played, pushing each other up and down the sidewalk on a stroller, and a man crouched in the field, speaking into his cell phone.

Since the COVID-19 lockdown first hit in March 2020, the Greek government had gradually whittled down the number of refugees and migrants living in Vial from north of six thousand to only a few hundred. Many had left the island, receiving asylum or transferring to other migrant facilities, and the number of arrivals who made it to camps like Vial was likely lower due to the boom in pushbacks. Now, they all lived in container homes inside the camp, surrounded by fences crowned with barbwire. Vasilis, who was thirty-eight, walked Vial's perimeter, his hands stuffed in his pockets. He had grown up in Chalkio and made a living farming olives, fruits, and herbs. Years back, he had helped some refugees slap together homes from scrap wood and sheets of metal.

But as weeks turned into months, months into years, he and many of his fellow villagers grew frustrated with the camp's presence in Chalkio. Tents had cropped up on a patch of land he owned, and like many farmers in the village, he still wasn't ready to start repairing his fields. He feared another spike in arrivals might see tents dot the fields once more. "We don't farm anymore here because we're afraid," he said, adding of migration: "There are political games being played on the backs of people."

Pushbacks and ramped-up patrols on land and sea had won the New Democracy government favor with many as sympathy for refugees and migrants deteriorated. But for Ayman, who tried and failed and finally reached Greece, the crackdown targeted those who needed help the most. Three years since his own crossing, he still heard stories from those who came after him. Some spoke of attempting to reach Greece dozens of times. Some mourned those who went missing. Many recounted beatings and routine humiliation. "In the end, [Greek politicians] consider this protecting their country," Ayman said. "But this isn't about protecting their country."

AFTER CALLS FOR new elections, on May 21, 2023, Greeks finally headed to the ballot box. It was for the first time since July 2019, when New Democracy had returned to power. Anger had been mounting for months against the government, in part thanks to a deadly train crash in late February 2023 that killed fifty-seven people. But New Democracy played the immigration card expertly. New Democracy and prime minister Mitsotakis had campaigned on a "tough but fair" migration policy. But only two days before the vote, the *New York Times* published a video of the Greek coast guard carrying out a pushback in the Mediterranean Sea. Filmed by an Austrian aid worker named Fayad Mulla, the video showed masked men moving a group of a dozen migrants, including children, from a van into a speedboat. The speedboat then carried the migrants away to a coast guard boat, which then set them adrift on an inflatable raft in Turkish waters. Naima Hassan Aden, a twenty-seven-year-old Somali mother who had reached Greece with her six-month-old baby, told the *Times*, "We didn't expect to survive on that day. When they were putting us on the inflatable raft, they did so without any mercy."[25]

Still, New Democracy swept the elections. Although New Democracy didn't receive a majority in the vote, some four in ten Greek voters cast their lot with the right-wing party, giving it a double-digit lead over Syriza. "The political earthquake that occurred today calls on all of us to accelerate the process for a final governmental solution," Mitsotakis said in a victory speech he delivered at the party's headquarters the night of the vote.[26] "The data from the ballot box is catalytic—it proves that New Democracy has the approval to govern independently and strongly, and they demanded it emphatically, in an absolute way."

Syriza lost fifteen parliamentary seats. MeRA25, the left-wing party led by Yanis Varoufakis, had failed to meet the 3 percent threshold and lost all its seats in the parliament. Mitsotakis had made history. Since the fall of the junta, no incumbent party had ever managed to gain voters in a general election. But New Democracy was now on a path toward an absolute majority in the second round. And several far-right parties had fared comparably well when compared with past results. Greek Solution, a pro-Russia party headed by parliamentarian Kyriakos Velopoulos, a longtime ultra-nationalist who had once sold copies of what he claimed were the original manuscripts of Jesus Christ, pulled in 4.5 percent of the vote, gaining an additional six seats in the parliament. The Democratic Patriotic Movement–Victory, a far-right party steered by founder and religion teacher Dimitris Natsios after the North Macedonia name agreement in 2019, won 2.93

percent of the vote, placing it within reach of entering parliament after a second round of voting.

But Mitsotakis still had to grapple with international criticism. After the *New York Times* report on pushbacks, he spoke to CNN's Christiane Amanpour.[27] After the prime minister boasted of his government's supposed "success story" in post-crisis Greece, Amanpour grilled Mitsotakis on the video. She asked him whether his government "illegally allowed setting adrift some migrants in the Aegean."

Mitsotakis claimed that he had already ordered an investigation into the incident, though he made no such claim of a probe into the thousands upon thousands of other allegations that Greek authorities had carried out pushbacks. He blamed smugglers for "putting people at risk at sea," and said Greece had respected European law as part of its effort to protect the EU's external borders. "I know that Greece has been getting its fair share of criticism when it comes to pushbacks, but very few people are actually addressing the issue of push-forwards. By push-forwards, I mean the activities undertaken by Turkey, the Turkish coast guard, to aggressively push people, desperate people, basically on inflatable boats that should never be seaworthy, to sea and pushing them into our territorial waters." Mitsotakis insisted his government had saved many people at sea.

THREE WEEKS AFTER the Greek prime minister made those claims, an Italy-bound boat from Libya, carrying hundreds of people, sank off the country's southern shores. Less than two weeks from the second round of voting, at least seventy-nine bodies had been retrieved after that boat capsized, but hundreds remained missing. The true death toll may never be known, but the boat was reportedly carrying up to seven hundred fifty people.[28]

Greek president Katerina Sakellaropoulou, who had recently been photographed in front of the border fence on the Greek-Turkish land border, rushed to southern Greece to meet survivors. Yanis Varoufakis blasted the president for her hypocrisy. "In Evros, Mrs. Sakellaropoulou goes—she's not a little shy—to be photographed in front of the fence, as if it's a good thing," he said. "And at the same time, they themselves, who build the fences and are photographed in front of them, preach national mourning, when it happens, the obvious thing that will happen when you build fences." Varoufakis claimed that almost none of the Greek political parties' leadership—including Tsipras, the former Syriza prime minister—had the right to mourn the deaths in the Mediterranean. "They have every right to believe in this solution, the fence solution," he added. "They don't have the right, hypocritically, to pretend at this moment, with national mourning."

The Greek government had initially claimed the passengers aboard the rickety fishing trawler refused assistance when offered. But a coast guard vessel, survivors would later insist, had tried to tow the boat before the moment it finally sank. The Greek government even alleged the passengers had blocked the coast guard from boarding the ship to gauge the potential danger it faced.[29] Activists rejected the coast guard's claims, insisting that the passengers had begged for help. The BBC, however, published an investigation that examined the tracking data of the coast guard vessel, and the findings were grim. The migrant boat hadn't moved for some seven hours, a fact that contradicted the Greek government's timeline and claim that the passengers weren't in danger until just a few moments before it went under. The UN called for an investigation into Greece's handling of the incident.

Even if the passengers had declined help, was Greece's record of pushbacks not a good enough reason to fear such offers?

The New Democracy government was quick to redirect blame elsewhere, and some party members attacked the passengers themselves. Spilios Kriketos, a New Democracy lawmaker up for reelection, lashed out at refugees and migrants in a racist tirade.[30] Speaking to the Kontra YouTube channel, Kriketos had insisted that Greece could not "tolerate" any more refugees and migrants.[31] If those who perished on the boat had survived, he claimed, they "wouldn't work," "would steal," and would live in cramped studio apartments packed with fifteen or more people. New Democracy expelled Kriketos, insisting that such opinions had "no place" in the party, a questionable claim.

ON JUNE 21, 2023, the day after World Refugee Day, I drove from Athens to Malakasa, a village in East Attica. It's home to not much more than a thousand residents. In 2016, the Syriza-led government erected a refugee camp on the site of a former military facility.[32] It was meant to be a temporary accommodation, but like so many of Greece's camps, it gradually evolved into another fenced-in semi-prison for asylum seekers.

Around noon, I found Javed Aslam near the camp's entrance, surrounded by reporters. Rows of mobile clinics sat in the parking lot, and reporters' cars lined the road in front of the camp. The sun pounded down, and the temperature topped ninety degrees. Police officers sat around drinking coffee and smoking cigarettes. The reporters stuck out their microphones, and Aslam said that survivors had told him the Greek coast guard had lashed a rope to the migrant boat and that caused it to capsize. Of the more than three hundred Pakistanis on the boat, there were only a dozen known survivors. "They say they're sorry they cannot talk today," he added, "because when they're talking about the boat and the dying [they witnessed], they feel [they] are inside the boat and this accident is happening again."

A week had gone by since the shipwreck, and each day that passed, there was less hope of finding survivors. Bodies were still turning up at sea. The Greek coast guard had found the water-logged cadavers of three men only a day earlier, around forty-seven nautical miles south of Pylos. Greek officials described the incident as "unexpected and encouraging."[33] No doubt, survivors and the relatives of those lost at sea would find some closure in knowing that their loved ones were located, but given the questions that had arisen after the shipwreck, it was hard to stomach.

Aslam was accompanied by Malek Shiraz, a thirty-seven-year-old Pakistani who lived and worked in Italy. Shiraz's brothers, forty-year-old Mohammed Tahir and forty-two-year-old Qasar Mahmood, had been on the boat. The last time he spoke with his brothers, Malik Shiraz had urged them not to go to Libya, a country known for its especially brutal conditions for refugees and migrants, including slave auctions, and told them the journey across the Mediterranean wasn't worth the risk. The summer heat sketched exhaustion across his face. His family told him they heard the boat went under, and he came to Greece to search for his brothers. He didn't have much time—his boss in Italy wanted him back to work after three days. "Until now we don't have any information. There are so many difficulties, and many things until now that I cannot understand," he said, adding: "I told my brothers this is too risky, and especially don't go to Libya, but they didn't [listen to] me. Then, they [went] to Libya without my knowing."

Malek Shiraz said one of his missing brothers had seven children, the other had two. Back in his hometown of Gujrat, his mother had already submitted DNA to help determine if it matched with any of the bodies that turned up. While his brothers were in Libya, he told me, he couldn't get a hold of them. Now, his family feared the worst. "Two people [in the camp] said my brothers were together on the ship," he said.

Aslam wore a suit and dress shirt despite the heat. Before he had gone to the camp, some survivors had told Aslam that "maybe [the Greek coast guard] was going to push us back," he explained. "This is what they were directly saying: 'We were not going to die. When [they attached] the rope, then our boat was [under] the sea.' These are the words of the witnesses who are in there."

One reporter noted that survivors had been willing to speak up until now. She asked whether the Greek authorities had pressured survivors to not speak with press. "Maybe," Aslam said, shaking his head. "Maybe. I don't know."

I set off back to Athens, my colleague and photographer Nick Paleologos riding with me. We took a detour through Oropos, a small beachside community located around thirty-five miles from the Athens city center. We pulled over at the shore for half an hour. Along the pebble-studded coastline, teens hit tennis balls back and forth with rackets. Others lay sprawled out on beach towels, and some waded out in the water. Across the water sat Evia, Greece's second-largest island. A ferry heading back toward Oropos nodded along in the blue waters, the sun burning high above.

THE NEXT DAY, Javed Aslam sat in his office fielding phone calls. In between staccato-burst conversations on the phone, he answered a few questions I had. Eight days had passed since the shipwreck, and he had worked nonstop the whole time, trying

to help families locate their relatives, trying to speak to the few
survivors, and dealing with his normal responsibilities at the
Pakistani Community of Greece. He struck me as gaunt and exhausted, thumbing through the notebook where he kept personal
details the families had sent him, phone numbers of survivors,
contact information for the relatives of those who were believed
to have perished.

I wanted to know more about what had happened the day
before at Malakasa camp, why the survivors had declined to speak
with anyone. Before he had gone there, he said, the Pakistani
survivors had wanted to speak to him. But when he showed up,
the handful of survivors who greeted him were nervous. It didn't
sit well with him. "I feel very strange," he told me. "They were so
afraid . . . There was something [wrong]. I cannot understand it
until now." As we spoke, his phone rang now and then: another
reporter, then a moment later, a Pakistani woman whose husband
had been arrested in Greece.

The Pakistani government had announced a probe into the
shipwreck. Official estimates put at least 209 Pakistanis on the
boat, but Aslam said he had already heard from more than 180
families who had sent him information about their loved ones
who, they believed, were on the boat. He and other advocates
estimated that at least 300 Pakistanis had been aboard.

Aslam had been in Greece for more than a quarter century. He
had organized to help migrants tossed into the deportation machine. He had witnessed the avalanche of attacks against migrant
workers, many of them Pakistanis, during the height of Golden
Dawn's violence in the streets. He had fought for justice after two
Golden Dawn supporters stabbed and killed Shahzad Luqman.
The shipwreck and the Greek coast guard's potential involvement in causing the deaths was different, though. Throughout his
twenty-seven years, the Pylos shipwreck "was the biggest tragedy"

to hit the Pakistani community in Greece. "I think it's a very big problem for Greece if this happened during [a] pushback."

After Luqman's murder, people had rallied behind migrants, and the authorities finally—but belatedly—cracked down on Golden Dawn. But it took the better part of the decade that followed Luqman's death for Golden Dawn's conviction to become a reality. The way Aslam saw it, the anti-fascist movement, the international media attention, and the efforts of other watchdogs and activists had helped keep the pressure on the government to push forward with prosecution. Save for comparably smaller demonstrations, no such reaction had taken place in the wake of the shipwreck. "I think that up until now," Aslam added, "it hasn't been enough pressure."

An Italian television crew came into his office and started to set up their equipment. Aslam had more interviews, more work to keep public attention on the lives lost in the Mediterranean. Before I left, he said, "I'm very tired, but it doesn't matter. This is real life . . . We have to do these things."

ON JUNE 25, 2023, Greeks headed back to the ballot box to cast their votes in the second round of elections. On that day I drove back to Malakasa. The streets in town were nearly empty. After a while, a colleague and I met two young Syrian men, both nineteen, at a café a short walk from the refugee camp. They had both survived the shipwreck and agreed to recount what happened, but neither wanted to use their real names. They had grown up together, and both had made the long journey from Daraa, their hometown in southern Syria, to Lebanon, then Egypt, and finally Libya. They had only passed through Lebanon and Egypt, but they spent two months in Libya before they boarded the boat. They told me that, among the hundreds of men aboard the ship, there were also five families with a handful of women and children. The conditions on the boat "were very bad . . . without much water or food at all." Hamdi, who asked me not to use his real name, echoed previous claims that the Hellenic Coast Guard had lashed a tow rope to the fishing trawler and caused it to tip, wobble, and eventually capsize. He said the Greek government's claim that the passengers had refused help was a lie. "We didn't refuse anything," he said.

Neither Hamdi nor his friend had ever wanted to stay in Italy, let alone Greece, and now they still wanted to continue onward to Germany. Hamdi had accepted that his relatives hadn't survived, but he was upset that Greek authorities had not allowed the survivors to see the recovered bodies to determine for sure.

Back in Syria, life had grown unbearable, he told me. A deadly earthquake in February that killed tens of thousands across southeastern Turkey and parts of Syria had only worsened an economy already decimated by more than a decade of civil war. For Hamdi, he had finished his studies and didn't want to carry out his mandatory military service.

Now, the teenagers said they could leave Greece relatively easily. They were likely to receive asylum, and even if they didn't, crossing the Balkan Route through North Macedonia, Serbia, and then back into the Schengen Area via the Hungarian border. But neither was ready to leave until they knew what happened to the bodies of their cousins and friends—if for nothing else, for their families back in Syria. "We saw death with our own eyes," he said. If the Greek coast guard hadn't tried to tow the boat, he said, "not a single person would have died."

Luckily, Hamdi knew how to swim. He guessed he spent three hours swimming up to the surface of the sea for breath. His friend, who didn't know how to swim, latched onto debris to keep afloat. "It was the first time in my life I was in the sea," his friend added. Hamdi leaned forward and said, "Thank God for returning us to life. The only thing we want from the Greek state and the European Union is to let us continue to Germany . . . There is no humanity here. There are no rights. The government is very hard on refugees."

Later that night, Greece's election results crept in. Voter turnout was the lowest since the fall of the military junta in 1974.[34] New Democracy had gained the votes of more than four out of ten Greeks, while the left-wing Syriza clinched even fewer votes than the first round. Meanwhile, the trio of ultra-right-wing parties—Niki, Greek Solution, and the Kasidiaris-backed Spartan Party—pulled in more than 12 percent, collectively.[35] Early numbers suggested that nearly one in ten voters between seventeen and thirty-four years old voted for the Spartans. Once the results became available, Spartans leader Vasilis Stigkas expressed his gratitude to Kasidiaris for endorsing his party, while Velopoulos said his Greek Solution had bested "the dirty war of the system." Less than two weeks had passed since the shipwreck that likely killed hundreds, and more than half of Greek voters cast their ballots for anti-migrant parties.

IN LATE AUGUST 2023, wildfires spread across northeastern Greece, in the Evros region that is home to the Greek-Turkish land border. Hospitals and nursing homes were evacuated, and residents had to flee their homes as the blazes continued to rip across the region. But it wasn't just locals who suffered. Attempted crossings on the land border, already a dangerous and deadly route for many who made the trek, were already on the rise again. Throughout the first three weeks of August, Greek authorities claimed that police and border guards had blocked an average of nine hundred migrant entries per day, and the police bragged of arresting "hundreds of traffickers."[36] This policy of deterrence—like in the US and elsewhere—effectively pushed refugees and migrants into yet more rugged and challenging routes across the frontier. When the latest wave of wildfires hit, it was no surprise that refugees and migrants were among the first ones to die.

On August 22, the fourth day of fires in Evros, firefighters near the village of Avantas found the charred remains of eighteen people believed to be refugees or migrants, including two children. Moving along the foothills of the Rhodope Mountain range, the group ended up trapped and encircled by the flames, authorities told local newspapers. Pavlos Pavlidis, the coroner who later examined the bodies in Alexandroupoli, told *Kathimerini* that the migrants' burned cadavers were found in two or three separate groups spread across an area of five hundred meters because they had "apparently [been] trying to flee."[37] Pavlidis added, "Some of them were in a barn when they burned to death."

But refugees and migrants weren't only among the first to perish in the flames—they were also among the first to be blamed for the fires. A video posted to social media the same day the news of the eighteen deaths broke appeared to show a group of vigilantes detaining a group of more than a dozen migrants in the back of a closed-in cargo trailer.[38] In the video, the man behind the phone boasts of capturing up to twenty-five people he accused of attempting to "burn us." He calls on others to follow his group's lead and hunt down refugees and migrants. "Get organized," he says into the phone. "Let's all go out and catch them." He opens the door to the trailer and the camera shows the frightened face of one of those detained.

Later, the police reportedly arrested three suspects, among them two Greek men and an Albanian national. The Supreme

Court prosecutor ordered an investigation into potential arson as well as into potential crimes like the apparent abduction of refugees and migrants.[39] The vigilantes, now facing charges, were placed under house arrest. But a prosecutor in the northeastern city of Alexandroupoli also accused the migrants themselves of crimes, including illegal entry and arson-related allegations. Greek media soon reported that the testimony that served as a basis for the migrants' arrests was provided by the very people who allegedly hunted them down and detained them.[40]

In a statement about the vigilante detentions, the Hellenic Police insisted that Greece was a "nation governed by the rule of law, built upon a solid democratic foundation, and guided by a humanitarian tradition," adding: "Any manifestation of vigilante justice remains unequivocally unacceptable."[41] But a separate statement put out by the new migration minister, Dimitris Karidis, who had taken over that ministry after the June 2023 elections, cast doubt on Greece's supposed commitment to a "humanitarian tradition." Although Karidis expressed "deep sadness" over the eighteen potential asylum seekers burned alive in Evros, he used the opportunity to push the government's anti-migrant propaganda line. "Despite the persistent efforts of the Greek authorities to protect the borders and human life, this tragedy stands as yet another reminder of the dangers of irregular migration," the statement read. "Against the backdrop of these tragic events, we highlight and denounce, once again, the murderous activities of criminal smugglers and those who facilitate them. Human trafficking endangers the lives of migrants, both on land and at sea, every day." In other words, their deaths were the faults of their own actions.

Of course, the eighteen people might still be alive had it not been for Greece's regime of border violence and pushbacks, which forced refugees and migrants into more dangerous terrains along the northeastern land border and into longer and riskier journeys at sea. As the anti-fascist group KEERFA said in a statement at the time, the New Democracy government had "opened the door to racist patrols and abductions of migrants in Evros," calling for "an end to the racist policies of closed borders and fences against persecuted refugees that Mitsotakis's ministers are defending on the same day they commit the horrific crime of incinerating dozens of migrants in Dadia."[42]

Incitement once again hit a fever pitch. Not confined to right-wing social media users, the anti-migrant hate speech and conspiracy theories found a home among some members of the Greek parliament. The Greek Solution's Velopoulos openly supported the alleged vigilantes, while fellow party member and lawmaker Paris Papadakis took to Facebook to up the ante. Papadakis claimed, with zero evidence, that refugees and migrants had been "obstructing" fire-fighting planes. He urged civilians to "take measures" against the supposedly nefarious foreigners, adding: "We are at war."[43]

Rights groups and aid organizations took notice, too. In a statement, the UN-backed Racist Violence Recording Network, an umbrella network of human rights monitors, warned that the incitement would "normalize, encourage, and ultimately escalate racist reactions" and could spur yet more violence in the streets.

The watchdog wasn't wrong. A week later, another video of self-styled militiamen rounding up migrants in the Evros region emerged online. In this clip, a man describes the four migrants he and another person have ostensibly detained as "investors," an apparently sarcastic jab at people fleeing war and poverty.[44] The man behind the camera says he called the police, but no one came. "Four more, four good investors," he says. "Do you see? It's midday, where are the authorities?"

Meanwhile, the border continued killing people. The same

day the second vigilante video spread online, five people died when two refugee boats sank on their way from the Turkish coast to Greek islands—four of the dead were children.[45]

True to his party's public-facing form, prime minister Kyriakos Mitsotakis condemned the vigilante violence in Evros but parroted some of the same conspiracy theories that helped fuel attacks. Without evidence, he addressed the parliament and hinted that refugees and migrants might be behind the wildfires in the country's northeast. "It is almost certain that the causes were manmade," he said.[46] "And it is also almost certain that this fire started on routes that are often used by illegal migrants who have entered our country. We don't know if it was negligence or deliberate."

The formula was in action once again: the Greek government didn't want a civilian to go out and attack foreigners, but it did need the country to know that refugees and migrants were the cause of its problems, whether wildfires or economic crises.

A little before noon on October 20, 2024, I drove over to the Sepolia neighborhood of Athens, where the Pakistani Community of Greece, KEERFA, and other anti-racist and anti-fascist groups had called for a march. A recent rash of racist attacks had prompted a few hundred people to turn out in the main square for the rally.

Near the front of the gathering I found Mohammed Aslam, who had spent the last eighteen years in Greece. He was helping others hold up a banner. At forty-three years old, he told me, he'd recently gone through a rough patch. His mother in Pakistan had died a little more than a month earlier, and although he had legal residency documents and paid his taxes in Greece, the government had recently rejected his application to bring his wife and children to the country. Worse still, after he had attended a protest for a Pakistani man who had died under murky conditions in an Athens police station, Aslam found himself on the receiving end of a racist attack for the first time in his nearly two decades in the country.

The previous Saturday, he'd walked away from the demonstration to search for an ATM. As he crossed the street, a car with two people nearly hit him at a stop sign. Aslam looked at the driver and said, "Sorry, but you have a stop sign."

"What are you, a smartass?" the driver shouted back. "Get out of here, you dirty Pakistani."

Aslam walked off, but only a few minutes later, he realized he'd lost his necklace. When he walked back to the area to look for it, three men swarmed him. They knocked off the motorcycle helmet he'd put on, and brass knuckles slammed into his face and head. As he told me the story, Aslam pointed to gashes on his chin, under his right eye, and on his skull. A doctor had to put ten stitches in his face and on his head to seal the wounds, he explained. Since the attack, Aslam had stayed inside his house whenever he wasn't working at one of his two jobs. "I've been very scared," he admitted. "I haven't gone out of the house at all. They had to call me many times to convince me to come here [to the protest]."

More than a year had passed since New Democracy again swept elections, since a trio of smaller far-right parties gained a notable presence in the parliament, and since ultra-nationalists and conspiracy theorists blamed the devasting and deadly wildfires in the country's north on refugees and migrants. Throughout that period, far-right violence had continued in ebbs and flows, the government continued to rail against people making the dangerous journey to Europe, and the coast guard and border authorities had continued to push back refugees and migrants at sea and on land.

Throughout that period, Nikolaos Michaloliakos, the former chief of Golden Dawn, had been granted early release from prison for good behavior. Amid public uproar, a council of judges rescinded his early release, and Michaloliakos was rearrested. Still behind bars, Ilias Kasidiaris, the former Golden Dawn legislator and spokesperson, had managed to win a seat on the Athens City Council, though he resigned not long after. Across the continent, far-right parties had made worrisome advances in the European Parliament, and ultra-nationalists had pulled off historic performances in elections from Portugal to Germany, from Austria to the Netherlands.

By the time I finished this book, I had spent the better part of a decade reporting on migration in countries around the world, the far right, and the fight against it. I had come to understand a lesson that people on the receiving end of incitement and violence knew intrinsically. Fascism cannot satiate itself targeting one group. Nationalists will never be satisfied by merely sealing off borders, as if that were even possible. There will always be a new enemy, a new demographic that must be confronted, fought, eradicated. When nationalists, xenophobes, and fascists speak of the harm they intend to inflict on refugees and migrants, they are also warning of their plans for anyone who doesn't fall in line with their vision of society. As vigilante violence and fascist conspiracy theories continued to find currency in Greece, now and then spiraling out of control, I was certain—knowledge that sank in like an anchor—that someone, somewhere, was already sharpening the knife.

That day in October 2024, sunlight splashed across the square. A few people took turns on the megaphone speaking out against the recent attacks. The demonstrators assembled, and columns of people prepared to set off. The march began. A banner up front read, In our neighborhoods, there is no room for fascists and racists. Locals crept out onto their balconies, watched the demonstrators inch through the streets. A cluster of riot police observed from a distance. The protesters turned down a side street and started to chant. "We work together, we live together," they sang in unison. "Locals and migrants, smash the fascists."

ACKNOWLEDGMENTS

My deepest gratitude goes to all my friends and colleagues who read portions of this book over the years—there are too many to name here. I thank my editor, Carl Bromley, and the entire team at Melville House for taking on this book. I'm grateful to my former writing teachers for reading portions of this book: Kevin Clouther, Patricia Lear, Jim Peterson, Kate Gale, and Marya Hornbacher. I extend so much gratitude to Jenny for the camaraderie, warmth, and company that she offered at the tail end of this manuscript. I could never have completed much of the reporting and research in this book without the help and friendship of Nick Paleologos, one of the finest photographers I have ever worked with. Thanks to Bill for always bringing beers and for all the friendship. Thanks to V for friendship and support. I'm also indebted to my mother, step-father, brother, and step-grandmother for their love and support. I'm deeply thankful for all the people who spoke with me over the years whose voices helped inform *You Can Kill Each Other After I Leave*. Some preferred not to be named, but here's to them. A book like this wouldn't be possible without the tireless work and input of so many Greek reporters and newspapers, refugees, migrants, researchers, activists, squatters, and advocates, among others.

CHAPTER ONE

1 Strickland, Patrick, "Refugee boats to Greece persist despite winter's chill," Al Jazeera English, December 2, 2015, www.aljazeera.com.

2 The United Nations High Commissioner for Refugees, "Over one million sea arrivals reach Europe in 2015," December 30, 2015, www.unhcr.org.

3 Constantini, Anthony J., "Understanding Europe's shift to the right," Politico EU, September 30, 2022, www.politico.eu.

4 Nakou, Georgia, "What brought down Golden Dawn?" MacroPolis, August 27, 2019, www.macropolis.gr.

5 Kazem-Stojanovic, Halima, "How Lesbos residents drove the far-right Golden Dawn party off the island," PRI, September 12, 2017, theworld.org.

6 Strickland, Patrick, "Life-jacket mountain a metaphor for Greece's refugees," Al Jazeera English, December 29, 2015, www.aljazeera.com.

7 Strickland, Patrick, "Greek anarchists organise for refugees as 'state fails,'" Al Jazeera English, January 19, 2016, www.aljazeera.com.

8 Barigazzi, Jacopo, and Matthew Karnitschnig, "EU and Turkey reach refugee deal," Politico EU, March 18, 2016, www.politico.eu.

9 Nallu, Preethi, "Greece outlines radical immigration reforms," Al Jazeera English, March 5, 2015, www.aljazeera.com.

10 Dinas, Elias et al., "Waking Up the Golden Dawn: Does Exposure to the Refugee Crisis Increase Support for Extreme-Right Parties?" *Political Analysis*, January 31, 2019, www.cambridge.org.

11 Squat!Net, "Athens: Announcement of Squat Notara 26 about the attack of August 24th," August 27, 2016, en.squat.net.

12 Strickland, Patrick, "Greek punk bands raise money for refugee squats," Al Jazeera English, February 7, 2017, www.aljazeera.com.

13 Strickland, Patrick, "Refugees in Greece's Chios fear violence from far right," Al Jazeera English, July 5, 2016, www.aljazeera.com.

14 Strickland, Patrick, "Anger on Greek island as refugee registration stalls," Al Jazeera English, June 18, 2016, www.aljazeera.com.

15 Strickland, Patrick, "Volunteers leave Greek island after attacks on refugees," Al Jazeera English, July 10, 2016, www.aljazeera.com.

16 IOM and UNICEF, "IOM and UNICEF Data Brief: Migration of Children to Europe," November 30, 2015, www.iom.int/sites/g/files/tmzbdl486/files/press_release/file/IOM-UNICEF-Data-Brief-Refugee-and-Migrant-Crisis-in-Europe-30.11.15.pdf.

17 Smith, Helena, "Shocking images of drowned Syrian boy show tragic plight of refugees," *The Guardian*, September 2, 2015, www.theguardian.com.

CHAPTER TWO

1 Kornetis, Kostis, *Children of the Dictatorship* (New York: Berghahn Books, 2013), 256.

2 Ioannidis, Sakis, "Documenting history as it happened for 30-plus years," eKathimerini, May 8, 2019, www.ekathimerini.com.

3 Aristotle Kallis, "Neither fascist nor authoritarian: The 4th of August regime in Greece (1936–1941) and the dynamics of fascistisation in 1930s Europe," *East Central Europe* 37, no. 2–3 (2010): 303–330, www.metaxasproject.com.

4 Weaver, Mary Anne, "Greece Probes Rightist Underground's Role in Violence," *The Washington Post*, April 9, 1977, www.washingtonpost.com.

5 Boukas, Phaedon, "Profile of a Greek extremist: Nikolaos Michaloliakos," Greek Reporter, September 28, 2013, greekreporter.com.

6 Counterextremism Project, "Nikolaos Michaloliakos," www.counterextremism.com/.

7 Baboulias, Yiannis, "Who is Nikolaos Michaloliakos?" *London Review of Books* (LRB Blog), October 3, 2013, www.lrb.co.uk.

8 Takou, Eleni, "The Rise and Fall of Golden Dawn," *The Brown Journal of World Affairs*, Spring/Summer 2021, Volume XXVII, Issue II, www.humanrights360.org.

9 Gregory Pappas, "Why We Refer to Greece's Golden Dawn Party as Neo-Nazi," *The Pappas Post*, January 5, 2016, accessed May 20, 2018, www.pappaspost.com.

10 Apoifis, Nicholas. *Anarchy in Athens: An Ethnography of Militancy, Emotions and Violence*. Manchester University Press (Manchester), 2016, pg. 147.

11 AP Archive. "L020185C," YouTube video, 6:28, October 4, 2018, www.youtube.com.

12 "Michaloliakos: Next year in Constantinople, Smyrna, and Trapezundi . . . ! The entire interview of the Golden Dawn chief [ΜΙΧΑΛΟΛΙΑΚΟΣ: ΤΟΥ

ΧΡΟΝΟΥ ΣΤΗΝ ΚΩΝΣΤΑΝΤΙΝΟΥΠΟΛΗ, ΣΤΗΝ ΣΜΥΡΝΗ, ΣΤΗΝ ΤΡΑΠΕΖΟΥΝΤΑ . . . !!! ΟΛΟΚΛΗΡΗ Η ΣΥΝΕΝΤΕΥΞΗ ΤΟΥ ΑΡΧΗΓΟΥ ΤΗΣ ΧΡΥΣΗΣ ΑΥΓΗΣ . . .]," *Stoxos* (newspaper), December 31, 2012, www. stoxos.gr.

13 Halikiopoulou, Daphne, and Sofia Vasilopoulou, "The Golden Dawn's 'Nationalist Solution,'" Reform and Transition in the Mediterranean, 4.

14 Ellinas, Antonis A., "Neo-Nazism in an Established Democracy: The Persistence of Golden Dawn in Greece," South European Society and Politics, 2015, Vol. 20, No. 1, 1–20, 1.

15 John Psaropoulos, "'Macedonia is Greek': A look back at the decades-old row," Al Jazeera English, February 4, 2018, accessed March 26, 2018, www. aljazeera.com.

16 Marlise Simons, "For the name of Macedonia, a burst of Greek pride," *New York Times*, 1992, accessed March 26, 2018, www.nytimes.com.

17 Giorgos Pitas, interviewed by Patrick Strickland and Nick Paleologos, Athens, Greece, April 20, 2018.

18 The Antifascism Project, "Χρονολόγιο Φασιστικής Βίας (1990–2013) [Chronology of Fascist Violence (1990–2013)]," October 18, 2013, left.gr.

19 Baldwin-Edwards, Martin, "Immigrants, Racism, and the New Xenophobia of Greece's Immigration Policy: MMO Working Paper No. 11, July 2014," Mediterranean Migration Observatory, migrant-integration.ec.europa.eu.

20 Harman, Diana, "Ignoring Pleas of Local Jews, Greece Swears in anti-Semitic Minister," *Haaretz*, June 9, 2014, www.haaretz.com.

21 The Press Project, "Makis Voridis: from axe-wielding fascist to Minister of Health," June 10, 2014, thepressproject.gr.

22 Smith, Helena, "Rise of the Greek far right raises fears of further turmoil," *The Guardian*, December 16, 2011, www.theguardian.com.

23 Demetis, Christos, "Όταν ο Κατρούγκαλος διέγραφε τον Βορίδη από τον Σύλλογο Φοιτητών της Νομικής [When Katrougalos removed Voridis from the Students' Union in Law School]," News 24/7, January 27, 2015, www.news247.gr.

24 Kapllani, Gazmend, "Under Greece's New Government, Its Future Remains Unclear," Balkan Investigative Reporting Network, July 15, 2019, balkaninsight.com.

25 The Press Project, "Makis Voridis: from axe-wielding fascist to Minister of Health."

26 Smith, Helena, "Rise of the Greek far right raises fears of further turmoil."

27 Psarras, Dimitris, *Golden Dawn on Trial*, 12, (Athens: Rosa Luxemburg Stiftung, 2015).

28 Golden Dawn Watch, "Day 209: The attacks were decided in the higher echelons of the organization," December 15, 2017, goldendawnwatch.org.

29 Βάλ' τους X [X Them Out], "In the ICU," retrieved September 6, 2023, valtousx.gr.

30 Psarras, *Golden Dawn on Trial*, 21.

31 Psarra, Ada, "Ποιος θυμάται τον δολοφόνο ρατσιστή Καζάκο [Who remembers the racist killer Kazako?]," EfSyn.Gr, October 19, 2018, www. efsyn.gr.

32 Mitropoulou, Marianna, "Παντελής Καζάκος: Ο δολοφόνος που πυροβολούσε όποιον μετανάστη έβρισκε μπροστά του [Pantelis Kazakos: The Killer Who Shot Any Immigrant in Front of Him]," Patris News, December 24, 2022, www.patrisnews.com.

33 Psarra, Ada, "Ποιος θυμάται τον δολοφόνο ρατσιστή Καζάκο.

34 The Athens News Agency, "Pantelis Kazakos-Murders-Life Imprisonment," February 28, 2001, Athens News Agency: News in English, 01-02-28 (hri.org).

35 Fotiadis, Ruža, "United against 'The Horsemen of the Apocalypse' and 'The Chessmen of the Devil': The Greek–Serbian Friendship during the 1999 NATO Intervention in Yugoslavia," Comparative Southeast European Studies, 2021, www.degruyter.com.

36 Michas, Takis, *Unholy Alliance: Greece and Milošević's Serbia* (College Station, TX: Texas A&M University Press, 2002), 48.

37 Fotiadis, Ruža, "United against 'The Horsemen of the Apocalypse' and 'The Chessmen of the Devil.'"

38 Michas, Takis, *Unholy Alliance: Greece and Milosevic's Serbia*, 23.

39 See also: "Unholy Alliance: Greece and Milosevic's Serbia." BosniaFacts, www.bosniafacts.info.

40 Konstantinidis, Petros, "The Greek Militiamen Involved in the Srebrenica Massacre," AthensLive (Medium), December 8, 2017, medium.com.

41 Golden Dawn Watch, "Day 185: Golden Dawn is a criminal organization using the guise of a political party," October 2, 2017, goldendawnwatch.org.

42 Psarras, Dimitris, *The Rise of the Neo-Nazi Golden Dawn Party in Greece: Neo-Nazi Moblisation in the Wake of the Crisis* (Brussels: Rosa Luxemburg Stiftung, 2013), 29.

43 Ibid.

44 Pierce, William Luther, "The National Alliance in Europe," The Legacy of Dr. William Luther Pierce (blog), March 27, 2012, accessed May 25, 2018, williamlutherpierce.blogspot.gr.

45 "National Alliance leader, William Pierce, seeks to build far-right alliances," *The Intelligence Report*, Southern Poverty Law Center, March 15, 1999, accessed May 25, 2018, www.splcenter.org.

46 "National Alliance," Southern Poverty Law Center, accessed May 24, 2018, www.splcenter.org/fighting-hate/extremist-files/group/national-alliance.

47 Ibid, note i.

48 Atlamazoglou, Stavros, "How the US defused a deadly showdown between 2 NATO allies' special-operations forces," *Business Insider*, May 8, 2022, www.businessinsider.com.

49 "Golden Dawn stage anti-US, Turkish and immigrant march past US embassy," Associated Press, February 3, 2013, newsroom.ap.org.

CHAPTER THREE

1 Maroufof, Michael, "Retracing the journey of Pakistani migrants to Greece," Irma, 2015, 4, www.eliamep.gr.

2 Ibid.

3 Clapp, Alexander, "Europe's heart of darkness," *1843*, October 24, 2017, www.1843magazine.com.

4 "Greece: The Roma and the preparation of the 2004 Olympic Games: ongoing violations of the right to adequate housing," World Organisation Against Torture, April 2004. www.omct.org.

5 Ibid, note i.

6 Javed Aslam, interviewed by Patrick Strickland via telephone, October 12, 2017.

7 "Three young men arrested for racist attack against Pakistanis in Aspropyrgos," Keep Talking Greece, October 13, 2017, www.keeptalking-greece.com.

8 "Three youths aged 17 and 18 arrested for attack on Pakistanis," AMNA, October 12, 2017. www.amna.gr.

9 Javed Aslam, interviewed by Patrick Strickland and Nick Paleologos in Athens, Greece, February 22, 2018.

10 Tina Stavrinaki, interviewed by Patrick Strickland in Athens, Greece, February 7, 2018.

11 Ibid, iii.

12 Ashfak Mahmoud, interviewed by Patrick Strickland and Nick Paleologos in Goritsa, Greece, February 2018.

CHAPTER FOUR

1 Howden, Daniel, "Refugees Caught Up in Child Prostitution in Athens," Refugees Deeply via The New Humanitarian, July 14, 2016, deeply.thenewhumanitarian.org.

2 Vogiatzakis, Stelios. "A . . . Fighter who Beats Women [Ένας... μαχητής που δέρνει γυναίκες]." Agonas tis Kritis, June 9, 2012, https://archive.agonaskritis.gr/enas-machitis-pou-dernei-gynaikes/

3 eKathimerini, "Golden Dawn spokesman to appear in court on Monday," June 6, 2012, www.ekathimerini.com.

4 Haynes, Gavin, "Ilias Kasidiaris Is the Playboy of the Greek Far-Right," Vice, June 6, 2013, www.vice.com.

5 "Far-right Greek spokesman assaults women politicians on TV," Reuters via France24, June 7, 2012, www.france24.com.

6 Savaricas, Nathalie. "Anti-fascist fury in Athens after far-right MP hit rival." The Independent, June 8, 2012, https://www.independent.co.uk/news/world/europe/antifascist-fury-in-athens-after-farright-mp-hit-rival-7831958.html

7 Druxes, Helga, and Patricia Anne Simpson, *Digital Media Strategies of the Far Right in Europe and the United States* (Washington, DC: Rowman and Littlefield Publishing, May 16, 2015), 204.

8 Tipaldou, Sofia, and Katrin Uba, "Golden Dawn: How the Greek far right wrote the playbook others now use to go mainstream," The Conversation, August 17, 2018, theconversation.com.

9 "MAT-Golden Dawn Collaboration [ΣΥΝΕΡΓΑΣΙΑ ΜΑΤ - «ΧΡΥΣΗΣ ΑΥΓΗΣ»]" Ios Press, 2008, www.iospress.gr.

10 Larson, Jordan, "Greek Farmers Accused of Shooting 28 Migrant Workers Have Walked Free," Vice, July 31, 2014, www.vice.com.

11 Smith, Helena, "Greece's migrant fruit pickers: 'They kept firing. There was blood everywhere,'" *The Guardian*, September 1, 2014, www.theguardian.com.

12 Amnesty International, "Greece: Despair pervades camps after 33 migrant workers shot in Manolada," April 22, 2013, www.amnesty.org.

13 "Yonous Muhammadi, Greece," Human Rights Watch, September 1, 2016, accessed March 24, 2018, www.hrw.org.

14 Yonous Muhammadi, president of the Greek Forum of Refugees, interviewed by Patrick Strickland, Athens, Greece, March 23, 2018.

15 Patrick Strickland, "Neo-Nazis Attack Afghan Community in Greece's Office in Athens," Al Jazeera English, March 23, 2018, accessed March 23, 2018, www.aljazeera.com.

16 "Day 175: 'An organized squad with motorcycle helmets and sticks was chasing immigrants,'" Golden Dawn Watch, July 19, 2017, goldendawnwatch.org.

17 Tsoutsoumpis, Spyridon, "The Far Right in Greece. Paramilitarism, Organized Crime and the Rise of 'Golden Dawn,'" *Comparative Southeast European Studies*, vol. 66, no. 4, 2018, pp. 503–531, doi.org.

18 Dinas, Elias et al., "From dusk to dawn: Local party organization and party success of right-wing extremism," Party Politics, 22, 80–92, www.researchgate.net.

19 Cosse, Eva, "What About Really Tackling Racist Violence in Greece?" Human Rights Watch, December 5, 2013, www.hrw.org .

20 Smith, Helena, "Greek socialists claim victory in election," *The Guardian*, October 4, 2009, www.theguardian.com.

21 Maltezou, Renee, "Secretive far-right party taps into Greeks' anger, fear," Reuters, April 25, 2012, www.reuters.com.

22 Borderline Reports, "Nikos Michaloliakos Nazi Salute at Municipal Council," YouTube video, 0:19, February 4, 2013, www.youtube.com.

23 Golden Dawn Watch, "Day 214: 'As if an invisible hand is conducting this terrible orchestra,'" January 12, 2018, goldendawnwatch.org.

24 "The 60 case files of the criminal organisation Golden Dawn," Jail Golden Dawn, August 24, 2014, accessed April 29, 2018, jailgoldendawn.com.

25 Human Rights Watch, "World Report 2013," 2013, www.hrw.org.

26 "Hate on the streets: Xenophobic violence in Greece," Human Rights Watch, July 10, 2012, accessed April 29, 2019, www.hrw.org.

27 "Golden Dawn financed its activities with protection rackets and blackmail, lawyers say," Jail Golden Dawn, November 14, 2014, accessed April 29, 2018, jailgoldendawn.com.

28 Ibid, note ii.

29 Inman, Phillip, "Greek debt crisis: timeline," *The Guardian*, March 9, 2012, www.theguardian.com.

30 International Monetary Fund, "IMF Survey: Europe and IMF Agree €110 Billion Financing Plan With Greece," May 2, 2010, www.imf.org.

31 Council on Foreign Relations, "1974–2018: Greece's Debt Crisis," no date, www.cfr.org.

32 Smith, Helena, "Greek bailout: Athens burns—and crisis strikes at heart of the EU," *The Guardian*, May 5, 2010, www.theguardian.com.

33 Blackburn, Bradley, and David Muir, "How Did Greek Economic Crisis Get So Bad?" *ABC News*, May 6, 2010, abcnews.go.com.

34 Allen, Katie, and Richard Wachman, "Europe's future in the balance as eurozone face its toughest test," *The Guardian*, May 9, 2010, www.theguardian.com.

35 Reuters staff, "Far-right drive for 'Greek' blood bank angers medics," Reuters, July 12, 2012, www.reuters.com.

36 BBC, "Golden Dawn nationalists hand out 'Greeks only' food," August 1, 2012, www.bbc.com.

37 IBTimes UK, "Neo-Nazi party hand out free food to 'real' Greeks," YouTube, August 1, 2012, www.youtube.com.

38 Ellinas, Antonis A., "The Rise of Golden Dawn: The New Face of the Far Right in Greece," *South European Society and Politics*, March 25, 2013, www.tandfonline.com.

CHAPTER FIVE

1   Strickland, Patrick, "What the fight against far-right violence in Greece tells us," Open Canada, June 12, 2019, opencanada.org.

2   Racist Violence Recording Network, "2013 Annual Report," April 2, 2014, rvrn.org.

3   Mezzofiore, Gianluca, "Golden Dawn Suspected of Stabbing 19-Year-Old Iraqi Man to Death," *International Business Times*, August 13, 2012, www.ibtimes.co.uk.

4   eKathimerini, "Counsel of men accused of fatal stabbing of Pakistani man say motive not racial," December 18, 2013, www.ekathimerini.com.

5   eKathimerini, "Luqman Shehzad's killers sentenced to life in prison," April 15, 2014, www.ekathimerini.com.

6   Smith, Helena, "Neo-fascist Greek party takes third place in wave of voter fury," *The Guardian*, September 21, 2015, www.theguardian.com.

7   Tahir, Usman A. Khan, "Pakistani community to be protected, envoy makes clear to Greece's Golden Dawn," Pakistan Today, October 20, 2017, archive.pakistantoday.com.

8   Omnia TV, "Δίκη δολοφόνων Σαχζάτ Λουκμάν (β΄ βαθμός) | 8η δικάσιμος [Trial of Shahzad Luqman's killers (B Grade) – 8th Trial]," April 2019, omniatv.com.

9   Fyssas, Magda, interviewed by Patrick Strickland on September 7, 2017, in Athens, Greece.

10 *Lifo*, "Δύο χρόνια από τη δολοφονία του Παύλου Φύσσα [Two years since the killing of Pavlos Fyssas]," September 18, 2015, www.lifo.gr.

11 Perrakis, Athanasios, interviewed by Patrick Strickland and Nick Paleologos in Athens, Greece. September 7, 2017.

12 Hallinan, Conn, "Golden Dawn: Fascists at the Gate," *The Nation*, March 25, 2015, www.thenation.com

13 Baboulias, Yiannis, "Blackmail, protection, money laundering: funding Golden Dawn," Channel 4 News (UK), November 19, 2014, www.channel4.com.

14 Malagardis, Maria, "Pavlos Fyssas, the hidden side of political assassination (2/2)," Voxeurop English, November 1, 2013, voxeurop.eu.

15 Strickland, Patrick, and Nick Paleologos, "Tapped phone calls further reveal Golden Dawn's police ties," Al Jazeera English, April 24, 2018, www.aljazeera.com.

16 Malagardis, Maria, "Pavlos Fyssas, the hidden side of political assassination (1/2)," Voxeurop English, October 31, 2013, voxeurop.eu.

CHAPTER SIX

1 O'Brien, Luke, "The Making of an American neo-Nazi," *The Atlantic*, December 2017 issue, www.theatlantic.com.

2 Telemachos, interviewed by Patrick Strickland, Athens, Greece, March 2, 2018.

3 Nastos, Vasilos, interviewed by Nick Paleologos, telephone, Athens, Greece, March 15, 2018.

4 Smith, Helena, "Greece's neo-Nazi Golden Dawn goes global with political ambitions," *The Guardian*, April 1, 2013, accessed May 22, 2018, www.theguardian.com.

5 Calligeros, Marissa, "Golden Dawn supporters clash with anti-fascists in Brisbane," *Brisbane Times*, May 2, 2014, accessed May 22, 2018, www.brisbanetimes.com.

6 Safi, Michael, and Helena Smith, "Greek neo-Nazi party Golden Dawn's visit slammed by community groups," *The Guardian*, September 3, 2014, accessed May 22, 2018, www.theguardian.com.

7 Mara, Darren, "Golden Dawn stops fundraising drive in Australia, refuses to impose blanket ban," *SBS News*, October 4, 2018, accessed May 22, 2018, www.sbs.com.

8 Leman, Jonathan, interviewed by Patrick Strickland, telephone, May 22, 2018.

9 "Besök hos Gyllene Gryning," *NordFront*, May 11, 2014, accessed May 22, 2018, www.nordfront.se.

10 Golden Dawn – Crete. "Τ.Ο. ΧΑΝΙΩΝ: Ομιλίες και επίσκεψη κλιμακίου Εθνικιστών από την Σουηδία (βίντεο-φώτο) [T.O. Chania: Speeches and Visit of Nationalists from Sweden (video-photo)]," May 5, 2014, xa-kriti. blogspot.com.

11 Papailias, George, "Nordic Resistance Movement Interview by Golden Dawn New York Division," *The Daily Stormer*, June 18, 2016, dailystormer. name

12 Ibid.

13 McDonald-Gibson, Charlotte, and Nathalie Savaricas, "Just what Greece didn't need: BNP leader Nick Griffin seeks Golden Dawn alliance," *The Independent*, January 10, 2014, www.independent.co.uk.

14 AP Archive, "Golden Dawn in joint briefing with leader of UK right-wing party," YouTube video, 2:09, posted July 31, 2015, www.youtube.com.

15 Dabilis, Andy, "French National Front flirting with Golden Dawn?" *Greek Reporter*, May 24, 2014, accessed May 23, 2018, greece.greekreporter.com.

16 Tsoutsoumpis, Spyridon, "The Far Right in Greece. Paramilitarism, Organized Crime and the Rise of 'Golden Dawn,'" Comparative Southeast European Studies, vol. 66, no. 4, 2018, pp. 503–531. doi.org.

17 "6,000 Nationalists at CasaPound's Annual Memorial Ceremony in Rome for the Dead Comrades – Golden Dawn was present," Popular Association—Golden Dawn, January 10, 2018, accessed May 24, 2018, www.xryshaygh.com.

18 "Golden Dawn in Moscow: We set the foundations of Greek-Russian cooperation," Golden Dawn New York (blog), May 15, 2014, accessed May 24, 2018, xaameriki.wordpress.com.

19 "'Natural allies'—The Kremlin connections of the Greek far-right," Political Capital: Policy Research and Consulting Institute, March 1, 2016, accessed May 24, 2018, www.politicalcapital.hu.

20 Ibid.

21 Shekhovtsov, Anton, "Greek neo-Nazi Golden Dawn criticizes Western 'usury' for supporting Ukrainian democracy," Anton Shekhovtsov (blog), February 27, 2014, accessed May 24, 2018, anton-shekhovtsov.blogspot.gr.

22 "Golden Dawn fosters ties with German neo-Nazis," *Spiegel Online*, February 4, 2013, accessed May 25, 2018, www.spiegel.del.

23 Psarras, The Rise of the Neo-Nazi Golden Dawn Party in Greece, 20.

24 Psarras, The Rise of the Neo-Nazi Golden Dawn Party in Greece, 37.

25 Baboulias, Yiannis, "Is Golden Dawn turning to terrorism to get their message across," VICE, April 2, 2013, accessed May 25, 2013, www.vice.com.

26 Dickson, Caitlin. "The Neo-Nazi Has No Clothes: In Search of Matt Heimbach's Bogus 'White Ethnostate,'" Huffington Post, February 2, 2018, www.huffpost.com.

27 Matthew Heimbach, "Sitting Down with Golden Dawn's Irene Pappas," *Praxis Mag*, December 8, 2014, accessed May 24, 2018, praxis-mag. blogspot.gr.

28 Matthew Heimbach, "Golden Dawn and the Traditionalist Worker Party: Nationalist Unity," I Stand with Golden Dawn (blog), December 13, 2015, accessed May 24, 2018, i-stand-with-golden-dawn.webnode.gr.

29 "Charlottesville: Race and Terror—VICE News Tonight on HBO," Vice News.

30 "Golden Dawn praises White supremacist rally in Virginia," eKathimerini, August 14, 2017, accessed May 24, 2018, www.ekathimerini.com.

31 Dickson, Caitlin, "The Neo-Nazi Has No Clothes: In Search of Matt Heimbach's Bogus 'White Ethnostate.'"

CHAPTER SEVEN

1 Strickland, Patrick, "Refugees fear winter at cramped and decrepit Moria camp," Al Jazeera English, December 6, 2017, www.aljazeera.com.

2   Strickland, Patrick, "Refugees in Greece's Lesbos left in the cold and rain,"
    Al Jazeera English, December 10, 2017, www.aljazeera.com.
3   Strickland, Patrick, "Refugees occupy Syriza party office in Lesbos," Al
    Jazeera English, December 8, 2017, www.aljazeera.com.
4   Left.gr, "Μόρια: Συνελήφθη ο 78χρονος που πυροβόλησε 16χρονο πρό-
    σφυγα [The 78-year-old man who shot a 16-year-old refugee was arrested],"
    July 10, 2018, left.gr.
5   Strickland, Patrick, "Far-right attacks increase tension in Greece's Lesbos,"
    Al Jazeera English, April 23, 2018, www.aljazeera.com.

CHAPTER EIGHT

1   "Greek far right burn squats, vandalise Holocaust statue," *Al Jazeera English*,
    January 22, 2018, accessed March 26, 2018, www.aljazeera.com.
2   Strickland, Patrick, "Tensions high in Athens ahead of nationalist rally,"
    Al Jazeera English, February 4, 2018, accessed March 26, 2018, www.al-
    jazeera.com.
3   Chrysopoulos, Philip, "When Greeks rallied against FYROM name in
    1992," Greek Reporter, January 22, 2018, greekreporter.com.
4   Ibid, iii.
5   Freedom, "Greece: Libertatia occupied centre burned by fascists," January
    21, 2018, freedomnews.org.uk.
6   Strickland, Patrick, "Tens of thousands of Greeks protest Macedonia's
    name," *Al Jazeera English*, February 4, 2018, accessed March 26, 2018, www.
    aljazeera.com.
7   "Threatening letter sent to Greek minister working on Macedonia issue,"
    Reuters, February 2, 2018, accessed March 26, 2018, af.reuters.com.
8   Dedoussi, Maria, "Σαν σήμερα: Η 15η Σεπτεμβρίου στην Ιστορία - Τι
    συνέβη το 1944 στο Μελιγαλά [Today: September 15th in history· What
    happened in 1944 in Meligalas]," CNN Greece, September 15, 2022, www.
    cnn.gr.
9   Kyriakidou, Dina, "Special Report: Greece's far-right party goes on the
    offensive," Reuters, November 12, 2012, www.reuters.com.
10 Ibid, iv.
11 Ibid, iv.
12 "Toskas defends police estimate of turnout at 'Macedonia' rally," eKathime-
    rini, February 5, 2018, accessed March 26, 2018, www.ekathimerini.com.
13 Kokkinidis, Tasos, "Macedonia will always be Greek, says Mikis
    Theodorakis at huge Athens rally," *Greek Reporter*, February 4, 2018, ac-
    cessed April 21, 2018, greece.greekreporter.com.
14 "Anarchists attack home of Mikis Theodorakis with paint ahead of

Macedonia protest," *Keep Talking Greece*, February 3, 2018, accessed April 21, 2018, www.keeptalkinggreece.com.

15 "Statement of the KKE regarding the developments with FYROM," Communist Party of Greece, February 5, 2018, accessed April 21, 2018, inter.kke.gr.

16 Ibid.

17 "Athens Occupied Theater EMBROS: Announcement about the Nazi attack during 04/02/2018 Greek nationalistic demonstration," *Void Network*, February 10, 2018, accessed April 21, 2018, voidnetwork.gr.

18 Marcos (pseudonym), interviewed by Patrick Strickland and Nick Paleologos in Athens, Greece, May 3, 2018.

19 Lomani, Nasim, interviewed by Patrick Strickland, Athens, Greece, March 29, 2018.

20 Ibid.

21 Kantouris, Costas, and Nicholas Paphitis, "Greek high school unrest amid fears of far-right resurgence," Ekathimerini, November 29, 2018, www.ekathimerini.com.

22 Jail Golden Dawn, "The Mafia of Golden Dawn (1): Christos Rigas [Η μαφία της Χρυσής Αυγής (I): Χρήστος Ρήγας]," January 31, 2015, jailgoldendawn.com.

23 eKathimerini, "Far-right extremists arrested in possession of weapons," June 28, 2018, www.ekathimerini.com.

24 eKathimerini, "Greek foreign minister seeks judicial intervention over death threats," June 28, 2018, www.ekathimerini.com/news/230144/greek-foreign-minister-seeks-judicial-intervention-over-death-threats/.

25 Reuters Staff, "Greek far-right MP arrested, investigated for treason over coup remark," Reuters, June 15, 2018, www.reuters.com.

26 Smith, John, "Greek Court Frees Treason-Charge Lawmaker on €30K Bail," Greek Reporter, June 20, 2018, greekreporter.com.

27 eKathimerini, "Photojournalist says demonstrator toted gun at name rally," September 12, 2018, www.ekathimerini.com.

28 Agence France-Presse, "Greeks reject Macedonia name deal in poll," France 24, July 8, 2018, www.france24.com.

29 eKathimerini, "Kammenos: FYROM referendum 'invalid,'" September 20, 2018, www.ekathimerini.com.

30 Strickland, Patrick. "Greece: FM Kotzias resigns amid tensions over Macedonia accord," Al Jazeera English, October 17, 2018, www.aljazeera.com.

31 Committee to Protect Journalists, "Far-right demonstrators assault reporter Thomas Jacobi in Greece," January 21, 2020, cpj.org.

32 European Federation of Journalists, "Greece: three journalists assaulted by far-right demonstrators," January 23, 2019, europeanjournalists.org.
33 Marusic, Sinisa Jakov, "Greek MPs Approve Historic Macedonia 'Name' Agreement." Balkan Insight, January 25, 2019, balkaninsight.com.

CHAPTER NINE

1   Tombatzaglou, Eleftheria, interviewed by Nick Paleologos and Patrick Strickland in Athens, Greece, on April 14, 2018.
2   Souliotis, Yiannis, "Five neo-Nazi suspects tied to bombing of leftist squat," eKathimerini, January 11, 2018, accessed April 17, 2018, www.ekathimerini.com.
3   Souliotis, Yiannis, "Two Piraeus squat attackers connected to Golden Dawn," *eKathimerini*, March 27, 2018, accessed March 27, 2018, www.ekathimerini.com.
4   Alizadeh, Taher, interviewed by Patrick Strickland and Nick Paleologos in Athens, Greece, April 19, 2018.
5   Ibid, chapter four, note i.
6   Elghandour, Naim, president of the Muslim Association of Greece, interviewed by Patrick Strickland at the Afghan Community in Greece in Athens, Greece, March 23, 2018.
7   Ibid.
8   Constantinou, Petros, national director of KEERFA, interviewed by Patrick Strickland at the Afghan Community in Greece in Athens, Greece, March 23, 2018.
9   See chapter one.
10 Kokkinidis, Tasos. "Racists attack home of Afghan student who marched in 'Oxi Day' parade," Greek Reporter, November 3, 2017, greece.greekreporter.com.
11 Tornos News, "Report: New Greek neo-nazi group threatens Muslims and migrants," January 21, 2018, www.tornosnews.gr.
12 Patrick Strickland, "Greek lawyer latest to be assaulted by far right," *Al Jazeera English*, November 30, 2017, accessed March 23, 2018. www.aljazeera.com.
13 Ioannou, Theo, "Neo-Nazi gang that attacked Amir threatens migrants with violence," Greek Reporter, November 8, 2017, greece.greekreporter.com.
14 Ross, Brandon D., "Krypteia: A Form of Ancient Guerrilla Warfare," *Grand Valley Journal of History* 1, no. 2 (April 2012): 1–10, accessed March 24, 2018. scholarworks.gvsu.edu.
15 Iefimerida, "Νέα χτυπήματα κατά μεταναστών από την ομάδα

«Κρυπτεία» σε Μπουρνάζι και Αγ. Αναργύρους [Translated title]," June 5, 2018, www.iefimerida.gr.

16 Iefimerida.gr, "Έξι προσαγωγές για την επίθεση της «Κρυπτείας» στην κατάληψη του πρώην ΠΙΚΠΑ Πετραλώνων [translated title]," June 25, 2018, www.iefimerida.gr.

CHAPTER TEN

1   Kitsantonis, Niki, "75-year-old mayor is attacked in Greece, and nationalists rejoice," *New York Times*, May 21, 2018, www.nytimes.com.

2   Erickson, Amanda. "Greece's most liberal mayor beaten by a bunch of far-right protesters," *Washington Post*, May 2, 2018, www.washingtonpost.com.

3   eKathimerini, "Argos mayor expelled over anti-Semitic rant," June 8, 2018, www.ekathimerini.com.

4   Kitsantonis, Niki, "75-Year-Old Mayor Is Attacked in Greece, and Nationalists Rejoice," *New York Times*, May 21, 2018, www.nytimes.com.

CHAPTER ELEVEN

1   eKathimerini, "After defeat, Greek PM calls for snap elections," May 27, 2019, www.ekathimerini.com.

2   Tidey, Alice, "Greek elections: Conservatives win power from Syriza," Euronews, July 7, 2019, www.euronews.com.

3   Souliotis, Yiannis, "Exarchia heading for ambitious makeover," eKathimerini, August 12, 2019, www.ekathimerini.com.

4   King, Alex, and Ioanna Manoussaki-Adamopoulou, "Greek police raid Athens squats and arrest migrants," *The Guardian*, www.theguardian.com.

5   Souliotis, Yiannis, "Riot police raid anarchist haunt in Exarchia," eKathimerini, August 20, 2019, www.ekathimerini.com.

6   Keep Talking Greece, "New Democracy member calls Iranian refugee a 'monkey,'" September 4, 2019, www.keeptalkinggreece.com.

7   Souliotis, Yiannis, "Judicial officials pave way for eviction of anarchists from Vox cafe," eKathimerini, September 9, 2019, www.ekathimerini.com.

8   Crowcroft, Orlando, "Police raid Joker screenings in Athens, turfing out 19 children," Euronews, October 22, 2019, www.euronews.com.

9   Bratsos, Nassos, "OLME for N. Tebonera – Private Universities – Corona virus in schools [Η ΟΛΜΕ για Ν. Τεμπονέρα – Ιδιωτικά Πανεπιστήμια – Κορονοϊό στα σχολεία]," ERT News, January 8, 2024, www.ertnews.gr.

10 Al Jazeera English, "Tight security in Athens before annual November 17 march," November 17, 2019, www.aljazeera.com.

11 eKathimerini, "Athens Mayor calls for peaceful demonstration this Sunday," November 15, 2019, www.ekathimerini.com.

12 Keep Talking Greece, "Police union spokesman calls migrants 'dust with annoying character,'" August 26, 2019, www.keeptalkinggreece.com.

CHAPTER TWELVE

1 Euronews, "Baby dies in Moria migrant camp, MSF reveals," November 17, 2019, www.euronews.com.

2 Rankin, Jennifer, "EU declares migration crisis over as it hits out at 'fake news,'" *The Guardian*, March 6, 2019, www.theguardian.com.

3 Bathke, Benjamin, "Greek villagers throw stones at migrant buses," InfoMigrants, October 10, 2019, www.infomigrants.net.

4 NewsIt, "Θεσσαλονίκη: Έδιωξαν πρόσφυγες και μετανάστες στα Βρασνά – Νύχτα έντασης με μπλόκα και μυστικά σχέδια – video [Θεσσαλονίκη: Έδιωξαν πρόσφυγες και μετανάστες στα Βρασνά – Νύχτα έντασης με μπλόκα και μυστικά σχέδια – video]," October 23, 2019, www.newsit.gr.

5 Touchtido, Symela, "Βρασνά: Οι πρώτοι που εκδίωξαν πρόσφυγες και μετανάστες [Vrasna: The first to expel refugees and immigrants]," Euronews, March 9, 2020, gr.euronews.com.

6 Likesas, Apostolos. "Η ξενοφοβία νίκησε στα Βρασνά [Xenophobia won in Vrasna]," October 23, 2019, www.efsyn.gr.

7 Kokkinidis, Tasos, "Greek islanders threaten to block migrant ship from docking," Greek Reporter, November 1, 2019, greekreporter.com.

8 Chrysopoulos, Philip, "Kos Residents Prevent 75 migrants form disembarking on island," Greek Reporter, November 2, 2019, greekreporter.com.

9 Keep Talking Greece, "Skydra: Priest in racist rant urges locals to take 'rifles' against refugees," November 1, 2019, www.keeptalkinggreece.com.

10 Racist Violence Recording Network, "2016 Annual Report," 2017, rvrn.org.

11 Carassava, Anthee, "Greece pork protest over transfer of migrants," *The Times* (UK), November 11, 2019, www.thetimes.co.uk.

12 Carassava, Anthee, "Smoke screen for Greek anti-refugee sentiment?" Deutsche Welle, November 11, 2019, www.dw.com.

13 EfSyn, "Έκοψαν κολώνες της ΔΕΗ και άφησαν χωρίς ρεύμα καταυλισμό προσφύγων [They cut down the DEH lines and left the refugee camp without power]," November 13, 2019, www.efsyn.gr.

14 Samos 24, "Γιώργος Στάντζος : «Θέλουμε λύση αυτή τη στιγμή» [Giorgos Stantzas: 'We want a solution this second']," December 17, 2019, www.samos24.gr.

15 Deutsche Welle, "Greek islanders strike against migrant camps," January 22, 2020, www.dw.com.

16 Strickland, Patrick, "Anger and 'fatigue' on Greek islands over migration limbo," Politico EU, February 25, 2020, www.politico.eu.

17 eKathimerini, "New Democracy ejects deputy governor from party over anti-Turkish comments," April 15, 2016, www.ekathimerini.com.

18 Hume, Tim, "Video shows Greek mobs attacking migrant boats and aid workers," Vice News, March 3, 2020, www.vice.com.

19 eKathimerini, "Mitsotakis says migrant crisis has become 'asymmetrical threat,'" March 3, 2020, www.ekathimerini.com.

20 Reuters staff, "Turkey prepares human rights case over Greece's treatment of migrants," Reuters, March 4, 2020, www.reuters.com.

21 Stone, Mark, "'They shot us with rifles': Migrants blame Greek authorities for border bloodshed," Sky News, March 5, 2020, news.sky.com.

CHAPTER THIRTEEN

1 Strickland, Patrick, "Golden Dawn: the rapid rise and even quicker fall of Greece far-right party," The National, November 24, 2019, www.thenationalnews.com.

2 eKathimerini, "Egyptian fisherman: We were attacked because we are Muslims and dark-skinned," October 14, 2019, www.ekathimerini.com.

3 3 eKathimerini. "Michaloliakos takes the stand in Golden Dawn trial." November 6, 2019, https://www.ekathimerini.com

4 Mandra, Ioanna, "Prosecutor seeks acquittal of Golden Dawn leader," eKathimerini, www.ekathimerini.com.

5 Hume, Tim, "Greek Neo-Nazis Swarmed and Beat This Journalist for 4 Straight Minutes. The Cops Did Nothing," Vice News, January 20, 2020, www.vice.com.

6 *Tagesspiegel*, 'Nach Doku über rechtsextreme Partei: Deutscher Journalist bei Rechten-Demo in Athen verletzt [After a documentary about a right-wing extremist party: German journalist injured at right-wing demo in Athens]," January 20, 2020, www.tagesspiegel.de.

7 Reporters Without Borders, "Greece: far-right activists attack German reporter during anti-migrant protest," January 20, 2020, rsf.org.

8 "Golden Dawn Press Release on the rally against illegal immigration [Δελτίο Τύπου Χρυσής Αυγής για την συγκέντρωση ενάντια στην λαθρομετανάστευση]," Golden Dawn, January 19, 2020, web.archive.org.

9 Reuters staff, "Greece opens detention camp for immigrants as election looms," Reuters, April 29, 2012, www.reuters.com.

10 Reuters staff, "Greece confirms first coronavirus case, a woman back from Milan," Reuters, February 26, 2020, www.reuters.com.

11 Reuters staff, "Greece says nightclubs, gyms, cinemas shut for 2 weeks as virus precaution," Reuters, March 12, 2020, www.reuters.com.

12 Human Rights Watch, "Greece: Move asylum seekers, migrants to safety," March 24, 2020, www.hrw.org.

13 Campana, Fahrinisa, and Patrick Strickland, "The looming refugee coronavirus disaster," Slate, March 23, 2020, slate.com.

14 Kakissis, Joanna, "Greece records first coronavirus cases among refugees, imposes quarantine on camp," NPR, April 2, 2020, www.npr.org.

15 eKathimerini English, "150 people test positive for Covid-19 at Kranidi refugee facility," April 21, 2020, www.ekathimerini.com.

16 Carassava, Anthee, "Greece sidelines thousands of asylum-seekers in national inoculation drive," Voice of America, March 7, 2021, www.voanews.com.

17 Squat!net, "Athens: Themistokleus refugee squat evicted," May 19, 2020, en.squat.net.

18 Hoffman, Cara, "The anarchist neighborhood of Athens," Daily Beast, August 23, 2020, www.thedailybeast.com.

19 Fallon, Katy, "Greece ready to welcome tourists as refugees stay locked down in Lesbos," *The Guardian*, May 27, 2020, www.theguardian.com.

20 Fallon, Katy, "Years ago a Greek refugee camp burned. Those blamed say they are innocent," Al Jazeera English, March 5, 2024, www.aljazeera.com.

21 "Greece: Moria camp will not be rebuilt," InfoMigrants, March 5, 2021, www.infomigrants.net.

22 Reuters, "Greece opens two more holding centers for migrants on islands," November 27, 2021, www.reuters.com.

23 Fallon, Katy, and Stavros Malichudis, "Greece says migration crisis over; refugees beg to differ," The New Humanitarian, October 5, 2021, www.thenewhumanitarian.org.

24 Smith, Helena, "Greece accused of 'biggest pushback in years' of stricken refugee ship," *The Guardian*, November 5, 2021, www.theguardian.com.

25 Amnesty International, "Greece: Authorities abusing power to trample on right to protest," July 14, 2021, www.amnesty.org.

26 Kakissis, Joanna, "Golden Dawn: Greek Court Delivers Landmark Verdicts Against Neo-Nazi Party," NPR, October 7, 2020, www.npr.org.

27 Al Jazeera English, "In Pictures: The day Golden Dawn was convicted," October 7, 2020, www.aljazeera.com.

28 Smith, Helena, "Neo-Nazi leaders of Greece's Golden Dawn sentenced to 13 years," *The Guardian*, October 14, 2020, www.theguardian.com.

CHAPTER FOURTEEN

1 Gatopoulos, Derek, "Greece: EU's external border is hardening, attitudes are too," Associated Press, December 23, 2022, apnews.com.

2 Greek City Times, "Evros: Greek-Turkish border fence to be extended by 80km," August 19, 2022,

3 Human Rights Watch, "'No one asked me why I left Afghanistan': Pushbacks and Deportations of Afghans from Turkey," November 18, 2022, www.hrw.org.

4 European Council on Refugees and Exiles, "AIDA 2021 Update: Greece," June 3, 2022, ecre.org.

5 Fallon, Katy, "The legal battle to stem the EU's border pushback boom," The New Humanitarian, January 9, 2023, www.thenewhumanitarian.org.

6 Forensic Architecture, "Drift-backs in the Aegean Sea," July 15, 2022, forensic-architecture.org.

7 Border Violence Monitoring Network, *Black Book of Pushbacks*, December 7, 2022, left.eu.

8 Papangeli, Iliana, Ottavia Spaggiari, and Isobel Thompson, "How European courts are wrongfully prosecuting asylum seekers as smugglers," The New Humanitarian, September 1, 2022, www.thenewhumanitarian.org.

9 Wallis, Emma, "Greece: Migrant accused of smuggling sentenced to 146 years in prison," InfoMigrants, May 14, 2021, www.infomigrants.net.

10 Kitsatonis, Niki, "He Saved 31 People at Sea. Then Got a 142-Year Prison Sentence," *New York Times,* June 25, 2021, www.nytimes.com.

11 Mitarachi, Notis (@nmitarakis), "Η λαθροδιακίνηση είναι μεγάλη φάμπρικα με πολλά λεφτά. Κάποιοι θέλουν η Ευρώπη να ανοίξει τα σύνορά της και κάποιοι να βγάλουν πολλά χρήματα. Κάτι τέτοιο με την κυβέρνηση @PrimeministerGR και όλα αυτά που συνέβαιναν επί ΣΥΡΙΖΑ, δεν θα συμβεί," Twitter, December 29, 2022, twitter.com.

12 eKathimerini, "Kasidiaris to run in elections with his own far-right party despite government ban," April 26, 2023, www.ekathimerini.com.

13 Global Project Against Hate and Extremism, "Ilias Kasidiaris' Neo-Nazi Party is too Extreme for the Greek Parliament, but not for YouTube," April 14, 2023, globalextremism.org.

14 Jakov, Marusic Sinisa, and Eleni Stamatoukou, "Golden Dawn Youths Invade North Macedonia Artist's Exhibition in Greece," BalkanInsight, April 27, 2023, balkaninsight.com.

15 eKathimerini, "New Democracy lawmaker ousted from party over anti-communist rant," October 5, 2021, www.ekathimerini.com.

16 eKathimerini, "Gov't issues warning to Bogdanos," September 16, 2021, www.ekathimerini.com.

17 Waters, Nick, "The Killing of Muhammad Gulzar," Bellingcat, May 8, 2020, www.bellingcat.com.

18 United Nations High Commissioner for Refugees, "Operational Data Portal: Refugee Situations - Mediterranean Situation - Greece," accessed June 27, 2023, data.unhcr.org.

19 eKathimerini, "Greece to receive additional 1.9 bln euros for migration, EU VP says," November 24, 2022, www.ekathimerini.com.

20 HIAS, "European Ombudsperson Opens Inquiry Into the Commission's Administration of EU Funding Used in Greece's Illegal Expulsion of Migrants," December 7, 2023, hias.org.

21 Ta Nea, "Βίντεο ντοκουμέντο από τη φασιστική επίθεση με θύματα Πακιστανούς μετανάστες [Translated title]," October 29, 2021, www.tanea.gr.

22 EfSyn.gr, "Ρατσιστική επίθεση κατά Πακιστανού στον Κόκκινο Μύλο καταγγέλλει η ΚΕΕΡΦΑ [KEERFA denounces racist attack against Pakistani in Kokkino Milo]," May 8, 2022, www.efsyn.gr.

23 Athens Magazine, "Συναγερμός στα Πατήσια: Οδηγός ταξί πυροβόλησε Πακιστανό μετανάστη φωνάζοντας «γ@μώ τους μουσουλμάνους!» [Translated title]," May 4, 2022, www.athensmagazine.gr.

24 EfSyn.gr, "Καταγγελία για νέα ρατσιστική επίθεση φασιστών [Complaint about new racist attack by fascists]," May 6, 2022, www.efsyn.gr.

25 Stevis-Gridneff, Matina, "Video shows Greece abandoning migrants at sea," *New York Times*, May 19, 2023, www.nytimes.com.

26 Stamouli, Nektaria, "Greece's conservatives achieve big victory but fall short of majority," Politico EU, May 21, 2023, www.politico.eu.

27 Protothema, "Μητσοτάκης στο CNN: Ισχυρή κυβέρνηση για να συνεχίσουμε το έργο μας στην οικονομία [translated title]," YouTube video, May 23, 2023, www.youtube.com.

28 Mogul, Rhea, Sophia Saifi, and Lizzy Yee, "Hundreds of Pakistanis dead in Mediterranean migrant boat disaster, official says," CNN, June 19, 2023, edition.cnn.com.

29 Beake, Nick, and Kostas Kallergis, "Greece boat disaster: BBC investigation casts doubt on coastguard's claims," BBC, June 18, 2023, www.bbc.com.

30 AFP, "Greek MP expelled from Mitsotakis' party over shipwreck comments," AFP via Arab News, June 17, 2023, www.arabnews.com.

31 EfSyn.Gr, "Διαγράφεται από τη ΝΔ ο Σπήλιος Κρικέτος μετά το ρατσιστικό παραλήρημα [Spilios Kriketos is removed from ND after racist delirium]," June 16, 2023, www.efsyn.gr.

32 Refugee Support Aegean, "Malakasa Camp," accessed June 27, 2023, rsaegean.org.

33 Smith, Helena, "Three more bodies found by authorities after Greek shipwreck," *The Guardian*, June 20, 2023, www.theguardian.com.

34 eKathimerini, "Voter turnout hits historic low," June 26, 2023, www.ekathimerini.com.

35 eKathimerini, "Kasidiaris-backed Spartiates party makes it into Parliament," June 25, 2023, www.ekathimerini.com.

36 eKathimerini, "Authorities apprehend suspect connected to migrant confinement video," August 23, 2023, www.ekathimerini.com.

37 eKathimerini, "Two children among 18 killed in blazes," August 23, 2023, www.ekathimerini.com.

38 Angelidis, Dimitris, "Κλείδωσε μετανάστες σε τρέιλερ φορτηγού και καλεί σε πογκρόμ [Immigrants locked in truck trailer and calls for pogroms]," EfSyn.Gr, August 22, 2023, www.efsyn.gr.

39 eKathimerini, "Supreme Court prosecutor orders dual investigation into arson and racist violence incidents," August 23, 2023, www.ekathimerini.com.

40 Telopoulos, Antonis, "Μόνο οι 3 ανθρωποκυνηγοί «είδαν» εμπρηστικό μηχανισμό [Only the three man-hunters 'saw' an incendiary device]," EfSyn.Gr, August 26, 2023, www.efsyn.gr.

41 "Authorities apprehend suspect connected to migrant confinement video," eKathimerini, August 23, 2023, www.ekathimerini.com.

42 EfSyn, "KEERFA: Kairides and Economou opened the door to racist patrols [ΚΕΕΡΦΑ: Καιρίδης και Οικονόμου άνοιξαν τη πόρτα σε ρατσιστικές περιπολίες]," August 22, 2023.

43 Staff, "Greek wildfires spur anti-migrant sentiment," AFP via France 24, August 25, 2023, www.france24.com.

44 eKathimerini, "Locals allegedly detain migrants in Evros region," August 28, 2023, www.ekathimerini.com.

45 Becatoros, Elena, "5 dead, including 4 children, in 2 migrant boat sinkings off Greek islands near Turkish coast," Associated Press, August 28, 2023, apnews.com.

46 Becatoros, Elena, "Greece: Firefighters rescue 25 migrants trapped in burning forest," Associated Press via ABC News, September 1, 2023, abcnews.go.com.